Blood, Sweat, Tears, and Prayers

Firefighting and EMS from Some of
the Toughest Streets in America

Gary Ludwig

ISBN: 978-1-4834-2654-9 (sc)
ISBN: 978-1-4834-2655-6 (hc)
ISBN: 978-1-4834-2653-2 (e)

Library of Congress Control Number: 2015902337

Because of the dynamic nature of the Internet, any web addresses or links contained in this book may have changed since publication and may no longer be valid. The views expressed in this work are solely those of the author and do not necessarily reflect the views of the publisher, and the publisher hereby disclaims any responsibility for them.

Any people depicted in stock imagery provided by Thinkstock are models, and such images are being used for illustrative purposes only. Certain stock imagery © Thinkstock.

Lulu Publishing Services rev. date: 02/27/2015

Dedication

To my wife Patricia, and my children, Nicole and Tyler who have supported me unconditionally and allowed me to grow in my career.

To my parents, Everett and Catherine who now basks together in God's glory. Their love and guidance helped make me the person I am. They are forever in my heart!

To the men and women in fire and EMS past, present, and future that unselfishly dedicate themselves everyday to saving others.

CONTENTS

FOREWORD

As firefighters, EMTs, and Paramedics we are all connected by experience. We all have a story to tell about the first gunshot wound we treated, the first defibrillation, the first intubation, the first extrication from a car crash, the first diabetic awakened, the first drug overdose miraculously revived, and the first baby we helped deliver.

Gary Ludwig is a lifelong fire department-based paramedic who has compiled his version of these shared experiences in such a way that you can visualize the reality of the streets. Descriptions so vivid that you will feel you are in the moment and on the scene.

For those firefighter/EMTs and Paramedics who have been in the streets for years or for those just starting out, Gary's detailed description of life in the streets, will remind you of the after midnight calls where you made a difference, as well as those frustrating calls where the adrenaline rush was wasted.

As you read, you will recall the names and perhaps the addresses of the 'regulars' you knew by heart, those you saw on a weekly and sometimes even a daily basis. Most of all, Gary's stories will remind you of your many colleagues in the fire and EMS arena. The crew members, the partners, the officers, and the rookies with whom you worked, served, and lived.

Take a ride in the streets and experience the encounters with Blood, Sweat, Tears and Prayers.

Dr. Lori Moore-Merrell
Assistant to the General President
International Association of Fire Fighters
Author of the IAFF Guide for Fire-Based EMS Systems, Co-Author of the Landmark Residential Fireground Report (NIST Technical Note 1661) & the High-Rise Fireground Report (NIST Technical Note 1797).

INTRODUCTION

I was just a young innocent 18-year-old kid when I walked through the door of my new employer—the City of St. Louis. Having never been north of Highway 40—the dividing line between north and south St. Louis—I was somewhat sheltered, and hadn't experienced much in my young life. I grew up on the near south side of St. Louis. My family wasn't rich, but my father and mother provided. We always had food on the table, clothes on our back, a bed to sleep in, and heat in the winter. We didn't get air conditioning until I was about 12 years old.

At 18, I thought I knew everything. That is, until my new-hire status meant I was assigned to work on an ambulance on the north side of the city. I discovered how much I *didn't* know. I had no idea the financial and social challenges some people faced in life. My heart hung heavy with some of the things I witnessed.

My very first call was in a nine-story, federally-funded, high-rise housing project for a woman having a baby. We had to walk up the stairs because all the elevators were broken. The dark and dirty concrete stairways with no lights smelled of stale urine in the summer heat as we made our way to the fifth floor. The apartment was not furnished well. It was obvious the family did not have much money. An older man by the name of Leonard was my driver. He thought of himself more like an airplane pilot. He drove with the side running lights on, wore a pilot's hat, and told me, "Only the pilot touches the controls and the radio."

I had no medical training to speak of. I had no EMT or paramedic license. In 1977, you did not have to be licensed to work on an ambulance in St. Louis. Bud Meyer was the lead first-aid instructor in the fire academy. He taught us how to stop bleeding with a compress bandage and to take a pen apart and stick it in someone's throat if they were choking—not much more than that. I was never taught how to deliver a baby, and I was certainly more at a loss on how to deal with the expectant mother's screaming and discomfort. I think I was in more of a panic than she was. From the back of the ambulance I kept pleading with Leonard to turn on the lights and sirens so we could get to the hospital faster but he refused to do it. He kept telling me everything was fine and to relax. The closer her contractions came the more I panicked. Thankfully, we got her to the city hospital before she delivered her baby, and I wiped the sweat from my brow. All Leonard did was laugh at me. This experience, and others, convinced me of the need to eventually go to paramedic school some two years later.

This first call started a journey of immense proportions that had me witnessing things I'll never forget, and see some things I wish I never had. The journey would have me cross paths with presidents, a pope, people who would forever be my friend, and many whom I'd first meet at the worst possible time of their life.

Over 25,000 emergency calls later, my journey was an experience only a few people will ever know, and even fewer have ever described in writing. I have worked a total of 34 years of my 37-year career in what the FBI statistically ranks every year as two of the most violent cities in the United States—St. Louis and Memphis. In 2014, the FBI ranked Memphis #3 and St. Louis #4 as the most dangerous cities with populations over 200,000. To illustrate the level of violence, during the last three years I worked in Memphis, there were a total of 11 police officers shot, two of whom were killed. During my time in St. Louis, a total of eight police officers were killed in the line of duty. When you work in these types of environments, it's hard to capture the emotions, the feelings, the smells, and the sights of what you see as a firefighter and a paramedic. This book attempts to capture all of those senses and thoughts as best it can.

This book's main purpose is to give the general public a deeper appreciation for what firefighters and paramedics do. The sacrifice is great in preparation, education, and training for the job. I have had the pleasure of working with some of the finest men and women possible. Their dedication, love of the profession, and commitment to their fellow human beings is second to none. I have seen many of them make sacrifices that the ordinary human being wouldn't consider or comprehend, and many do not even get a thank you. This book is for them.

I started my career in 1977, just two months out of high school. I was baptized by fire with some of the things I saw and experienced in my first month working in a big city. Thirty-seven years later, I had spent 25 years working in St. Louis, holding various positions. I started working in EMS and I am proud of that. That is the majority of what fire departments do these days. Eventually, I retired as the chief paramedic from the St. Louis Fire Department. After St. Louis, I served as the director of emergency services in Jefferson County, Missouri, and spent some time starting up a paramedic education program for a college in St. Louis County. Then I was blessed to work for nine more years in another big-city department when I was hired as a deputy fire chief in Memphis, Tennessee. I now serve the City of Champaign, Illinois as their fire chief.

All along the way, no two days were ever alike. Likewise, no two fires, accidents, or shootings were ever the same. And things that were unusual—like tornados, floods, and presidential visits—were no longer a surprise.

My career has given me an education no university or college could ever provide. I've taken a few artistic liberties in order to emphasize different points of what I've learned, and to paint a clearer picture of some scenes, situations, or circumstances. However, the overwhelming majority of events described in this book are factual and accurate.

My career has left me with physical and mental scars. Almost anyone who has worked any length of time in this profession has been hurt or has seen things they would like to forget. In my case, I almost got killed in a backdraft. I almost fell from high buildings twice, and I dislocated my shoulder once when we were making a rescue on a natural gas tank that rose some 200 feet in the air. We were working some 60 feet in the air on a narrow platform, trying to extricate a worker who was overcome by fumes when I stepped into a wrong spot and slipped, causing me to fall forward. When I stretched out my arms as a normal defensive reaction to my fall, I dislocated my shoulder when my hand impacted the ground. Years later, my shoulder and arm still hurt during normal usage, and the rotator cuff has now torn and needs to be fixed.

However, one of the most serious challenges to my health came when I was diagnosed with Hepatitis C on a routine physical examination. My world was devastated! At the time of the diagnosis in 2001, there was no known cure and no vaccine for Hepatitis C. You could only hope you responded well to the treatment to keep the viral load low. If you did not respond well to the treatment, you would eventually need a liver transplant or you would die. I know of firefighters and paramedics throughout the United States who have died from contracting Hepatitis C on the job. Many others live with Hepatitis C, and some have received liver transplants.

I do not know how I contracted Hepatitis C. I am almost positive I contracted it on the job. I just know that I did not have any of the risk factors for contracting the disease except one. I did not have any blood transfusions or organ transplants before 1992; I was not an IV drug user; I do not have tattoos; and I am heterosexual. What I did do was treat victims of gunshots, auto accidents, stabbings, assaults, and other trauma that were covered in blood, and I did it without gloves. When I started in 1977 it was unheard of to use gloves and other protection in the field to shield yourself from someone's body fluids. I can remember coming back from calls covered in blood from head to toe. Many times, my hands and the lower part of my arms would be blood-soaked. Many of my colleagues would look the same way. Some considered it a sign of honor, or a battle scar. The more blood you got on you, the deeper you were in the fight to save someone's life. Then sometime in the mid-1980s the warning came that we needed to start protecting ourselves, and at least wear rubber or latex gloves. There was this disease called non-Hepatitis A and B—which would eventually come to be known as Hepatitis C. But the main catalyst was a disease that mostly gay men were dying from called AIDS. We were warned that it was a blood-borne disease and you could get AIDS if you got blood on you. Initially, there was panic. Later, we would learn that it would have to be through an open sore, cut, or through mucus membranes such as the eyes, and it was called HIV. If you had HIV it could eventually lead to AIDS. But it would be too late for me! Somewhere in my career, on some call, probably in some dark alley, a vacant home, or some terrible crash, I got someone's contaminated blood into my system and I contracted Hepatitis C.

The good news is that now I do *not* have Hepatitis C. God was watching over me. I am in the small percentage of people who contract Hepatitis C and their immune system is able to fight the disease off. Today, I have the antibodies for Hepatitis C. That is why the initial test on the physical exam showed I had Hepatitis C. It detected it because of the antibodies. Further and deeper testing showed I was clear of the disease. This was not the only time God would watch over me, as there were other close calls in my career.

Some may consider me a hero after reading of my experiences. One thing is clear in my mind, and I wish to make understood—I am no hero! I have seen some firefighters and paramedics do some extraordinary and brave things. I have heard and read of feats of courageous US soldiers in combat. *They* are the heroes. They are the ones who have performed heroic and valiant actions. Anything I have done is because I was doing my job and fulfilling my goal of helping others.

There are names listed in this book, but I'm not disclosing any privileged information. All of the events I write about were already published in a legal document or a newspaper in St. Louis or Memphis. I would never disgrace the memory of a victim or cause more pain to the family by revealing the victim's name. If I list no name, it's because the newspapers had it omitted, it was never published, or I chose to leave the name out for personal reasons.

The important thing to remember is that many of the events that I describe happened to real people—people just like you and me. Their dreams and future were dashed and taken away. Their expectations of what life would be like in the future were changed suddenly and forever, sometimes in the most callous, brutal, or devastating ways. Many left their homes thinking they would be back to take care of that little undone matter that could wait. They never returned to finish it.

When things like this happen, there's usually a firefighter or paramedic there to see that the victim is given any chance of survival and, above all, that they're treated with respect. We try not to judge people. Sometimes they are innocent victims. Other times, their choices brought about their circumstances. Someone may have been drug dealing or robbing someone when they were shot, but we treat them as we would any other shooting victim. We don't condemn.

We do a dangerous job. We know that when we sign up. We reach out to each other in difficult times. We are there for each other—all the time! You can replace my name on the cover of this book with thousands of others who chose this profession. They are remarkable and incredible people. They all have stories to tell—maybe even more dramatic than mine. They are the true professionals, and this book tells their story also.

CHAPTER 1

＋

A SIMPLE SOUND CAN MEAN SO MUCH!

It's amazing how a simple click—a sound most of us hear every day—can mean so much. The click of a pen, the click of a switch when you turn on a light, or the click of a lock when you turn the key. But the click on the speaker hanging from the fire station ceiling is usually the telltale sign you're about to go from zero to one hundred in a matter of seconds. The speaker notifies us of a fire, an emergency medical call, or some other emergency; the click happens when the Fire Alarm Office opens the speaker to make the announcement. The dispatchers don't even have to say a word. The click is enough to make you sit up in bed if you're sleeping, stop eating, get up from a chair, stop drinking a cup of coffee, or halt whatever else you're doing. Chances are high you'll enter someone's life you've never met, and at what very well could be their worst moment.

This time as the speaker clicked open, the fire alarm dispatcher gave three sharp alert tones. *Beep! Beep! Beep!* then barked over the speaker, "Engine 5, Medic 8, respond to a report of a shooting at the corner of Jefferson and 18th Street in front of the liquor store. We have a report of a one male who has been shot in the abdomen, time out 1833 hours."

At this point in my career, I was one of two paramedic captains covering half of St. Louis on a shift that operated from a station wagon equipped with all kinds of life-saving equipment. I heard the call go out over the radio in my car, and since I was near the assignment, I informed the dispatcher I'd also be responding. I've been on an estimated 3,500 shooting calls in my career; unfortunately, this was just one more I could add to the tally board. I have no memories of the majority of them, but I do remember some that were more unusual, or significant. Shooting calls are routine to me now. Sometimes, somebody will try to remind me of one that I totally forgot, and something they say will trigger my memory. Others, no words will ever trigger a memory. I just don't remember because of how many there have been.

It was early evening in the summer, and that meant the sun was still high. In mid-summer, the sun doesn't set until just after 9:00 p.m. in St. Louis, and these hours before sunset have always been a unique time for me. I call it the calm before the storm; you could sense what was coming once the sun went down. There always seemed to be a burst of calls through the afternoon heat until rush hour was over. Then there's a calm period when everyone makes it home, eats their evening meal, and maybe watches a television show. Then, they head out. After dark is when the city comes to life and the call volume picks up again. Except this evening was different; we were handling a shooting call with the sun still high in the sky.

Acknowledging that they'd received the call and were en route, the firefighters and paramedics mounted their fire engine and ambulance that were sitting side by side in the fire station, similar to soldiers getting into their tanks, ready to roll into battle. Smoke and exhaust spewed from the tailpipe as the driver started his rig, which even sounded like a battle tank as the noise echoed off the walls of the fire station. The ambulance didn't sound much different. They were both well-equipped, and very expensive pieces of apparatus, with thousands of dollars' worth of expensive and unique equipment designed to save a life, rescue someone trapped in a car, or put out a fire.

Both of the fire station's bay doors rose in unison, as if the fire station had come to life, its eyes opening from a deep sleep. The drivers of both vehicles flipped on their emergency lights as they waited for the doors to rise to their highest level and lock in an open position with an all-too-familiar click. The emergency lights and flashers were clearly visible as they flashed against the walls of the fire station, and of the cars and building windows outside. Then, both raced out the doors with sirens and air horns blaring, about to enter the life of someone who has had violence forced on them.

Knowing the route they will probably take, I met them at an intersection and joined the convoy. Winding our way through the cars that had pulled to the right, and those that had just come to a dead stop in the middle of the road in the wake of the siren, the fire engine and ambulance proceeded to a staging area several blocks from the scene.

***

When there is a shooting, the staging area is necessary for the safety of firefighters and paramedics. The police must respond to the scene first, and secure it before the firefighters and paramedics can treat the victim. The shooter may still be on the scene or, in some cases, may even be the person who was injured. Anything is possible in this field; but the safety of firefighters and paramedics is imperative. Before St. Louis adopted the practice of setting up a staging area, we'd get to the scene of a violent crime and sometimes the assailant would still be on the scene, holding a gun—with no police in sight. It had happened too many times before in my career. In the early 1980s, the Missouri state EMS director, Ken Cole, was almost shot when he and I walked into a shooting scene in the 3900 block of Russell in south St. Louis.

Ken was riding with me that day. I remember pulling up slowly and scanning for trouble. Everything on the street seemed calm—kids were playing on the sidewalks, and people were sitting on their porches. It looked pretty quiet and innocent. As I pulled up at a snail's pace with the car lights and siren off, we could see the wife open the storm door of her house and yell for us to come inside. I yelled back, asking if the shooter was gone. She said he was, and waved for us to come in. I grabbed my jump kit from the back of the station wagon and headed inside, Ken trailing behind me.

It was a "shotgun" house, with three small rooms. As you entered the front door, you'd be in the front room. If you kept walking straight, you walked into the middle room, which is typically the bedroom. If you keep walking further, you'd enter the last room of the house, which was the kitchen. The bathroom is usually a small room off the bedroom.

After we passed the wife at the front door, she told us her husband was in the kitchen. We walked straight to the last room in the house where we found the victim, near death, lying on the floor, shot multiple times in the abdomen and chest. He was unconscious, and slumped upright against the back door of the house.

I turned to ask the wife who shot him. She was standing there, pointing a gun at us. "Let the motherfucker die," she said.

I've had guns pointed at me before—I've even been shot at before—but a gut feeling told me this was a very ugly situation that was going to take some skill to get out of. I could see the rage and hatred in her eyes. We had no way out, since the victim was lying against the back door of the house, and the woman stood between us and the front door. I had to negotiate with her to hand the gun over before we could begin treating her husband, who would die without some type of intervention. Sometimes it's not only your medical skills, but your negotiating skills that can get you out of trouble.

Ken and I joked many times about it later that I almost got the EMS director for the state of Missouri killed. I guess it would have been grounds to pull my Missouri paramedic license.

Another time—I wasn't on the scene, but was working that shift—a person was shot six times and killed while lying on the stretcher in the back of the ambulance.

Clarence Stallings and Charlie Antoni got dispatched to a shooting scene at 20th and St. Louis Avenues and arrived before police. They found the victim lying in the street, surrounded by some people trying to help him. They loaded the patient onto the stretcher and put him in the ambulance. He was still conscious and alert. They left the back doors of the ambulance open as they put him on oxygen and started IVs in both arms, because the ambulance air conditioner was not working that well. Charlie squatted between the stretcher and the bench seat of the ambulance and worked on the man's left arm, and Clarence got between the wall of the ambulance and the stretcher in an attempt to put an IV in the victim's right arm.

Without warning, a man stepped onto the back step of the ambulance and asked, "Is he going to make it?"

The patient lying on the stretcher recognized the voice and raised his head to look. His only words were, "Oh shit!"

Seeing that the patient was still alive, the man calmly and matter-of-factly removed a gun from his pocket and fired six more rounds into the patient as he lay on the stretcher.

Charlie was able to escape out the side door of the ambulance, but Clarence was trapped between the wall and the stretcher. The shooter calmly placed the gun back in his pocket, looked at Clarence, and walked away. Clarence was lucky to only have his uniform splattered with the victim's blood. The victim, of course, died.

Today, fire and EMS personnel can only enter a scene *after* police have secured it. This is common procedure in most cities and communities now. I know sometimes it doesn't seem logical to respond to a scene quickly only to sit and wait several blocks away until the police arrive, but it's necessary for the protection and safety of the firefighters and paramedics.

***

Back on the shooting scene at Jefferson and 18th; only after being cleared to proceed into the scene by the dispatcher, the engine, ambulance, and I began the short trek to the shooting victim. We pulled up with the engine leading the procession. As I got out of my car, I could see pandemonium and chaos everywhere. Family members and bystanders at any shooting are always a challenge for firefighters and paramedics. Family members are usually in a panic, as bystanders stare at the chaos trying to take in all the activity whirling around them. It's human nature to be curious. The public has an insatiable curiosity to know everything; except, sometimes, what is worth knowing. Usually, the police arrive there ahead of us. They have either taken the assailant into custody, or verify the assailant isn't there. The police also move the bystanders away from the scene and have them far enough back that they can't interfere with us. It's important to keep them away from the scene, not only for our safety, but because it's a crime scene. This means there may be evidence in or around the victim. The more people who trample through the scene, the more evidence can be destroyed. The O. J. Simpson murder trial of Nicole

Simpson and Ron Goldman in the 1990s proved the need to preserve crime scenes.

As the firefighters and paramedics disembark from their tank-like fire engine and ambulance, they must take all the necessary equipment needed to save a victim. Airway equipment, drugs, bandages, and IV fluids are just some of the tools that are used when a shooting victim's life hangs in the balance.

Slumped against the building on the concrete sidewalk was the male shooting victim. It was hot outside, and the pungent smell of blood and sweat permeated the air. I've never smelled anything like it. It's not terrible, like a decaying body, but it does have its own unique, overpowering smell that words cannot describe.

Sweat poured down his head and around his neck. He was either running when he was shot, or is in shock. Almost like a pit crew at a NASCAR race, six firefighters and paramedics began to go about their job, without saying a single word. Everyone knows what to do without being told. Sometimes it's like watching a well-rehearsed, choreographed dance. Rick, a paramedic, checked the body for entrance and exit wounds while asking the victim where he was shot. Before the victim could answer, Rick announced to everyone, "Got one here in the right abdomen." Checking further, he leaned the victim forward and examined the back. "I don't see an exit wound anywhere." Chances are, the bullet is somewhere in the abdomen, and it hit one or several major organs.

Bill, a firefighter, took a blood pressure reading and announced to the group, "100 over 65." This was a sign the patient was in shock, probably due to internal bleeding. Kevin, another firefighter, prepared a bag of fluid because an IV would be started in the victim's arm to replace the blood he's lost. Maurice, another firefighter, went back to the ambulance to retrieve a backboard and stretcher, while yet another firefighter put a pressure bandage over the entrance wound and taped it down to control the bleeding.

In the meantime, police officers patiently had their notebooks out, taking down the name of the victim and the names of any witnesses. I'd seen it hundreds of times, but its funny how many people never witnessed anything but were there when it happened. After a shooting in a bar in north St. Louis one night, it just so happened at least 30 people said they were in the restroom at the time of the shooting and didn't see anything. That must have been one large bathroom!

In less than five minutes, the victim had an oxygen mask on his face, an IV in place, his wound bandaged, an EKG monitor hooked to his chest monitoring his heartbeat, and had been placed on a long, hard backboard to move him to a stretcher. He was now ready to be moved to the ambulance and rushed to a trauma center commonly known as City Hospital #1 on the near south side of St. Louis.

This is how I spent 25 summers in the city of St. Louis, when violent crimes usually peak. Summertime in St. Louis is like no other place: heat with such stifling humidity that you can almost see it hanging in the air. The humidity just sticks to you, and you feel miserable. Making it worse is that St. Louis is like a brick jungle. Almost every home is made of brick. Even the alleys, the old sewers, and the streets were made of brick before they were paved over. Many homes also have a flat, black tar roof—I call these the "hotboxes." During the summer, the bricks heat up and the flat black tar roof prevents the bricks from cooling down at night. When one was on fire, the bricks would stay hot for hours, never seeming to cool off.

Regardless of what city I have worked in or title I have held, I am, before anything else, a firefighter and a paramedic.

Whenever an elderly person falls, or a child chokes, or a man gets shot, or a woman gets beaten, or anyone has a stroke or heart attack or asthma attack; whenever an illness or injury suddenly threatens someone's life, or your house is on fire, firefighters and paramedics are the first to respond—many times in less than four minutes in most major cities and suburbs.

At a time when some politicians want to cut funding to fire and EMS agencies, what is it worth to you to know that help is coming when you have a massive heart attack? What is it worth to you to know that when your child has fallen off playground equipment, drowned in a pool, is having uncontrolled seizures, is choking, been abused or beaten, or been ejected from a car that firefighters and paramedics are coming? What about when your house is on fire? Firefighters and paramedics do everything we can to stand between you and all the evils of the world so you don't have to see or acknowledge them— we've seen so much death and destruction that some of us will never, ever be the same again. We know the smell of burning bodies, and it will haunt some of us to our last days; some of us have lost our families through divorce, committed suicide, abused alcohol, or used drugs because we didn't know how to cope with what we've seen and experienced.

You should know that firefighters and paramedics are cursed, struck, spit on with saliva and blood, talked down to and treated as lowly sub-humans sometimes, only to arrive at the station the next day to do it all over again.

In exchange, the pay range for these dedicated servants can be as low as $20,000 a year with some benefits. Your salary can vary depending on where you live, but according to the Department of Labor, the average annual salary for a firefighter who is also a paramedic is $55,000. That's a pretty good bargain for the public, when you consider what some other government employees are paid.

A firefighter/paramedic working in a big city, over the course of his/her career, will probably be shot at, threatened with knives and other weapons, attacked by dogs, yelled and cussed at, all for trying to keep their end of the bargain. I should know—all of those things and more happened to me.

In the seven years since the downturn of the economy in 2008, most firefighters and paramedics have gotten little or no raises, and their health insurance premiums continue to rise. In many places their pensions are under attack and may be taken away. Part of the reason pensions were put in place for firefighters is because no one wants a 70-year-old firefighter trying to rescue them out of a burning building. In the 1930s, St. Louis had a 96-year-old firefighter working for the department because there was no pension system and he had nothing to retire on.

But this is the career I have chosen, and I spent most of it working in St. Louis.

I grew up on Nebraska Street on the near south side of St. Louis, with its predominantly German ancestry. We lived approximately one mile from the huge Anheuser-Busch Brewery, and if the wind was blowing the right way, you could smell hops and barley brewing as strong as if you were standing next to the kettles. From the windows of our third-story attic, I could see most of downtown St. Louis. My mother was a first generation German-American, and proud of her heritage. Sunday afternoons in our house consisted of my dad watching football or baseball on television, while my mother listened to a German polka show on the radio while she prepared the evening meal in the kitchen. Once in a while she would grab me and we would dance to one of her favorite songs. I still remember summer evenings as a child when practically everyone on the block sat on their porches, because no one had air conditioning and the houses were too hot. The kids played on the sidewalks and only went indoors when it was time for bed or the street lights came on. We hoped our huge window fan would pull cooler air into the house at night.

I started my career with the City of St. Louis two months after graduating from high school, at the age of 18. Some in my profession would call me a dinosaur, but I'd like to think I've got quite a few good years left in me. I got my paramedic license in 1979 and my firefighter certification in 1982. But it doesn't matter: Whether you have one year or 37 years, anyone who's been in fire and EMS—who has brought a new life into this world, restored life to a dying patient, or had a life slip through their fingers no matter how hard they have tried to save it—knows this profession we live is a calling. It is not a career, and it is not a job.

We do what we do because we're here to help our fellow man, no matter how rich or poor, no matter their skin color or nationality, no matter their choices that bring us into their lives, and no matter if we agree with those choices or not. We're here to aid our community in its time of need. Many of us thrive off the excitement of the job and the adrenalin rush that comes from what we do, but there's also a sense of satisfaction and reward.

In my case, I have had the honor to work and serve the people in two major cities the majority of my career.

Many of the circumstances are the same. You could take the name off the fire trucks and ambulances in Memphis and put St. Louis on the side and I wouldn't know the difference if I was at an emergency scene somewhere else. The fires are the same. The shootings are the same. The heart attacks are the same. And the pain and suffering we see is the same. Sometimes someone loses all their prized possessions. Sometimes they suffer physically and mentally. Other times, they suffer because they've lost a loved one.

Many firefighters and paramedics enter this profession because there's something that draws them to it. Some are adrenalin junkies—there's a lot of excitement driving through the streets at high speeds with a siren wailing, and blowing your air horn as you pass through intersections. It is all part of raising your blood pressure for the adrenalin junkies. Fighting fire, treating a shooting victim, rescuing someone who is trapped in a car after an auto accident, rappelling off the side of a building, standing on top of a burning building cutting a hole in the roof—this all feeds the need of the adrenalin junkie. I think part of me is an adrenalin junkie also: I have never tired of it after 37 years.

But there is another side of me and others in this profession. The vast majority of firefighters and paramedics decide to take a career in the fire service or in EMS because they have a deep need to help their fellow man and make a difference. There is tremendous satisfaction that comes from helping others who are sometimes facing the worst moment of their life. As I like to tell new recruits, an 80-year-old lady has lived approximately 29,000 days. And of those 29,000 days, you may be the one standing there, trying to help her on the worst one. She will look to you to alleviate her suffering; comfort and treat her as if she was a member of your own family. Firefighters and paramedics are so trusted that they are the only ones who can walk through someone's back door at three in the morning and enter the bedroom of a young girl in her pajamas without parents giving it a second thought.

This profession has shown me the good, the bad, and the unfortunate. The good is the camaraderie among the firefighters and paramedics inside the fire station, on the scene and off the job. That's why they call it a brotherhood and sisterhood. One of my favorite pictures is of White, Black, Hispanic, and Asian male and female firefighters. The caption under the picture reads: "Brothers and sisters do not always come from the same mother." When a firefighter or EMS professional dies in another part of the country, the word goes out nationwide through numerous sources. We all know about it, and we all feel it. Thousands of firefighters will show up at the funeral of a firefighter who's died in what I call a "battle death"—when they suffered a traumatic death while fighting a fire.

I have love for my family, my wife, my children, and my parents. But I also love the members of my other family—my brother and sister firefighters and paramedics! I love to go to fire stations and visit. We usually sit around, bond, tell stories, laugh, and sometimes bitch about things. Sometimes I am the brunt of a practical joke. Even though I am a chief, and in some circles that is taboo, I laugh with everyone else. It's part of the brother and sisterhood.

They are a unique group of people who make sacrifices in their personal lives to give back to a community. The sacrifices started when they went to school to learn their profession, and the other sacrifices occur when they are away from their family for 24 hours at a time. Some miss Christmas, birthdays, little league games, and other significant events because they work 24-hour shifts. Some don't get off work on time. A call will come in right before the end of your shift and you have to take it, even though you're the one who's supposed to get the kids to school because your better half works. This is inevitable, and you learn to dread hearing those tones go off close to shift change.

Every shift firefighters and EMS may respond to some call where all their skills, training, and education will be put to the test. Maybe not on every call, but some will be beyond the realm of anything they've experienced before.

I can remember a call in Memphis when I was working as a deputy fire chief. Three workers were cleaning and repairing a venting spout at a refinery. You might be familiar with these when you see an orange flame burning brightly whenever you drive past a refinery. This particular day, the venting stack had been shut down, and supposedly all fumes and other products had been removed so there was no possibility of fire. When the workers lit a cutting torch, a fire erupted and burned all three men. One man was burned severely: over 95 percent of his body suffered third degree burns. He was so severely burned that not only was the skin burned off, but tissue had been burned away on his legs to the point I could see bone in some places. He was still conscious because he had worn a face piece for breathing since he was going to be in an enclosed environment. When he was carried down from the platform by firefighters in a stokes basket to the waiting ambulance, I could see the "deer-in-the-headlights" look on the firefighter/paramedic's face. He was a new firefighter/paramedic, so his reaction didn't surprise me. I am sure I had that look early in my career. We in the profession commonly refer to this as the "Stare of Life" as a play on the phrase "Star of Life."

They placed the man on the stretcher and loaded him into the back of the ambulance. The firefighter/paramedic climbed into the back of the ambulance by himself and closed the ambulance doors with a thud of uncertainty. To make sure he was okay, I walked over to the ambulance, opened the back doors, climbed in, and closed the doors behind me. I asked him if he needed anything. He shook his head no as he removed burn sheets and examined the legs and torso. He kept saying, "Oh my God," "Gosh dang," and, "Oh no." He even threw some periodic "tssks" in there for good measure. Finally, I tapped him on the arm and made him look at me. I put my right index finger to my mouth in a gesture to be quiet. The patient was hearing everything he was saying, which doesn't bode well for the patient or their mental status. I told him to load the guy up with some morphine and I would get him some help. I left the ambulance, saw a seasoned firefighter/paramedic, and told him to get in the back of the ambulance, help the other guy, and go to the hospital with them. The man died within a day of being taken to the hospital.

I went to the fire station several days later to check on the firefighter/paramedic and to see if he needed anything. He said he was fine, and I believed him. He'll be much better the second time he encounters something like that. Experience is the best teacher!

The bad is that, no matter what our efforts to save a life or a building on fire are, it's sometimes out of our hands. Sometimes the damage is beyond our control. Even if the patient were in an operating room when they were injured, it wouldn't matter. The wounds would have been mortal. They would have died. The same is true of building fires. A fire almost doubles in size every minute, so the longer the delay before the fire is discovered, the longer it has an opportunity to destroy an entire building or take a life.

It does not matter how much training we have, how much expensive equipment we carry, or how many other resources are available: Sometimes things are only in God's hands. I firmly believe paramedics and firefighters are an instrument of God and He works through us to carry out His will. I always pray that whatever His will, that if the person does pass from this world, that He allows that person to enter Heaven and enjoy His glory and give strength to those left behind to deal with the loss of their loved one. I truly believe God has a master plan and we will never understand it.

The unfortunate are some of the most horrific things I've witnessed. Some I will describe in this book, others I don't want to think about. Being a firefighter and paramedic leaves you many times with haunting dreams that wake you in the middle of the night. Sometimes you see scenes in your head over and over. Sometimes you wake in a cold sweat. On many occasions you find yourself driving down the street with your mind totally immersed in some of the horrific scenes you've seen. Sometimes you find yourself sitting at the stoplight engrossed in things you wish you never witnessed. Someone has to tap their horn behind you to get you moving.

Sometimes I wish my brain could forget the things my eyes have seen. Especially the children! That's what hurts the worst, and what keeps me awake sometimes at night. It's the disastrous things that happen to innocent children who have no control over their destiny that made me rush home to hug my own children when they were small. Some nights they got an extra hug and a stronger and longer squeeze than they expected. They knew something was wrong, but they were too young to realize.

One particular call where I had to "extra hug" my children after I got home occurred on July 17, 1985. Jim McDonald and I, the paramedic-captain who handled the other side of St. Louis, were eating at one of our favorite places on the south side. Our favorite restaurant was Hodaks, a small restaurant and bar on the near south side of St. Louis at the intersection of Gravois and McNair.

As we were just sitting down to some of the best chicken I have ever eaten, our portable radios crackled with information about a shooting in the 4900 block of Magnolia. The dispatcher had the mother on the phone, who had requested three ambulances for three children who had been shot. At one point during the phone conversation, she admitted she had shot them. The dispatchers believed the call was a false alarm since the caller was calm during the entire phone conversation. However, it immediately raised alarm bells in my head. Any mother who would shoot her three children would most likely be mentally unstable, and might very well be calm on the phone. I suspected there was a good probability the call was real.

Jim and I raced to the scene, where we arrived with the first police car and ambulance. At the time of the incident, St. Louis did not have the staging policy for shooting events described earlier.

As I got out of my car, I could see a small boy of about four years old standing at one of the windows of the four-family brick apartment building, screaming out the window. I thought, *My God, my fears are realized. This is a real call.*

Scurrying as fast as I could, I helped the ambulance crew by grabbing some of the medical equipment and carrying it into the building and up the stairs to the second-floor apartment. As we entered the worn, green tile in the hallway and neared the wooden steps leading to the second floor, we passed the boy, who was still screaming and crying at the window of the landing halfway up the stairs to the second floor. Unfortunately, I had seen the look in this boy's eyes many times, and in many situations. I knew what awaited me through the doorframe of the apartment would be horrifying.

My instinct was correct. The first thing I saw was a blonde-haired girl about the same age and size as the boy, lying on her stomach in the front room. There was a small pool of blood around her head and it tinted part of her hair red. She was unconscious, and thankfully didn't know what was going on around her.

The police officer entered the apartment before us and was leading a young, handcuffed woman into the hallway as we were walking in. She had a blank stare on her face and looked straight ahead with no expression as she closely passed me. I took a quick glance and saw two more children lying in the middle room, which is a bedroom. Both also appeared to be shot in the head, as blood similarly dyed their blonde hair. I stood there for a second. I couldn't help but think they looked like my daughter, who was about the same age. My daughter also has blonde hair.

I immediately radioed the dispatcher requesting two more ambulances, since we had three critical victims. The two paramedics who responded on the initial ambulance began triaging. We had three females ages 1, 4, and 7, all shot in the head with a rifle. As I continued to stare in disbelief at these children who'd been shot for no apparent reason, my anger rose. How could any person do this to children who were probably doing nothing but playing? How could a mother do this to her own children? I'd seen too many gunshots to the head, and knew that since they were unconscious, with brain matter showing, their chances of surviving were about zero.

Our first priority as paramedics is to establish an airway and make sure air is flowing through that airway. We have a saying, "Air goes in and out. Blood goes round and round. Anything different is bad." It sounds simple, but it's so true.

All three children were shot in the head and unconscious. All three were still alive, but were obviously in critical condition.

Gunshot wounds to the head usually do not have a good outcome. Either the person dies, or they suffer some type of serious brain damage. But I have come to learn in 37 years and some 3,500+ shooting calls that bullets can do strange things—including the cab driver I treated who was shot point blank in the face in a robbery attempt, and the bullet never entered his skull. It hit just to the right of the nose and below the eye, followed along the surface of the skull to the right side and exited by the ear without entering the skull. That cab driver certainly had his guardian angel riding with him that night.

Or the woman who was found by her husband with another man, and her husband shot her six times in the head with a .44 Magnum. I found her sitting in her car, calm and lucid, having a normal conversation with me as I was treating her. The shape of her head was so disconcerted that it did not look like a normal-shaped skull anymore, but she was conscious and having a normal conversation with me. She survived!

I started working on the 4-year-old girl, who was starting to show bruising and swelling around her left eye—a bad sign. She was having trouble breathing, and was in a fight for her life. As I tried to stabilize her, my thoughts returned to my daughter, and my anger rose again. But I couldn't let my emotions take over. I needed to concentrate. I had to remain calm. I had to remain a professional. I wouldn't do this child any good if I lost control.

I stabilized my emotions and focused on saving her life. Shortly thereafter, Susan, a police officer whom I had known for a while, leaned over and asked, "Gary, is there anything I can do?" I looked up to see her red hair and friendly face.

"What the hell happened?" I asked.

Susan said the mother shot her children because she was worried about going on welfare. What? She's worried about going on welfare? No way! Now I got angry again! Who the hell shoots their own flesh and blood because they're worried about going on welfare? I'd heard that people who plead mental insanity on criminal charges spend a little time in a mental hospital, and then get released. I'm not a mental health expert, but it's hard for me to comprehend that they can't rationalize between right and wrong—especially when you murder your three children. I would think maternal instinct would override insanity, but I am neither a psychiatrist nor a psychologist.

The first ambulance took off with one of the girls while Jim and I remained on the scene trying to stabilize the others. There wasn't much we could do except maintain the airway and make sure they kept breathing. They needed an operating room as soon as possible. Just like if your arm or foot was subjected to trauma, the brain swells when damaged. But unfortunately, the skull acts like a sealed container, and the brain has nowhere to go when it swells.

Eventually, almost simultaneously, the two other ambulance crews arrived. I told them over the radio not to bring a stretcher—just bring a backboard and we'll strap them down. The girls were small enough we could carry them down the stairs, so it would be a waste of time to try and bring a stretcher upstairs. We needed to get them to a hospital as soon as possible.

I picked one of them up. As I looked at her face, I couldn't help but wonder what moments of pure panic she went through after her sister was shot and she saw her mother coming toward her with a gun. Maybe she was the first to be shot and never saw it coming. The way the children were scattered around the apartment, it looked like they were running to get away. This poor child! As I had done many times before, I said a short, silent prayer to myself: "God, please grant this child healing and peace, and allow her to live the life that she should have enjoyed."

As I headed down the steps with the child strapped to the backboard, me at the head and another paramedic at the other end, I noticed that the small boy who was originally crying at the landing on the stairway was gone. I wondered who he was. Was he in the apartment? Why was he spared? Was he able to get away?

I reached the front door of the apartment building and saw lots of bystanders from neighboring homes who had gathered in front of the apartment building to see what the commotion was. When you look out your window and see three ambulances and multiple police cars, you know something big has happened. Behind me was one of the ambulance crews, and behind them was the other crew and Jim, who was carrying the last child to the ambulance on the backboard. As we headed down the sidewalk, I saw some of the women bystanders clasp hands over their mouths as they saw the small girls with bandages on their heads being whisked to the ambulances, and us trying to breathe for them by squeezing a bag to put air into their lungs. I'm sure they recognized the girls, and probably saw them playing outside in the past.

We got into the back of the ambulance and laid the backboard onto the stretcher. The other paramedic helped strap her down with the stretcher straps. While I maintained the airway, the other paramedic hooked up the heart monitor and got equipment to start an IV. The other paramedic slammed the back doors of the ambulance after announcing we were heading for Children's Hospital, which is about five minutes away. I shouted at the paramedic, "Give us a nice, smooth ride!"

The paramedic put the ambulance in drive, turned on the siren, and headed to the hospital. The paramedic in the back of the ambulance with me called in a radio report to Children's Hospital to let them know we were en route, and to give the patient's condition. This allows the hospital to prepare for our arrival and get a team in place that will take over patient care from us. The voice on the other end of the radio acknowledged our transmission and let us know they would be ready.

By this point, the small child was struggling for life, and still unconscious. Her chances, along with her two sisters, weren't promising. Her breathing was obviously slowing; the only thing separating her from death was the bag-valve mask I hooked up to an oxygen tank. With every squeeze of the bag with my hand, the oxygen gas was pushed into her lungs. I gripped it tighter over her face to make sure no air could leak out.

As we raced down one of the major streets of St. Louis, riding in the back of an ambulance is like an amusement ride—although there was nothing fun about this particular trip. The sensation is different. You have no visual of where you are going, and many times you find yourself rocking from side to side. You can only look out the back window and see where you've been. And if the person driving the ambulance suddenly slams on the brakes—and you can't see *why* he is slamming on the brakes— you immediately brace yourself for impact. Unfortunately, when you're working on a patient in the back of an ambulance, you're not wearing a seatbelt most times. You're either sitting on the bench seat, leaning over to treat the patient, or you're standing as the ambulance moves at speeds usually above 50 miles per hour. If the ambulance hits something and suddenly stops, you're still going 50 miles per hour or more. This usually isn't a good outcome for the paramedic standing, as he suddenly becomes a flying projectile. More than one paramedic has been killed or seriously injured this way.

We arrived at the hospital and removed the stretcher with the small, lifeless child, who still looked like my daughter. It was hard to look at her. The blood had now soaked through the bandage we'd secured to her head and continued to tinge her blonde hair ever more red. We headed inside the emergency department, all the time trying to ventilate the child who had now stopped breathing.

A nurse immediately met us at the door and directed us to Room 3. As we moved swiftly down the hall, I could see a team of doctors and nurses in Room 1 already working on the sister taken in the first ambulance. Unfortunately, they were doing CPR, which isn't a good prognosis.

A second team of dedicated doctors, nurses, and other technicians were waiting for us in Room 3. They all had donned gowns, gloves, and surgical masks, ready to do battle to save this girl's life.

We moved the girl from our stretcher to the hospital bed as I immediately rattled off a report for the doctor. "Four-year-old female, shot once in the head, no exit wound found, no other history that we know of, blood pressure is 80 palpable, pulse is 56, and respirations upon our arrival were 16 but she has now stopped breathing. The left pupil appears blown." The small girl was suddenly and completely surrounded by a team who would use everything they have learned and every piece of equipment they possess to save this poor, unfortunate girl's life.

The two paramedics and I grabbed our equipment and immediately left the room to give them space to work. Our job was done! Her outcome still remained in God's hands.

Tragically, none of these three little beautiful girls survived.

I finally learned their names in the newspaper the next day—Melissa, age 21 months; Danielle, age 4; and Crystal, age 7. Their mother's name was Lavenia Goree,[1] and she was 25 years old.

It was Danielle with us in the back of the ambulance. What I didn't ever know was her favorite color, teddy bear, television show, or food. But

I was at there at the end for Danielle; the most she ever did wrong in life was probably fight with her sister over a toy.

I also learned that her mother said on the 9-1-1 call that she didn't want to go back on welfare because she was concerned she couldn't continue caring for her children. She had no history of mental disease and took great care of the girls, according to neighbors, which included always dressing them in pretty dresses, and buying them treats when the ice cream truck came by. One neighbor said in a newspaper article the girls were "always well-dressed and well-fed and showed no signs of abuse."

Today, Danielle would have been about thirty-three years old. Chances are she would have had children of her own, and would be enjoying life. Her sisters would have had children, and they would play together. Unfortunately, that never happened. Instead, their mother was convicted of three counts of first degree murder without the possibility of parole.

The St. Louis community poured their hearts out to these three girls. People came forward and donated cemetery plots. Funeral homes and cemeteries offered caskets and other services for free. Churches offered to conduct religious services. The outpouring of support for three little girls that no one knew until their mother took their lives was overwhelming.

This job hardens you. If you took in all the pain and suffering we see it would just destroy you, so we try not to let it affect us. But every so often a call, like this one with the three little girls, just breaks your heart! These you never get rid of. This is one of the hardest calls of my career. The sights, the sounds, and the smell of the blood still haunt me. While everything at the time seemed to happen so fast, it also seems like I can relive it in slow motion. Paramedics who were on this call still vividly remember it 29 years later, and it torments them to this day. I was not the only one affected by this loss of innocence. Every paramedic and police officer on that scene experienced untold emotions. Paramedic Charlene Jansen still tells me how deeply she was affected by this call. Like me, she has seen far worse situations and terrible things in her career, but this was one of the worst for her. Another paramedic, Tim, visited the three girl's graves every year on the anniversary of their deaths, even though he wasn't on the call. And I know a nurse at Children's Hospital who worked on one of the little girls who never wore that set of hospital scrubs again. We carry many scars from the calls we have handled, and many times they are not physical scars.

These days I am used to seeing death. But, there are great moments also—like the times you deliver babies. The first baby I ever delivered was by a policeman's flashlight on the third floor of a cold, vacant home in north St. Louis. A homeless family was squatting there. Not only did I deliver the baby, but since we would have trouble getting her down the stairs, I decided to stay and deliver the placenta.

There is also joy when you track one of your patients after you deliver them to the hospital and find out they were released to go home. There are the occasional letters of thanks; someone who stops by the firehouse to leave their appreciation in the form of cookies or cake, or just someone who says thank you when they see you somewhere in uniform. However, no amount of good moments can make you forget the really bad times, since they vastly outnumber the good times.

One of the proudest moments in my career happened in 2007, when I was not even working. My parents had just celebrated their 60th wedding anniversary in the Cathedral Basilica in St. Louis. Afterward my family, including my brother and his three sons, went to the Bevo Mill restaurant in south St. Louis for some good German eating. The Bevo Mill restaurant sits on the corner of where Gravois, Morganford, and Delor Streets meet, and is a familiar landmark with its rather large windmill on the front of the building, and architectural design of a Dutch mill. Built by the Busch family of the Anheuser-Busch brewers in 1916 as a banquet hall, it conveys German heritage with a large, open hall for restaurant seating, which is where my family sat to celebrate.

On this particular Sunday afternoon, the whole family was together and eating our meal and chitchatting. Suddenly, I heard a commotion at the table next to us and I saw the restaurant manager trying to do the Heimlich maneuver on a man who looked to be about 65 years old, slumped over at his table. The Heimlich maneuver is used on choking victims to squeeze the diaphragm, which then expels the air pressure in the lungs to dislodge the foreign body object in the throat. There were five other people at his table; it looked to be three couples who went to dinner. They looked concerned and alarmed as they watched the restaurant manager valiantly attempt to dislodge whatever the man was choking on. Two of the women were visibly crying and, every so often, let out a scream.

The screams were what alerted me to what was happening, but by this point, most of the restaurant had been alerted to the distress.

I immediately got up and asked the restaurant manager what was wrong. He told me the man was choking on some beef, as he tried another Heimlich maneuver with the man sitting slumped, unconscious, over the table. In front of him was his plate of roast beef, some mashed potatoes and green peas. The restaurant manager asked if I was a doctor. I told him no, I'm a firefighter/paramedic, and to let me try.

I got behind the man and put my right fist on his chest just below his Xiphoid process and above his navel. I grabbed my fist with my left hand and forcibly pressed in his abdomen with thrusts in an attempt to use the air in his lungs to push the obstruction out. It wasn't working! I told the restaurant manager we needed to get this man to the floor. I grabbed the upper part of his body and the manager grabbed his legs. By this time a crowd had gathered around us, including some of the waitresses. One of them leaned forward and said she had called 9-1-1 and the fire department was on the way.

After we got the man on the floor, I could see he was in serious trouble. He was unconscious, blue, and not breathing. All the signs that is inconsistent with life. The women at the table remained in their seats and continued crying as one let out an occasional agonizing scream that pierced your soul. The two other men also remain seated, as though they were awaiting permission from someone to get out of their chairs. One of the men kept coaching the unconscious man, saying, "Come on, Herman, you can do it."

With Herman on the floor I was able to do abdominal thrusts. This procedure again uses the air pressure in the lungs to push out the lodged material. This was also unsuccessful, so I started suspecting, based on his age, that he might not be choking, but merely had a heart attack and slumped over while eating. Sometimes, people who are eating and have a heart attack are mistaken for a choking victim. I checked. He still had a pulse, but he was not breathing.

I asked his companions what happened, and they said he was eating and started choking. I asked them to describe what happened, since I wasn't sure they'd know how to tell if someone was choking versus having a heart attack. One of the men told me that he was eating and suddenly dropped his fork and grabbed his throat. I asked the man if he said anything, and he said no. I asked this question purposely since a person who is choking cannot talk or say anything since the airway is blocked. No air can move past the vocal cords, which make the sounds we hear when someone talks.

At this point I was truly suspecting choking as the main culprit. I asked the restaurant manager to help me sit him up, since I wanted to do some back blows. We sat him up and I delivered four sharp cracks to the center of his back. We laid him back down and I checked his airway. He still wasn't breathing. I checked for a carotid pulse, which he still had, but I knew it wouldn't last long, because after someone stops breathing for a while, the heart will eventually shut down.

I opened his mouth and reached in as deeply as I could with two fingers. I felt some foreign material and grabbed it with two fingers to pull it out. Sure enough, it was unchewed roast beef.

I did another abdominal thrust but he still wasn't breathing, so I reached into his mouth again. I opened his mouth and reached deep inside with two fingers again and pulled more roast beef from his mouth. I put my ear close to his mouth and heard air moving, albeit slow and shallow. However, his breathing became deeper and more rapid as I continued to monitor him, and his color returned from blue to pink.

I looked over and my entire family, including my dad and mom, were watching me. I gave them the thumbs up with a smile.

By this time I could hear sirens, which I assumed belonged to the engine company coming as the first responder. The sound stopped just outside the restaurant door. As I continued to monitor the man who was now breathing normally and starting to wake up, a lady bent down and told me she was a nurse. She asked if there was anything she could do. I told her everything was under control and he was breathing again.

Herman was starting to wake up, so I bent down next to his ear and told him to relax and breathe normally. I kept my fingers on his radial pulse, which was beating good and strong, and told his dinner guests he was breathing again. One of the ladies started thanking God out loud while the other lady was still crying; this had been terribly emotional for her.

The four-person engine company came in with all its medical equipment, and I thought how ironic this was.

***

On the orders of Fire Chief Neil Svetanics back in 1994, I'd started the first-ever first responder program in St. Louis. Prior to this, no fire engines responded to medical calls. We had to train over 700 firefighters to the emergency medical responder level, put medical equipment on the fire engines, and change procedures. This radical change didn't come easy, since most people are resistant to change—especially one that involves doing more work. Before the start of each training session (which totaled 48 hours of training), I spoke to the class of firefighters for about an hour and talked about the need for medical training, and to get more involved in medical responses. I'd like to think I won over and convinced almost everyone of the need to save lives through medical response on first responder runs, but I know there are those few who would resist change no matter how noble it was.

But eventually the first responder program started after everyone was trained, and on this day, if I had not been there, medically trained firefighters would have been at this man's side within four minutes of being dispatched.

As a result of the success of the first responder program, I was nominated by Chief Svetanics for the Mayor's Award for Improved Level of Service in 1996, and was honored to become its only recipient of nearly 4,500 city employees.

***

As we waited for the ambulance in the restaurant, the man was now fully conscious. I told him to lay still and just relax. One of the firefighters put him on some oxygen by putting a nasal cannula around his ears and nose. The ambulance arrived with the paramedics. They took the man's blood pressure and hooked him up to their EKG machine. His blood pressure was fine, and his EKG was looking great. The decision was made to sit him up. We helped him raise up his head and upper body so that he was sitting on the floor. When asked how he felt, he told us that he felt fine. The decision was then made to sit him in the chair. Two firefighters grabbed him under his armpits and raised him to his feet. He stood there for a second, and the paramedic again took a set of vital signs and asked him how he felt again. He indicated he felt fine, so they sat him in the chair, still hooked up to the oxygen and the EKG monitor. The five people at his table started talking to him. "Herman, we thought you were dead!" I thought to myself, "He *was* dead five minutes ago."

The paramedics fully explained to him that he was choking, and his airway had to be cleared out since he wasn't breathing, so it might be best that he go to the hospital and get his throat checked out.

The paramedic asked him if he wanted to go to the hospital to get checked out and he said no. He just wanted to go home. They offered a trip to the hospital to him one more time. Again, he refused. When a person refuses a trip to the hospital, they have to sign a refusal form that's mainly a legality to protect the paramedics and the department if something later happens to the patient. If they drop dead later or suffer some complications, the burden is on the patient, since they refused to be transported to the hospital, if they were fully informed of what may happen before signing.

Nonetheless, Herman signed the refusal form. I would like to suspect he was embarrassed by the whole situation and was looking for a fast exit, since all eyes in the restaurant were on him. He put on his coat and his remaining party of five people got up from the table and they all left together. I stood there in astonishment—he was dead less than 10 minutes ago, and now he was walking out the door. I didn't see anybody pay a bill, but I know this wasn't faked to get a free dinner. He was definitely blue, not breathing, and had roast beef lodged in his throat. Besides, nobody had finished their meal.

The excitement was now over. The firefighters and paramedics packed up their equipment. I gave them a business card with my name on it for their report. We said our good-byes, and they headed out the door. The waitresses began clearing their table and the restaurant manager turned to me, shook my hand and said thanks. I thought his appreciation came from the fact that he was in a dire situation and I was his cavalry coming over the hill. If I had not been there, he would have been hard pressed to know what to do. I'm sure he probably had taken some basic CPR course in his training to be a restaurant manager, but it might have been two years ago, and he had never been put in a situation to use his training. I could tell he was deeply thankful for my efforts. I was sure the restaurant didn't need the publicity of someone choking to death in a crowded dining hall in the middle of a Sunday afternoon.

I returned to the table where my family was. They had seen me in action—had seen what the many years of training, education, and years of going on thousands of calls had given me the gift to do. I am sure my dad and mom felt immense pride during that moment. My son, who was just a teenager at the time, told me he was so scared he was shaking while he was watching what was transpiring just one table over.

Shortly after I returned to the table, the restaurant manager came over to the table with a $100 gift certificate to come back and eat at the restaurant anytime we wanted. I tried to give it back to him, but he would not hear of it. He was insistent that I take the gift certificate. It was at this point that I truly knew how appreciative he was for my intervention.

There is no other feeling like it in the world when you know that you have saved someone's life. God made the final determination, and I was merely an instrument of him. I sought no recognition for what I did. I considered it something I was trained to do. I was in the right spot at the right time, and I did nothing that any other firefighter or paramedic would have if they'd been in the same situation.

This was not the only life I have saved in my career. If I had to count them up, I would not even know the number, since I don't keep track of them. It's something I'm trained to do and, put in the right situation, I would perform as trained. But this saved life was unique in the fact that my family was a witness.

Even though I don't know the number of lives I've saved, there have been moments that I will never be able to shake from my memory. There was an older lady whose husband died, and several months later we got called back to her house where we found she had committed suicide by hanging herself from a door transom, wearing her wedding dress.

Equally as bizarre was the suicide call I had on the south side of St. Louis where a person shot themselves in the head in the confessional of a Catholic church. The priest went to the confessional on a Saturday afternoon to hear confessions, opened the door, and found the dead man where the priest would normally be sitting.

Another lady, whose husband suddenly died in their home, was in such shock and disbelief she was more worried who was going to keep the grass so beautifully cut. It's all she talked about the whole time we were there. Apparently, the husband was very particular about his yard, and would manicure the lawn perfectly each day in the summer. I have to admit, the lawn was absolutely beautiful. It looked like a carpet with its deep, green grass, no weeds, and perfectly trimmed and contoured blades. Some 20 years later, my travels sometimes took me past that house. The house and yard sat next to an alley I could drive down, look to my left, and see the yard behind the wire cyclone fence. These days, it looks absolutely terrible, with weeds and grass growing over the sidewalk and between the cracks. The garage shingles were starting to fall off the side also. Thankfully, the man who lived there does not have to see what has become of his beautiful lawn.

Then there was the man who set himself on fire one day, even drinking the gasoline to make sure he burned internally. Someone shot some pictures of the scene and gave me copies. You can see me, and other firefighters and paramedics, in the several series of pictures, tending to the man. The burns are ghastly, and beyond anything I can describe. He was still alive when we got to him but I could never tell if he was unconscious, because, although he was non-responsive, his body would badly jerk from time to time, almost like he was responding to pain.

He eventually died, and we never found a suicide note. It always seems like those intent on committing suicide seldom leave a note, and never call or tell anyone. We just find their body—sometimes much later than we should.

That happened in 1982. The St. Louis Cardinals were making their run toward the pennant race when we got a call for a jumper on the MacArthur Bridge over the Mississippi River. Since I was already in the downtown area for the ballgame, I got to the bridge relatively fast. We pulled up on Wharf Street below the bridge and saw a man sitting on the superstructure some 60 feet or more above the car deck. Just as we stepped out of our vehicles and looked up at him some 250 feet or more above us, he propelled himself off the steel where he was perched. As he was falling, his leg hit the handrail on the car deck and detached from his body. He and his leg both tumbled into the river. He came up for a brief moment, and then disappeared below the waters. We never did recover his body, even after searching the river until dark. I asked Homicide Detective Sergeant Steve Jacobsmeyer for months afterward if his body was ever found. Steve would tell me that they had not recovered his body.

This guy was determined to commit suicide, but never left a note. If he'd had reservations, he would have talked to us for a while. I watched others jump from the different bridges along the river over the years, but this one was the most dramatic.

Jumping from a bridge of this height is like hitting concrete. I can remember being on the St. Louis fireboat one day when we pulled a jumper from the river who had just jumped. We found him slightly downstream from the bridge, and he was already dead. As I and some firefighters pulled him into the boat, I started to examine him, and I found the entire right side of his chest caved in. It was clear where he had hit the river with his body. As I said, it looked like he had hit concrete.

The Mississippi River is good for swallowing up bodies and never giving them back. There were quite a few bodies that were never recovered from the Mississippi River after we knew the person had drowned, committed suicide, or were thrown into the river after being murdered.

One of the stranger incidents of disappearance included a helicopter with a student and an instructor who crashed into the river, right next to the bank of the river, after taking off from getting fuel at the foot of Biddle Street in St. Louis. Numerous witnesses told us the helicopter went into the river after lifting off from a fuel depot at the river's edge. They swore it had crashed at the water's edge. The student and the instructor were strapped in their seats. The helicopter, along with its passengers, disappeared into the river, and nobody swam to the surface. Searches with divers and sonar never found the helicopter or its occupants. It just disappeared, and has never been found to this day.

Of course, there was the time a letter arrived at our administrative headquarters written by a man who lived in the Dogtown area of St. Louis. The letter said he had committed suicide, gave his address, and noted his back door was unlocked. He wanted someone to come and get his body. We sent paramedics and police to the address and found the man inside, already dead. He just wanted to make sure his body didn't decompose for days or weeks before he was discovered. He also left final instructions on whom to notify, and final preparations for his body.

But there was one call in the Dogtown area of St. Louis that will always gnaw at my memory. It's one of the estimated 5,000 fire scenes I've been to—but this one I will never forget.

One crisp fall morning in St. Louis, we got dispatched to a house fire in the Dogtown area, with a report of people trapped. Dogtown is in the western section of St. Louis, and just south of Forest Park—a large city park with lots of attractions, including the St. Louis Zoo. Dogtown supposedly got its name because of the dog-eating Igorot tribesmen from the Philippines who camped in that area during the 1904 St. Louis World's Fair. The tribesmen would sneak into the yards of the sparsely populated area at the time and steal the dogs. Another story says the name stems from the workers from the old steel and brick works, who kept many dogs around for security purposes.

Even though there were scattered homes throughout the area at the time the stories emerged as to how this area got its name, the area now is mainly filled with one-story wood-framed houses and duplexes that were built after World War II to accommodate the population explosion. The home on fire was such a structure. A duplex is a single building divided into two different homes on the same floor. They are usually no larger than 1,500 square feet. Try picturing two small apartments in one building on the same floor.

As I was driving there as a paramedic/captain in my station wagon, it was evident there was a working fire, which was confirmed by the first-arriving engine company. The plume of black smoke could be seen from a distance. When I arrived on the scene, the first thing I saw was a man sitting on the curb, with a small boy who looked to be about two years old under one arm, and cradling a small infant in the other arm. But this was no ordinary man, boy, and baby. This man had no clothes on, and his body was burned from head to toe. Burns covered over 90 percent of his body. Much of his skin had already burned off, and in other places the skin was sloughing off, like when you would pull off a glove and it is hanging half-on and half-off your hand.

Nothing is more ghastly or has more of an impact on me than seeing a burnt body. The pain and suffering they must have endured and still may be going through is beyond any description. However, usually when they're burnt this badly they don't feel much pain, because all their nerve endings are destroyed. They seem to function just like an ordinary person, just a burned person.

He was sitting there on the curb with what appeared to be his children, because the engine companies were making valiant efforts to get inside the blazing home. Nobody was tending to him because there was still a report of more children trapped inside.

Like his father, the small boy who he had his arm wrapped around also had very little clothing on and was severely burned. The baby had some burns, but was not as bad as the other two. They were all alert and fully conscious of their surroundings. When people are burned from head to toe, they have no body hair left, and their head is mainly bald. Sometimes there's a small patch of hair left on the head, or you can see where the hair has fizzled in the heat. There's evidence of charring on their body, and in some places you see patches of red from the lower layers of skin. It would be the same if you badly scraped off the outer layer of skin and all that was visible is the red of the lower skin layers.

The small boy stared straight ahead with a 1,000-yard stare as his small body shivered either from the shock, the coolness of the morning, or both. He never said a word. He sat on the curb and virtually stared in disbelief at what he had gone through. I am sure it seemed surreal.

As I walked up to the man and what were apparently his two children, the man looked deeply into my eyes. His only words to me were, "Take care of my children." I can still see him looking at me and saying those words. That look, those words, and that image of them sitting on the curb have not left my memory after all these years. He cared nothing about himself. His main focus was only for his children, one of which was suffering from ghastly burns.

That scene and his words have haunted me for over 25 years, mostly because of the backstory I learned later. Apparently the man was a divorced father of four, with full custody. He was in the backyard doing some work, and heard the children hollering for him in the house. As he turned around, to his shock and horror, he saw flames and smoke coming from the small duplex home. Without hesitation and without any regard for his safety, he ran through the back door of the home, into the flames, and searched until he found one child. He carried that child through the flames to the outside and returned back to look for the other children. A passerby also made entry and found the 2-month-old infant near the door and carried him outside. The father ran back into the flames looking for the other children! Apparently when the father could no longer stand the pain from his burning flesh, he returned outside without the children. It was at this point he gathered the 2-year-old boy and his infant son and sat on the curb, awaiting the firefighters, and knowing he probably lost the two children who remained in the home.

We later found the other children in the home severely burned and dead. One child was near the kitchen door, and was just a few small steps from the freedom of the flames.

It takes tremendous courage and perseverance to run into a burning home not only once, but multiple times. Each time the heat from the fire and burning of his flesh must have been severe, but he pushed on. Don't be fooled by what you see on television. The heat from a fire can be unbearable. Try getting close to a blazing bonfire and see how long you can stand there—and that's only a small fire. Imagine the heat of an entire house on fire.

The more fuel (wood and contents of the house), the higher the BTUs being produced.

I didn't have to tell him what happened to his other boys. He already knew! He didn't ask, and I didn't volunteer. His only concern at this point was for his two remaining children, who still hadn't spoken a word. The baby was not even crying. When the ambulances arrived, they were all loaded separately and transported to local burn centers in St. Louis. I learned the next day that the two-year-old boy died later that evening, and the father died within 24 hours. The infant baby survived. I said silent prayers for all of them, also.

Unfortunately, the cause of the fire was ruled as one of the children playing with matches. The remnants of a burnt mattress were found outside the home, and some burnt diapers were found in the bathtub. It appeared that there'd been previous fires and other forms of combustion had been ruled out, including electrical.

It's rare for someone to survive long-term after being severely burned. If they survive and die early, like this father and his son, it is because all the fluid from their cells shifts to the area outside the cells and, in essence, they die from loss of fluid volume in their body and from shock. Some die from damaged lungs after breathing in super-heated smoke and gases. If they do survive this initial critical period, their biggest danger is dying from infection months later. Sometimes it's a blessing that they die early and don't have to endure the months of treatment and operations, only to die from an infection.

The mental impact these types of calls have on you can be devastating. I still talk to the paramedic who transported the father and the small baby to the hospital. For purposes of this book, I will not use his real name; I will call him Bill. Even to this day, over 25 years later, Bill can describe almost every second of that scene, and every action he took en route to the hospital to save their lives. He vividly describes looking into the father's blue eyes. Bill knew the father would eventually die, and that the father knew he was eventually going to die—and the father knew looking into Bill's eyes that Bill knew he was going to die. Even then, the father kept saying, "Take care of my children."

When Bill requested some type of intervention in the form of a critical incident stress debriefing, the chief told him debriefings were only for the timid and the weak. Bill was so deeply affected by this that he eventually turned to drugs as an escape mechanism to deal with the pain he was experiencing. He wanted to forget everything he saw, smelled, and heard that day. The pain was too much for him. It took him years to kick his addiction and find peace, but eventually he would do just that.

But it is small things that you remember. The first time you did CPR. The first family or person you had to tell their loved one was dead. I still remember working a cardiac arrest on a mother in a home in south St. Louis, and all six of her children and the husband were kneeling in the room saying the "Our Father" prayer out loud over and over as we tried in desperation to save the lady's life. Unfortunately, she didn't make it.

I've had people kiss their loved one as we transported them out the door during a cardiac arrest. We stop so they can give them one final kiss. It almost gets to a point where you stop looking at the faces, because you don't want to remember.

CHAPTER 2

I SEE ADDRESSES AND INTERSECTIONS!

I always think of the movie starring Bruce Willis called *Sixth Sense* and the line by the little boy: "I see dead people." I don't see dead people—I see intersections and addresses. Although I silently think of those intersections and addresses, I get irritated sometimes when someone asks me about my job.

It usually happens at a party or get-together. It happened at a wedding reception with some people at my table, just as this book was being edited. Usually someone will walk up to me with a wine glass or beer in their hand and say, "So, you're a fireman, right?"

I start to rattle the ice in my glass, since I'm sensitive to the term *fireman* because it sounds sexist. I'll usually say, "Well, I'm a firefighter and a paramedic, yes!"

Then they'll say something stupid like, "You guys just sit around all day, eat, watch television, and sleep, right?" And then to emphasize their point, they'll make a fist and lightly give you a fist bump to the upper arm near your shoulder—as though we are bonding in some fashion.

At this point I usually give a look of "You have no clue, do you?" But I usually say, "You're right. In fact, we even find time to work out when our personal trainers come into the fire station, and the lobster tail we eat every night is to die for!"

Not taking the hint that I really do not want to have this conversation, this person will go even deeper by asking, "You guys earn a lot of money, too, don't you?"

I usually give a slight little grin and look to where I can escape to a bathroom or to refresh my drink. I tell him "No, we don't earn a lot of money. Most firefighters and paramedics have to work second and third jobs on their off days to make ends meet."

But usually before I can get away, the atomic bomb question comes: "So, what's the worst thing you've ever seen?"

Trying to get out of answering the question, I typically answer by saying, "I have seen so many horrible things I don't even know which one is the worst."

This usually prompts them to say, "Come on, man, tell me," as those within earshot usually start inching closer like those E. F. Hutton commercials from the 1980s, or those who rubberneck past an accident to see if they can see something gory.

Okay, you want to hear it? Here it goes! I can't drive through an intersection or past certain streets without thinking of calls I've been on or the things I've seen there. I try to forget them, but they're constant visible reminders to me every time I drive past them. For instance, I can't drive down Interstate 55 in south St. Louis and not think of everything I have seen from the city line to downtown. The distance between these two points is about eight miles, and I can't drive more than one mile without a reminder of some call I have been on along the stretch. At the start of the city line, at River des Peres and Interstate 55, I'll never forget the man whose tractor trailer crashed over the rail and he was about to plummet 60 feet below. He attempted to jump out of the cab but missed, and went over the rail with the tractor trailer, which landed on his head. All we initially saw was his body from his shoulders down sticking out from underneath the trailer.

A little further north down the highway at Holly Hills, I can't help but think about the guy who committed suicide by jumping out from behind concrete pillars in the center of the highway while a tractor trailer was barreling down the highway. He got hit by several other cars and at least one other tractor trailer. The different parts of him had to be picked up off the highway with shovels.

Further north on the highway, I remember two guys on their motorcycles who were riding to work when a van crossed over the grassy median of the highway and turned on its side and was sliding down the highway the wrong way. One of the motorcycle riders hit the windshield straight on. He was decapitated from the door post of the van and the motorcycle was propelled inside the van, killing the two front passengers. This was before they put concrete barriers in the center. Back in the day, the only thing that separated northbound vehicles from southbound vehicles was a grassy median.

Further down the highway at Bates, I can't forget the car that ran off the highway and went down the middle embankment between the north and south lane bridges, finally landing on Bates Street, killing the driver. It took at least 45 minutes to cut the dead driver out of the car.

Going further north, I can't stop thinking about the three kids in a car that went off the highway between the north and southbound lanes of the highway and crashed through a narrow gap between the elevated sections of the north and southbound lanes over Zepp Street. They landed some 60 feet below in a vacant lot. Witnesses said one person was hanging out the passenger car window, peeing, when the driver lost control at a high speed, turned on its right side where the guy was hanging out the window, and then ping-ponged between guardrails before slipping through a narrow crack between both elevated sections of the highway. While we were on the scene trying to extricate the victims from the car, a police officer pulled up and said a driver reported hitting part of a body on the highway. The driver was right. It was part of the guy who was hanging out the window, trapped between the car and the pavement when the vehicle turned on its side. The biggest part of him we found was a portion of his upper chest torso. There was tissue parts scattered all over the highway.

Further north on the highway in front of the Anheuser-Busch Brewery at Arsenal Street, there was the fatal and fiery crash of a man I knew and worked with many times. He was the St. Louis Parks Commissioner. He was rear-ended by another car, which caused his car to catch fire while he was trapped inside the car. He burned to death. Ironically, I had treated him earlier in my career when he was shot in the leg during a robbery at his home in the Lafayette Square area of the city.

I also remember working a call at Arsenal Street to extricate Don Miller [2] from a helicopter. Known as Officer Don Miller, he was a local celebrity who worked as a helicopter traffic reporter for the highest-rated radio station in St. Louis at the time. His daily reports came from a helicopter, and he would routinely report morning and evening traffic flows throughout the metropolitan area over the radio station. He and his pilot crashed in the middle of the interstate in 1978 during rush-hour traffic.

A picture the next day showed up on the front page of the *St. Louis Post Dispatch* with me working inside the bubble of the helicopter to free Don Miller, who suffered a broken back.

Half a mile down the highway at Sidney Street, an off-duty police officer in uniform collided head-on with three teenagers. I recognized the dead officer from being on calls with him before. One of the teenagers had also died, but two were still alive. I was angry at the teenagers on the scene, since I assumed they were probably drinking and going the wrong way on the highway on a Friday night. As it turned out, the police officer was a heavy drinker, and was the one to drive the wrong direction down the highway. The teenagers were outstanding students who were just driving to the Muny Opera in Forest Park to pick up one of their friends who worked there. I really felt bad about that later, and decided I would try not to judge people when an incident happened.

About this time, those who've gathered are sitting with their mouths open, not even capable of taking a drink for fear they'll miss something. Others constantly drink to compensate for their uneasiness. A few can't take it, and usually drift away.

I continue down the highway with my stories. I tell them about the guy on the motorcycle who hit the metal guardrail with such force he was cut in half where Interstates 44 and 55 come together. Or what about the poor girl from France who was only here a couple days? The people she was in the car with were caught in such a ferocious thunderstorm they pulled off the side of the highway near Park Avenue to wait it out. Unfortunately, they parked just below a seven-story brick building that butted up next to the fence of the highway. The bricks were loose near the top and the fury of the thunderstorm made about three stories of bricks collapse directly onto the car. It crushed the car like a pancake. As we attempted to dig them out, loose bricks continued to fall from the building. The two other people in the car survived, but the young girl from France died on the scene.

I ask them if they want to hear more, since I can take them up and down any street in St. Louis and tell all kinds of stories like I just told. Usually they don't want to hear more.

I can give stories for the other three interstates that go through St. Louis, or the highways that transverse through Memphis. One interstate call I haven't forgotten occurred on Interstate 64 in front of the St. Louis Zoo one December evening in 1980. We got a call for people trapped in an automobile accident on westbound Interstate 64 at the Tamm Street overpass. It was late evening, around 9:00 p.m., and I knew we had a bad accident because the traffic in the westbound lanes was at a complete stop as I tried to make my way to the scene. I had to snake my way along the emergency lane on the left with my right wheels on the pavement and left wheels in the grassy median.

When I got to the scene, I found out why traffic was stopped. In front of me was a horrific crash with debris, oil, gasoline, glass, and other wreckage strewn all over all. Some emergency vehicles were already there, and I could see people standing on the Tamm Street overpass looking down at the action below. In the lane closest to the grassy median was a car that appeared to have had its entire top ripped off. There was another car resting nearby that also appeared to be in the crash. Most everyone was gathered around the car with the top severed off. I walked up and saw two small children and an adult who appeared to be dead with mortal wounds. The driver of the other car was being tended to and had injuries that also put her in serious condition. Witnesses began to tell us the woman was driving eastbound on the interstate when her car started throwing sparks from underneath and began swerving. The car then crossed over the grassy median and went airborne, shredding off the top of the car that was going westbound.

There was not much for us to do after the lady was transported from the car. We placed white sheets over the top of the car and the bodies, since people could stand on the overpass and almost look right down into the car. The social impact and the dignity of the people should always be of a concern to those of us in our profession.

By this time the news media had made it to the scene. Someone from the news media I saw on a routine basis was Herb Humphries. Herb was a news reporter for a CBS affiliate in St. Louis at the time. He always worked the evening shift, and his traditional line whenever he closed a live report from a scene was: "Herb Humphries, Nightside."

I saw one of the police officers call Herb over to the car with the three bodies. They were looking at something in the trunk.

Soon I learned it was some personal items of another reporter from Herb's news station. The dead adult in the car was a news reporter. I knew the reporter from working on other stories with him. I took a look at the adult laying dead in the car and, quite frankly, I didn't recognize him. Another police officer started digging through the back pants pocket of the man in the car. When he got his wallet, the officer looked at the driver's license and confirmed who it was. Obviously I was stunned. I knew this man. I'd dealt with him many times. Herb was also upset. This was one of his colleagues from work.

We again covered him. All we could do was wait for the medical examiner to come and take the bodies away. We waited for what seemed an eternity until we finally learned the medical examiner's van was stuck in the stopped traffic that had come to a complete stop in the westbound lanes of the highway. The police commander on the scene asked if we could transport the bodies to the morgue by the ambulance that was still there. This isn't something traditionally done by an ambulance in St. Louis and even Memphis, but I knew I had an unusual circumstance on my hands. There was the social impact of these three people lying dead in a car while people stood on an overpass and looked down. I also felt a sense of obligation to the news reporter and his two children. I ordered one of the ambulance crews still on the scene to load the bodies and take them to the morgue in downtown St. Louis.

It took about 10 minutes to place the news reporter and his two sons into the ambulance. I was standing there at the back of the ambulance, watching it pull away, and it was not 30 seconds after the ambulance left that a lady ran up to me in a frenzied state and said her husband and two children were in that car, as she pointed to the vehicle with the top sheared off. She then pointed to the ambulance that had just pulled away and she wanted to know what hospital they were going to. I asked her name;

her first name escapes me, but she did tell me the last name of the news reporter.

What a dilemma! I couldn't just blurt out that they're en route to the morgue.

I told her to come with me as we walked toward Herb Humphries. It was a stall tactic. The whole time I was walking I was searching for a way to tell her that all three were dead. How do you find the words to say that? Herb was pretty emotional also. But as soon as he saw her, he grabbed her and hugged her and said he was so sorry. She stepped back and asked what he meant. That's when he told her that they were all gone. She stood there and looked at him as though he was trying to make some small conversation. His initial words didn't seem to sink in. She asked him, "What do you mean, they're all gone?" He had to explain it to her again.

This was another one of those nights when you go to bed and can't sleep. I tossed and turned all night. The next day I read in the paper that after the news reporter got off work he joined his wife and three children at a recital in the midtown of St. Louis. When the recital was over, they decided to split the children into the two cars. His two sons went with him, and their daughter with the wife. The wife was driving ahead of the reporter and his sons, and never saw what happened in her rearview mirror. When she got home she waited for her husband and two sons to come home—but they never did. After waiting for a long period of time and out of concern, she decided retrace the route. That's when she discovered the accident. Although there was no pleasure in this call, I was always happy I made the decision to have them transported to the morgue. It would have been terrible for her to come to the scene and to see them in the condition they were in.

One would probably ask, why would anyone do this job that subjects you to such horror? It's certainly not easy in a physical and intellectual sense, and we certainly don't sit around the fire station drinking coffee, watching television, and eating all day, like my friend at the party thought.

Becoming a firefighter is hard physically. Becoming a paramedic is even harder intellectually. There is lots of studying and several years of lectures, labs, and clinical time riding on ambulances, spending time in hospitals, watching surgeries, and even watching some autopsies. Paramedics can read EKGs, start IVs, decompress a collapsed lung, administer medications, and do advanced airway procedures such as intubation, plus other advanced skills such as intraosseous infusions where we actually drill into a bone to establish an IV. Basically, you're the eyes, ears, and hands of the doctor in the emergency room, but you're doing it at 55 miles per hour in a small compartment—the back of the ambulance. Sometimes you're treating a patient who is wedged between the toilet and the bathtub. Sometimes it's a dark alley and the only light you have comes from a police officer's flashlight. That's how I delivered that baby one cold evening on the third floor of a vacant house in north St. Louis. Sometimes we wish all our calls were in a well-lit emergency room where you could close the door and keep everyone out. Instead it's in some dimly lit room, or the patient is on the top floor of a three-story building and stairs are winding.

When I went to paramedic school in 1979, it was only about six months long. We didn't have any standardized textbooks to study from. Everything was copied from articles from medical journals, and we had to rely on what we were being taught in class. You hoped what they were teaching you was going to be on the exam when you took the test for your state practicing license. There was no national standard curriculum for paramedics like there is today.

Today's paramedics don't have it as easy as I did. Today's paramedics first have to take an EMT course, which is roughly six months long, depending on where you take it. Then you have to take anatomy and physiology, English comp, sociology, algebra, and interpersonal communication as pre-requisites for paramedic education. Then you have to be accepted into a paramedic program. The paramedic program itself is around 16 months long, during which you have lectures, labs, and clinical time that you do by riding on ambulances and working in hospitals. The textbooks are well over 1,200 pages, and there's a lot of studying involved.

When you get done with paramedic school, all you have is a certificate saying you completed the program. Now you need to become licensed before you can treat your first patient. In order to obtain a license, most states require the paramedic to pass the National Registry test. The National Registry of EMTs is a national testing and certification agency that currently 46 states recognize and use to register EMTs and paramedics. If you pass the skills and computer-based testing, you obtain certification as a Nationally Registered paramedic.

Most US states recognize this certification, and will grant you a license to be a paramedic in their state. The first-time pass rate taking the National Registry test hovers around 68–70 percent. Those trying to obtain National Registry can take the test up to six times before they have to repeat the entire paramedic education program again. But those who don't pass after six attempts usually move on to some other career instead of repeating the entire program.

Many paramedics take education programs at community colleges, then use their paramedic education credits towards obtaining an associate's degree. Many also move on to bachelor degrees and more after finishing paramedic school.

Firefighting school can be challenging, also. There's a lot to study, and it can be very physical. For those who think firefighting is just putting wet stuff on red stuff, it goes a lot further than that. There's an entire science behind fighting fires, fire prevention, and ensuring the safety of the general public and fellow firefighters.

Before becoming a firefighter, you'll spend anywhere from 12–16 weeks in training. Usually that comes out to over 600 hours if you go to school 40 hours a week. Firefighter training usually occurs at a fire academy operated by a fire department, but many community colleges also provide the training.

Some apply to a fire department before they obtain the training. Once hired, the fire department puts them through the training. This is especially true in large urban departments, and because of this it can be competitive. When I worked in St. Louis and Memphis, it wasn't uncommon for thousands to apply for a firefighter position. But if you were selected, you would have a career that, in most cases, would earn you a decent living, and provide you with a pension at the end of your career. Unfortunately, many cities are claiming pensions are too costly and are trying to move away from them, attempting to put firefighters into a 401A or 457 plans. Would you want a 70-year-old firefighter trying to rescue you from a burning building because they can't afford to quit working, because their retirement account didn't do that well? Many politicians seem to think that is OK.

Most fire departments will provide you with all the training you need. At the Memphis Fire Department, we even provided EMT and paramedic training. This additional skillset makes you very marketable to other fire departments or jobs—especially if you have a paramedic license. Some smaller fire departments that pay well and have a good pension plan have a very competitive process for obtaining a job, including requiring you to already have your firefighter certification and paramedic license.

Most fire departments want you to be at least 18 years old (sometimes 21), have a high school diploma or equivalent, be physically fit, have a clean criminal record, and have 20/20 vision, with or without correction.

Before getting hired by a fire department, a written test and a Candidate Physical Ability Test (CPAT) is required.9 The written test is usually about 100 questions or more, and covers spatial awareness, reading comprehension, mechanical reasoning, logic, observation, and memory. The CPAT measures your physical ability to do the job. During the CPAT, you're physically and sometimes time tested on your ability to perform certain firefighting evolutions, such as dragging a certain length of fire hose a certain distance, reaching an aluminum ladder and moving it from one set of hooks to another (this simulates reaching up and grabbing a ladder off the side of a fire truck), climbing five stories while carrying a donut role of hose, or using a rubber sledge hammer to move an object a certain length (which simulates chopping a hole in a roof), all while dressed in firefighter gear.

Unfortunately, many people have the smarts to become a paramedic and a firefighter, but their physical capability is just not there. In other circumstances, they have the physical ability, and not the academic ability.

Many women are excellent firefighters and paramedics. However, by percentage of those taking the CPAT, many women get washed out. It seems to me this occurs during the evolutions that may require testing upper body strength. As an example, many women I see fail the CPAT during the hose drag. Instead of wrapping the hose around them and driving forward with their legs and their head down, they try to use their upper body to pull the hose. The weight of the hose with the friction of dragging it across the pavement is too much of a physical challenge for someone who doesn't have the upper body strength. This also happens for men who don't have the upper body strength, and I've also seen many men fail during these stations.

I've seen excellent male and female firefighters, and I've seen terrible male and female firefighters. Unfortunately, since this is a male-dominated profession, if one female is a terrible firefighter, it puts a label on all female firefighters—which is unfair. In the case of the terrible male firefighters, their inabilities don't put an entire stigma on all male firefighters. Unfair as it is, females are put in a position to prove themselves more than their male counterparts in the firefighting profession because of prejudices.

Firefighting is a highly competitive field. Thousands of applicants apply every year across the country, but most are rejected, or sit on a waiting list that expires. Many larger fire departments hire every two years, and typically give positions to about 30–50 applicants at a time. While some fire departments only require applicants to hold a high school diploma, many look for applicants with at least an associate's degree from a college or university. Firefighting is so competitive, in fact, that many applicants obtain EMT or paramedic certifications before applying to become a firefighter so they'll be more desirable to hiring departments. Today, more applicants than ever before have four-year degrees in fire science, paramedicine, or related fields, which have made the field even more competitive.

After you become a certified firefighter and a licensed paramedic, your education isn't done. There is continuous training and ongoing education. This is especially true for paramedics who are required in many states to relicense every two years. In order to relicense every two years, you must have a certain number of hours of continuing education. In some states, it can be as much as 150 hours of continuing education every two years in order to be able to relicense in the state.

In the old days, the person who worked on the ambulance was called the "ambulance driver," because that's what they did: drive the ambulance. They had no skillset to treat a patient, and probably knew nothing about medicine. Many times, there was nobody in the back of the ambulance. That was certainly the case when I grew up in St. Louis. When I was little, I can remember the police "paddy wagon," which was a truck-like police vehicle that would haul prisoners and injured patients. They would put the patient on the canvas stretcher on the floor of the paddy wagon and race to the hospital as fast as possible. There was no attendant or police officer in the back with the patient. When I look back on it, I wonder how many patients died by choking on their blood or bled to death because there was no one to tend to them when they got injured or ill, and they had to rely on a police officer to race them to the hospital. I still hear that term "ambulance driver" from time to time and it drives me nuts, but thankfully it's becoming more obscure.

Besides the paramedic license, there are also additional certification classes you can take to bolster your skills in certain areas, like Advanced Cardiac Life Support and Pediatric Education for Pre-hospital Professionals. Like a paramedic license, those certifications are usually good for about two years, and then you have to retake them in order to maintain the certification.

You are constantly re-educating yourself and taking classes in firefighting after you graduate from firefighter school. Many times it's learning how to use a new tool, how to do a new procedure, training on your apparatus, studying the construction of the buildings and the hazardous materials in your territory, memorizing where all the fire hydrants are, or sitting in a classroom covering the latest developments in firefighting for railroad tank cars. The days of movies that portrayed firefighters sitting at the fire station playing checkers while waiting for a fire are gone.

That firefighter training is put to the test many times.

While I have been to more medical calls than fires in my career, I have certainly been to my share of fires. My estimate is over 5,000 fires during my 37-year career, the majority of which have been house fires. But the more spectacular fires are the ones in large buildings, high-rises, or warehouses.

One of the most impressive, largest, and hottest multiple-alarm fires I've ever seen in St. Louis history was the Royal Paper Company that sat at the intersection of Chouteau and Vandeventer. It was a Sunday evening in February 1988.

I heard the fire go out on my radio as a first alarm for a building fire. The first-arriving engine, which was Engine 29 from the fire station at Vandeventer and Forest Park, reported on the scene and said nothing. Rescue Squad 2, which is also stationed at Forest Park and Vandeventer, also reported on the scene but, with urgency in his voice, the captain reported a five-story commercial building with heavy smoke showing. I'd heard the captain's voice on the radio many times before. Usually it was calm and cool, with never a hint of excitement. This time it was different. The captain was clearly talking faster than normal, and his voice was raised slightly above its normal pitch. Surely what he was looking at wasn't good.

I immediately responded in that direction, all the while looking for a glow in the sky. In February, the sun is usually setting around 5:00 p.m., so it was already pretty dark when this call came in around 7:30 p.m. If it had been daylight, I might have seen the smoke rising, but I saw nothing until I pulled up. When I did, I knew why I saw no glow in the sky. The only fire I saw was coming out of the windows on the bottom floor, on one side of the building. But it was the rest of the building that caught my attention. From every floor, on every side of the building, heavy black and brownish smoke was pushing out of every window frame or crack where it could find its way out.

It was evident, the building was heavily charged with smoke, gases, and heat. Usually when you see buildings at this stage, there is no recovery. The building will be lost, and it's best to retreat, stay out of the collapse zones of any walls that will fall, and try to throw water on the fire. I soon learned this was a warehouse that covered an entire square city block and was full of paper products on every floor. Whenever you have paper products such as cups, paper plates, and napkins stored in boxes on every floor that is a tremendous amount of fuel. It will make any fire burn large and hot. The more fuel, the hotter and larger the fire!

I soon learned how hot this fire would become. Fire trucks that were too close to the building had to be moved back because of the heat and the danger of collapse. Eventually the building would lose its structure and support, and the brick walls would collapse. You have to plan for these collapses and make sure all firefighters and apparatus are out of the way. Walls will usually fall about a third of their height, and you have to build in enough of a buffer zone beyond that.

It didn't take long for the fire to start breaking out of windows on different floors and on different sides of the building. When glass breaks, the fire behind it has reached above 500 degrees Fahrenheit. It will crack at about 200 degrees Fahrenheit, but needs the pressure of hotter temperatures to start falling apart.

The fire raced from floor to floor and from room to room, starting on the ground floor and working its way to the top. Some of the ladder companies that were too close actually had the flashing lens covers on their fire apparatus melt from the heat emanating from the building.

Fire was now coming from every window on every floor of the building, and had even vented through the roof. What was a freezing February evening in St. Louis now became a toasty warm spot. A block away, you felt nice and warm. Any closer to the building and you got a first-degree sunburn on your face. The flames were easily reaching over 100 feet.

I'll never forget what I saw next, and made sure to remember every detail. I never wanted to forget watching a tornado of fire at the top of the building—a 150-foot-high swirling cyclone of flames. Picture the same type of tornado that you see spinning at 200 miles per hour or more across the plains during the spring of the year, except that it is made of fire at the top of a five-story building, and you know the image that I have locked into my memory. It even made the sound of a freight train that so many people describe with a regular tornado. I had never seen that before, and haven't since. I stood there in complete awe and amazement of such a sight.

Eventually, Fire Chief Neil Svetanics arrived and took command of the fire. Knowing he was going to have problems with blowing embers through the surrounding residential neighborhoods, he ordered extra alarms that brought every available fire company in the city, along with apparatus from 30 different fire departments outside of St. Louis. Some of those fire departments from outside the city came to the fire, while others were sent to staff the city's now-unmanned fire stations.

Some fires did break out in the surrounding residential neighborhoods as embers traveled in the air from the conflagration and landed on buildings, cars, garages, and bushes. Fire companies were dispatched, and thankfully there wasn't much damage to a house on McRee Avenue and a commercial building on Central Industrial Drive.

The fire burned for over 12 hours; eventually the floors and the walls collapsed as their support members were burned. It's an amazing sight to see an entire five-story section of brick wall collapse. When large sections of the wall collapse, they don't fall straight down—they typically fall outward about a third of their height. So, a 60-foot building will fall about 20 feet out from the building. This is customarily called the collapse zone and, when operating at a large fire like this, you need to be operating with staff and fire equipment at a minimum of 20 feet away from the building. I'm quick to point out that this is the minimum, and traditionally fire officers will keep manpower and fire apparatus much farther away.

You also need to take into consideration that a wall collapse may pull electrical lines down. Hopefully the local utility company has shut off power to the pole, but if they haven't, someone standing a good distance from the fire can still be impacted by charged electric lines coming down.

This building collapsed into one large pile of brick, wood floors, and beams. Century-old warehouses like the Royal Paper Company are called heavy timber (Type IV) construction, also known as mill construction, because of the substantial size of the wooden structural elements. These buildings are found in many old cities like St. Louis, when the manufacturing age created population centers. This type of structure does not typically collapse early in the fire because of the large cross-sectional lumber used in walls, ceilings, floors, and roof assemblies. Some of these wood beams are sometimes two, three, and four feet thick. The brick masonry exterior walls can be 60–80 feet high. Depending on the structure's height, the extra-thick walls can be 36 inches thick at the foundation. Usually the floors are large and open, like a warehouse, and are also made of plank wood. The floors are usually supported by solid timber trusses or wooden columns that are at least eight inches thick.

After the building collapses, all you can really do is keep throwing water on the mass of bricks and wood timber. There will always be hotspots under the pile that continue to burn. The only way to put out the fire is to get construction equipment to slowly and eventually remove the debris to expose the hotspots so more water can be poured on to the fire.

Eventually the fire would be put out, and relief crews would be sent home. Investigation into the fire showed that three neighborhood boys, ages 10, 13, and 14, were picked up and questioned after they were seen running from the paper company slightly before the fire started. After being questioned, the 10-year-old admitted to sticking a lighted book of matches through a broken window in the foyer area on the north side of the building. According to a newspaper account, the sister of one of the boys overheard her brother and the two boys plotting about setting fire to the "cup company."

The owner of the company estimated the cost of replacing the building at $1 million, and the inventory at $1.5 million—and those were 1988 dollars. To his advantage, the building and the contents were fully insured.

Thankfully, no firefighters and no civilians were killed. One firefighter did suffer a minor arm injury and was treated at the hospital. Six other firefighters suffered minor injuries when they slipped on some ice that formed from the tons of water that had been poured onto the building.

I later read a letter to the editor in the newspaper from a lady who was wondering why a building had to burn to the ground when 200 firefighters were on the scene. She wrote, "Instead of the knee-jerk Feb. 9 follow-up on the heroics of the firefighters during the Royal Paper fire, the *Post-Dispatch* (*St. Louis Post-Dispatch* paper) should ask some tough questions. All those firefighters did not control the blaze; they just poured water on it until the flames burned themselves out. Why didn't this task force of some 200 get inside the building and stop the blaze from devouring all the paper inside instead of standing outside and watching?"

I chuckle when I read comments like this, and I also shake my head. Like many citizens, the writer of the letter has no clue about how and why we contain fires the way we do. The fire was well advanced by the time we arrived on the scene. Do you know how much water is needed to put out a fire of this magnitude? If you wanted to get complicated, multiply the length of one floor of the building by the width and divide by three—this gives the number of gallons of water needed *per minute* to extinguish the fire. So a building like Royal Paper that covers one square city block, probably 500 x 300 feet, would be 150,000 square feet on one floor. Divide by three and you need 50,000 gallons of water per minute. Multiple it by five floors and that's 250,000 gallons of water per minute to extinguish the fire.

Considering the average fire engine pumped 750–1,000 gallon per minute in 1988, it would take over 250 fire engines pumping water into ladder companies with water turrets, hose-hand-lines and deck guns on top of the fire engine to extinguish this fire. This doesn't take into account that the water mains running underneath the city streets probably wouldn't be able to supply that type of water flow, let alone have enough fire hydrants in the area to support that many hoses.

Sending firefighters into this building that was already well advanced with fire would have certainly gotten them killed. On a Sunday evening for a business of this type, chances were that no one was in the building, so the only reason to send in a firefighter would be to save property. Putting firefighters into a building of this type with this amount of fire would have been to only save property that—as it happened—was already fully insured. It makes no sense for fire incident commanders to put firefighters in tremendous risk to save property. If any firefighters had been killed at this fire, all that would have remained at the end of the day would have been a vacant lot—and I doubt they would even put the firefighter(s) name on a plaque at the vacant lot.

The fire service has evolved, with new philosophical thinking over the years. This Dynamic Risk Assessment model is designed to put fire incident commanders in a position to continually evaluate the risk versus the reward in an emergency situation. The model that is followed is: "(1) We will risk our lives a lot, in a calculated manner, to save SAVABLE LIVES; (2) We will risk our lives a LITTLE, in a calculated manner, to save SAVABLE property; and (3) We WILL NOT risk our lives at all for a building or lives that are already lost."

In the case of a business like Royal Paper Company, there's a great chance there were no savable lives. When you consider there was already heavy smoke pushing from all floors of the building when the first companies arrived, it's natural for a firefighter to assume the fire is well advanced. Therefore, it doesn't make sense to risk firefighter lives to save a building that's already lost. Even if someone was in the building, chances were it wasn't a savable life.

In the case of the World Trade Center and the subsequent collapse of both towers, 343 New York City firefighters lost their lives. Those who were in the towers were mainly concerned with the savable lives of the people still inside. When the first tower collapsed, an evacuation of the firefighters from the second tower was ordered because the risk was too great to the firefighters. Still, it's estimated that the New York firefighters saved over 25,000 people from both towers before they collapsed.

Until recently, the United States fire service had been losing over 100 firefighters a year to deaths. Through concerted efforts, awareness, training programs, and other efforts, such a near-miss reporting systems like the airline industry has, that number has been reduced to less than 100 over the last few years.

Hopefully one year I'll hear there were no line-of-duty deaths of firefighters or paramedics.

CHAPTER 3

✚

BURNING DESIRES

Picture this scenario. I would like to drive you to a house that you have never seen or been inside before. It is a rectangle-shaped, two-story wood white frame home sitting in the middle of the block about twenty feet from the curb of the street. The house extends about 100 feet deep into the lot. There are two homes on either side that have the same type of construction, and they sit about 10 feet apart from each other. There are some shrubs in front of the house, and a little walkway that snakes to the porch steps. The house has a large, gray-painted wooden porch that runs the entire length of the front. There are five gray-painted wooden steps with a banister leading up to the porch. The porch has a slanted shingle roof over it to protect it from the elements. Above the slanted roof of the porch are two other large-sized windows that are on the second floor, each with white painted frames around the windows. You could actually step out of the second floor windows onto the slanted roof of the porch. The front door is in the center of the porch, and on either side of the door are also some large-sized windows with their white frames and curtains. There is an aluminum storm door and a dark green wooden paneled front door. The roof of the house is slanted, and the two sides rise to a peak in the center of the house with its asphalt shingles.

I walk you up the five wooden steps of the front porch and you find yourself standing at the front door of the home. Now, I put an air mask on your face and black out the glass so you cannot see. It is completely pitch-dark, and you cannot see any light with the mask on. Why would I black out the mask so you could not see? You would have the same conditions in a fire. You would have zero or near-zero visibility. Don't be fooled by what you see on television or in the movies. Usually those fires are burning nice and bright and there is no smoke. The pyrotechnicians that work for the movie industry are experts at making fire without smoke. If there was as much smoke in the movie as there would be in a real fire, you probably would not be able to see what was going on, since the smoke would fill the room and make visibility zero. You might have a chance, though, if you got close enough to the floor, if you were crawling. Generally, the lower to the floor you get, there might be a chance you can see something. It is also cooler down there.

Now, I want you to get on your knees and crawl while you search every room of this house for a child who is reported to be inside. Chances are the child will not be making any noise. You have never been in the house. You do not know the layout, the hallways, where the bathrooms are, or even how many rooms there are. Don't forget to check under beds, closets, and sometimes even the toy box. Children will hide virtually anywhere when they are scared.

Based on your experience, knowledge, and training, you probably know this two-story has bedrooms on the second floor, and there is living space on the first floor, including a kitchen, dining room, and a front room or family room. The kitchen is probably in the rear of the home, and the dining room is probably right off the kitchen. Probably! But I have seen homes that don't fit this mold. I have seen the kitchen in the front of the house and the family room in the rear of the house. I have even seen kitchens in the basement, as some nationalities think it is cooler down there for cooking purposes. So when they built their homes, they built the kitchen in the basement. Speaking of basements, does this home even have a basement? It all depends on what part of the country you are in. If you live in the north, there is a good chance it has a basement, since it needs to sit on a foundation that goes below the frost line. If the home did not sit on a foundation that goes below the frost line, the home would shift during the winter. If this home was in the south, there is a good chance it will not have a basement.

So now you have entered this home on your knees and you are searching for a child who does not even whimper. You have a pretty good idea how the home is laid out and where rooms would be.

Even if the child was whimpering or crying you might not hear him if the house was on fire. There would be lots of other noises that would drown out the child, including lots of other firefighters entering and leaving the structure. Houses make strange noises when the structure's integrity is being challenged. Creaks, groans, and bangs almost sound like the house is crying out in pain from torture of the fire.

During quiet periods, or when you get close, you might even hear the fire. Generally it has been my experience that small fires pop, medium-size fires crackle, and large fires seem to roar. So if you're inside the building and you hear roaring, you might want to be thinking where your exit points are so you get out right away if conditions deteriorate.

Now you only have so long to search this home—the home you cannot see your way through, or even know the layout of. You will not have all day.

If you are fortunate, a ladder truck company may have gotten on the roof and cut several holes to let the heat and smoke out of the building. It might give you a little better visibility.

Picture a firefighter in the same scenario. You pull up to the house on your fire apparatus and you have never seen this house before or been in it. People outside the home are screaming that there is somebody inside. I have always been amazed at how many times you arrive at a scene and someone shouts that there is someone inside but after a thorough search, it was discovered that no one was inside the building.

When you search for the child someone says is inside, you do it in zero visibility, and there is a stopwatch on you. You only have so long. Now in reality, if you worked in a big city like me, chances are you are going to have plenty of resources on the scene, and you will not be the only one searching. Chances are your entire fire company of three or four firefighters has been assigned to search the building, and you'll work in conjunction with another firefighter.

The search should always be in the direction of where you believe the victims would be. If it's during the night, chances are they are in the bedrooms. If it's during normal waking hours, chances are they may be in rooms that are not bedrooms.

Firefighters search houses and rooms in different ways. No matter the technique, there should always be two firefighters working together to perform the search for victims. With the first technique, the firefighters get on their knees and the first firefighter leads, starting either with a left-handed or a right-handed search. That means they are using either hand to stay along a wall and reach out with the other hand and a tool to search. The second firefighter should be right behind the first. The second firefighter should be able to periodically touch the first firefighter's leg. They should be talking to each other. The first firefighter should be telling the second firefighter everything he is seeing and touching. "I got a chair here," or, "I'm pushing the chair out into the middle of the room now," are some of the things the first firefighter should be saying. But, many times the second firefighter is searching the same area, and some people found this method totally inefficient.

To be more efficient, another technique used by two firefighters to search a home is to use voice contact. Using this method, they do not have to touch each other, but they constantly verbalize to each other so that by sound they can tell where the other firefighter is. Using this technique, the first firefighter starts off with the right- or left-handed search, but the second firefighter follows and searches away from the wall out into the center of the room. This allows both firefighters to cover a larger area, twice as fast.

Sometimes firefighters have to split duties. In some cases, the first firefighter can search the room, while the second firefighter controls the door with a hose-line. That second firefighter has the ability to protect the other firefighter's position and any victims they might find, should fire conditions deteriorate quickly. Using their voices and verbalization, the first firefighter can find his way out of the room by listening for the second firefighter at the door.

I love fighting fire! When I say I love fighting fire, it is not because I get a sense of joy or pleasure, but it is an opportunity to help someone else who is in need. It is the opportunity, even with a vacant building, to keep it from spreading to someone's home next door.

But the problem with fire is that it can be very devastating. There is nothing that can be more destructive to another person's life in terms of emotional or physical pain. If someone loses their home, they may have insurance, but they will probably lose things that insurance cannot replace. Family pictures and sentimental things that mean so much to someone is something no insurance company can ever think of replacing. I had one lady at a fire some years ago crying uncontrollably because every picture she had of her dead husband went up in flames after she lost her home. I tried to console her, and I told her that some relative probably had a picture somewhere that she could make copies of. She assured me that their family circle was very small and there were no other pictures. I believed her, since this was at a time when taking pictures was not done with phones, and you had to actually take film to a store and get it printed. The only picture she will ever have of her husband is what is in her memory.

Fire can also be devastating physically. The pain one endures when all or some part of their body is burning must be unspeakable. I speak from experience. I severely burned my hand some years ago when I dumbly grabbed a log on a fire that I thought was not burning, in an attempt to put it deeper into the fire. The pain and blistering went on for several days as I attempted every possible means I knew of trying to diminish it.

Of the hundreds of burn victims I have seen and dealt with over the years, nothing has affected me deeper than hearing the screams of a man who burned to death in a tractor trailer accident one night in St. Louis because he was entangled in the wreckage. The crying and screaming pierced my soul. The fire was too intense to extinguish with the water that was in the tank of the engine, and there was no hydrant anywhere in sight to provide a water supply. By the time a second engine got there, he had been consumed by the flames. We desperately tried to get him out but he was trapped in the wreckage, and all our efforts were in vain.

Unfortunately, I saw the same scenario play out on a bridge over the Wolf River in Memphis when a pickup truck collided head-on with another truck in the center of the bridge. The two occupants in the pickup truck were trapped and the pickup truck was on fire, including the cab where the people were trapped, when the first engine company arrived on the scene. They were able to quickly pull a hose-line, and using the water from their tank began extinguishing the fire enough to be able to pull the man out, who was still behind the steering wheel of the vehicle. He was severely burned and unconscious. His wife, who was still trapped in the passenger seat, was also unconscious, and severely burned. As the firefighters worked to free her from the pickup truck, the smoldering fire of the vehicle began to ignite again. The firefighters began to use what water they had left, but it was not enough. Seeing he was going to need more water, the lieutenant on the engine company called for another engine to respond. I pulled up in my chief's vehicle about three minutes later. I could see the plume of heavy, thick black smoke as I was approaching the scene. I had no idea they still had someone trapped in the pickup until after I got out of my car and approached the scene.

As I walked up I knew something was wrong, just by the looks on the firefighters' faces. Long, grim faces with no one talking is usually a hint of something being wrong. I knew they had a water supply problem when I heard them call for another engine. They were in the middle of the bridge, and there was no hydrant in sight for them to get more water. What I did not know was that someone was still in the pickup truck. The firefighter/paramedics on the scene already had the husband packaged up and in the back of the ambulance. As I approached the scene, the lieutenant scurried over to me and said he still had someone trapped in the pickup truck and they had run out of water. The lieutenant had a deep look of concern on his face, almost as if to say, "You're a chief—do something!" The first thing I asked was if we had a hydrant anywhere on either end of the bridge. I tried to look in both directions to see if I could see a water supply source. There was nothing. The bridge was over 800 feet long, and both ends of the bridge were nothing but mostly vegetation that sloped down to the river some 60 feet below. This is the most helpless feeling you can imagine—a firefighter watching a fire burn, someone in the fire, and there is nothing you can do about it. All you can do is stand there. The pickup was so consumed in flames that you could not see the person inside.

Eventually, after what seemed like an eternity but was actually some five minutes later, the other fire engine showed up, and the fire was extinguished. On the passenger seat sat the charred and blistered body of the woman. When bodies are burned that badly, you cannot tell if it is a male or female. You might be able to tell by looking at the hip structure, since females generally have wider hips than males because of child-bearing anatomy. She had obviously burned for a while, and the fire was intense.

All you can do is call for the police and leave her in the pickup truck, since the scene will have to be processed by the accident investigation team.

They'll need to photograph the scene and document everything, including where the occupants of the vehicle were sitting. A firefighter took a white sheet from the ambulance and slowly walked back across the street so he could show some dignity to the lady and cover her body from anyone who wanted to look.

This is a solemn time, and every firefighter on the scene is affected by what happens. Usually no one says a word. Everyone is in deep thought and reflection as they ponder what they just witnessed. Many times you keep asking yourself if it was real, or if you will wake up and realize it was all a nightmare.

Eventually all the firefighters on the scene received professional counseling through our critical incident stress debriefing teams, or CISD teams. CISD is a program designed to help firefighters deal with something traumatic they were involved in, by allowing them to talk about the incident without judgment or criticism. The program is peer-driven by trained CISD counselors with a mental health counselor on call or retainer. In regions where there are smaller fire departments, there may be a conglomerate of departments that share counselors.

The process includes all the people who were involved in the traumatic event sitting in a circle. The counselor gives some preliminary ground rules about talking about the incident and how to speak. All sessions are confidential unless the counselor feels the person(s) being helped is a danger to themselves or others. The process allows people to talk about their feelings regarding the incident. The theory is, it allows them to deal with the traumatic event by releasing their inner thoughts and emotions.

There are differing schools of thought on whether this process really works or not, and each side has their data showing their side of the argument. I pretty much liked the old method, before CISD came about. We sat around the kitchen table at the station and did our own method of CISD by talking about it, and sometimes in a perverse way to non-firefighters and paramedics, joke about it at times, to ease the tension in the room. Personally, I have only sat through one CISD debriefing, and it came 36 years into my career. I wasn't even there when the incident happened or when the person's body was found. It happened when I was working in Memphis, and one of our secretaries was found dead of natural causes while sitting in her car on the Mississippi riverfront.

Working in such fields as firefighting and paramedicine is a challenge psychologically. Soldiers who are in battle situations are eventually rotated after a period of time back to non-combat duty. This is not the case for firefighters and paramedics! They endure these stresses for multiple years, shift after shift. There are only the occasional vacations and the lull between calls that gives the mind some rest. Many in our profession, although they will not admit it, are on anti-depressants and mood-elevator drugs to help them deal with the stresses they experience day in and day out. Some experience irrational thoughts that they cannot explain.

I listened to one excellent paramedic describe how he was holding his new-born daughter and he kept having recurring impulses to take a knife and repeatedly stab her. He eventually had to put her down, walk out of the room, and seek professional help. He said he was at a low point in his life and needed professional intervention to deal with all the things he had seen throughout his career.

Suicides among firefighters and paramedics are not uncommon. In both St. Louis and Memphis where I worked, I knew of firefighters and paramedics who had committed suicide.

One of the more notable paramedic suicides involved the rescue of baby Jessica McClure in Midland, Texas, in 1987, after she fell down an 18-inch-wide well. CNN was a fledgling news station at the time, and there was almost round-the-clock coverage of the rescue attempt that lasted 58 hours. Robert O'Donnell [3] is the paramedic who is mostly credited with saving baby Jessica. Mr. O'Donnell received tremendous media coverage as a result of the rescue. In 1995, eight years after the incident and suffering from post-traumatic shock disorder from the rescue, he committed suicide. *USA Today* did an article in 2003 and found that at least 100 police officers and paramedics committed suicide while on the job between 1992 and 2001. They did their research by delving into Occupational Safety and Health Administration (OSHA) records.

The fire where I watched a man burn to death in the cab of a tractor trailer and the fire I responded to where the lady burned up in the pickup truck were not the only fires where I encountered someone burning.

In about 1984, I was paramedic-captain responsible for the south side of St. Louis when a call went out for an auto accident with someone trapped at Interstate 55 at the Poplar Street Bridge entrance in downtown St. Louis.

When you get an address like this, it could be anywhere. Usually people do not know what address to give, since Interstate 55 and the Poplar Street Bridge have multiple on and off ramps—one of those conglomerations of concrete that twist over the top of each other in all kinds of directions.

The normal "person trapped" response on an interstate in St. Louis is one engine from each direction, a ladder company, a rescue squad, a battalion chief, an ambulance, and a paramedic-captain. In my case, I was already rolling down Interstate 55 and was only about a mile out from scene. Geez, I thought, I'm already rolling in that direction, and it's right in front of me. I'm going to be the first one on the scene. Sometimes that's a good thing, and other times that can be a bad thing; you're doing a "John Wayne" all by yourself.

I notified the dispatcher that I received the assignment and I was already northbound on Interstate 55 at Russell. My ETA was one minute. As I was approaching the downtown area and the scene, the traffic was already starting to back up. This is a good indication that the accident you are responding to is probably in the same lanes you are traveling, and it's bad enough to narrow the lanes down to one, or might even have traffic stopped.

In this case, the traffic was stopped, and was not moving in all three lanes. This was not a good sign at all since, this meant the accident was bad enough to block all lanes of traffic. The only way to the scene was to take the emergency lanes on the side of the highway.

As I gingerly made my way up to the emergency scene next to the concrete divider in the middle of the highway, I could start to see it come into sight. From my vantage point, the Gateway Arch was clearly visible through the web of other entrance and exit ramps that overlap each other in the downtown area of St. Louis.

As I drove into the scene, there were debris and bystanders everywhere. My first glimpse told me an 18-wheeler tractor trailer had rear-ended a car and was virtually on top of it. The front of the car was pushed into the rear of another 18-wheeler tractor trailer. Before I could bring my station wagon to a stop and get out, people were frantically waving for me to come as fast as I could to where the car was smashed between the two tractor trailers. The looks of desperation on their faces was quite evident.

One civilian ran up next to my window and was running alongside as I crawled to a stop. He couldn't wait to tell me something. He was trying to tell me something through the car window, and to emphasize the point, his hands waved wildly in front of him. But rolling the window down would be a waste of time, so I tried to open the car door; but he wouldn't move back away from the car to let me out. He was emphatically trying to tell me something. With my hand, I motioned for him to move back and let me out. He backed up and before I could step fully out of the car, he was telling me that someone was trapped in the car and the car was on fire.

I walked briskly toward the accident scene to get a better assessment, and again I was confronted by numerous bystanders—all who looked too hyped up on caffeine. One bystander who looked like a truck driver approached me and said the engine compartment was on fire. As I looked at the car sandwiched between the two tractor trailers, it was even hard to distinguish it as a car. Steam rolled off the front of the car from either a fire or from the radiator being cracked—or both. It was nothing but one big heap of metal crushed like an aluminum can. Just one quick glance told me the traffic was stopped on the entrance ramp from northbound Interstate 55 onto the Poplar Street Bridge that would have taken you across the Mississippi River into the state of Illinois. Since the traffic was stopped, the tractor trailer that was virtually on top of the car smashed into it at a high rate of speed, and pushed it into the other tractor trailer. The rear of the car was crushed by the tractor trailer and had been pushed all the way up to the front seats of the car. The engine compartment was a crumbled mess and was almost pushed back to the passenger compartment.

As I was standing on the driver side of the vehicle, trying to get an overall assessment, I was again bombarded by about five citizens who were standing on the passenger side of the vehicle, motioning me to where they were standing. I could see steam and light smoke still coming off the engine compartment area, and some truck drivers were hitting the smoking areas with their fire extinguishers. It would be tough navigating to the passenger side of the vehicle without having to walk around or crawl underneath either tractor trailer. So I told the driver of the tractor trailer in the front of the vehicle to move it forward, since his truck looked drivable. He promptly did so, and I was able to maneuver around to the passenger side of the vehicle.

As I arrived at the passenger side, I peered into the vehicle and the first thing I saw was a man in his middle 30s, laying across the seat, virtually on his back but turned slightly to his right, with his head on the passenger seat and from his waist down, I could not see anything. The bottom part of his body was entangled in the wreckage of the car, and nothing was visible below the waist. With his arms outreached to me and with a look of desperation on his face, he screamed for me to get him out. "I'm on fire!" he cried out loud. "Please help me! Get me out! I'm on fire!" he continued to holler. I bent down and in my calmest voice tried to reassure him that the fire was out and he was not on fire. But it did little good, since he continued to scream that he was on fire.

By this time I could hear the sirens coming in the distance. *Thank God,* I thought. Being first on the scene is sometimes a helpless feeling. All I had was a station wagon with some medical equipment in it. I don't carry water like a fire engine, and I don't carry extrication equipment like a rescue squad. I suspected it was Engine 11, since the sirens were coming from the south of me, and that is where their station is located. I reassured him he was not on fire, and the car was no longer on fire. I told him, "We'll have you out of here real soon."

At that point, I was close enough that he reached out and grabbed my left hand, and with a death grip he tried to pull himself out of the wreckage. But he couldn't. He was literally entangled to the point where he and the car were one. Nothing was visible from his waist down. Again, he pleaded for me to get him out since he was on fire. Again, I tried to reassure him that he was not on fire, and we would have him out of the car soon.

I was correct! About this time, Engine 11 was pulling up, and parked slightly in front of the accident scene. I could also hear more sirens in the distance, and they were coming from both directions. Whenever I was on a scene by myself, those sirens always reminded me of the old Western movies when the cavalry comes over the hill and saves the day. Just replace the bugle call with the wail of the siren.

The engine company captain jumped out of his front passenger seat and walked briskly toward me. He asked what I got, and I gave him a quick size-up of the situation. I told him he probably needed to pull a line, since the engine compartment was on fire before I got there. The evidence of it being on fire was readily apparent from the charring and the white powder of the fire extinguishers that were sprayed onto the exterior of the car and the engine compartment. I didn't have to tell them the bystanders told me the car was on fire. It was pretty obvious.

The engine company captain ordered his crew to pull a line and check the engine compartment. Afterward he came back to me as I continued to remain with the man trapped in the car, who continued to plead for us to get him out since he was on fire. I told the captain the rescue squad was the only way we were going to get him out. He was entangled with the car, and they were going to have to cut him out. Even though it was daylight out, the captain tried shining his flashlight into the twisted wreckage to see if he could see the victim's legs somewhere in the twisted and crumbled vehicle. No legs were visible. It was almost as if he was in a cocoon of bent and contorted metal, plastic, and other assorted debris.

Shortly thereafter, Rescue Squad 2 pulled up from their engine house on the near north side of downtown. I recognized some of the members getting out of the apparatus, including Bruce Williams and Terry May. The six-person heavy-rescue squad vehicle was some 40 feet long and over 12 feet high, and carried every conceivable piece of rescue tool known to the fire service. Whether the victim is in a car, high on a building, in a confined space, involved in a collapse, or in the water, the tools and firefighters are on that piece of apparatus to get them out. The firefighters assigned to the rescue squad are some of the highest trained firefighters on the job because of the special certifications they must possess for unique types of rescues.

As the firefighters from Rescue Squad 2 disembarked from their monster vehicle, they took one glance and knew what they were going to need. They immediately, as if rehearsed over and over like some orchestra, started opening just the right cabinets and taking out the necessary rescue tools they were going to need. The captain of the rescue squad made his way over to the captain of the 11s and me next to the passenger side of the car, where we continued to try and reassure the man he was not burning. Again, in a terrified voice, he screamed that he was on fire, and pleaded for us to get him out. Now both of his arms and hands are outreached to us, almost like a baby would reach out to be picked up by an adult, as he pleaded for us to get him out. The rescue squad captain took one look at the inside and the outside of the car. His keen eyes took everything in and he started formulating a plan in his head on the strategy for cutting this car apart.

As the extrication process began, we had to cover the victim with a blanket to protect him from flying debris, shards of glass, or maybe even sparks from some of the cutting tools. As I suspected, this terrified him, so I stuck my head under the blanket to try and console and calm him. He still cried that he was burning and wanted out.

The extrication process took at least 15 minutes, as the car was methodically and surgically taken apart. Paramedics had moved a stretcher behind me with a backboard so that once the victim was free, we could slide him onto a backboard and then put the backboard onto the stretcher. Whenever extrication procedures are taking place to free a victim from a car, it is standard procedure to have a firefighter standing ready with a hose-line in case a fire erupts.

As the firefighters from Rescue Squad 2 got down to the last couple of steps before the victim was freed, a firefighter pulled back a large section of the metal enveloping the man with a special tool with chains called a Come Along. As the metal was pulled back to expose the area where the man's legs were, there was a sudden pop, and flames began to shoot from the newly exposed area underneath the wreckage. Immediately, the man began to scream again that he was on fire. This time he really was on fire! The area where his legs disappeared down under the wreckage now had the metal pulled away to create a void, and air had rushed in and ignited a smoldering fire. Flames were now leaping out of the void space and the man screamed at the top of his lungs while trying to push himself out.

The firefighter who was standing by with the hose-line dragged it, with the assistance of other firefighters, over to where I was standing, and immediately sprayed water into the void space to douse the flames. They continued to pour water in until there are no more visible flames, and only a scant trace of smoke and steam. We were done trying to extricate him cleanly. It was time to just grab him as best we could and pull him out onto the backboard before another fire erupted. We couldn't risk another ignition, with even worse consequences.

I and some other firefighters grabbed whatever parts of him we could, including under his arms, shirt, or belt to pull him out.

As we began to pull him out, I suddenly glanced at the area where his legs were coming out of the void space. He virtually had no legs left. They were burnt almost down to the point where bone was showing in some areas. He was right. He was on fire. The fire was smoldering and burning down in the void space, and the wreckage was so tightly crunched together that no air could get to the flames. But there was enough oxygen to keep the fire burning, and also to consume his legs. The fire just smoldered. His legs were literally charred black from the continual flame and heating process. We moved him to the backboard, and then the backboard with him was moved to the stretcher. I couldn't believe how damaged his legs were. His legs literally cooked for the entire amount of time he was trapped in the wreckage.

I felt sorry for this man as I watched him wheeled away to the ambulance. He was no doubt going to lose both legs, and I doubted he'd survive. Major trauma like that to the body back in the early 1980s did not bode well for survival rates. I never did find out if he survived or not. I never knew his name. I just know that unforeseen circumstances brought our lives together at a critical point. I don't know if he was from St. Louis, or just traveling through town. I never checked the newspaper the next day to see if the story was even in the paper. I just prayed that everything worked out the best for him that it could.

***

The majority of fires that I have been to are house fires. At some point they all run together, and one home looks like another. In St. Louis they were mostly one- and two-story brick structures, and in Memphis they were mostly one-story and sometimes two-story frame homes. It did seem to me, though, that St. Louis had a far greater percentage of larger and multiple-alarm fires than Memphis. I don't necessarily know why, other than St. Louis has massive warehouses that were built before the turn of the last century, when St. Louis was a stopping place for those heading west. Being a stopping point, a lot of trading was done.

Some of the old mercantile mill construction warehouses rose up more than 10 stories and covered an entire square block. Some have been converted to hotels, apartment buildings, and condominiums. When the conversions occurred, they had to be brought into compliance with the fire code and as a result, fire sprinklers, doors with burn ratings of two hours or more, and alarm systems had to be installed that would prevent fires, or at least hold the fire in check until it could be extinguished.

One of the largest fires I have ever seen in St. Louis history occurred about a year before I came on the job. It was April 2, 1976, and it started in the old seven-story Heyday Shoe Company building at 21st and Locust. The building took up the entire city block, and had those high floor-to-ceiling windows to let light and ventilation in that is typical of buildings built in the late 1800s and early 1900s. Lighting was a luxury, and there was no such thing as air conditioning, so factory workers had to see and get ventilation through big, open windows.

On the day of the fire, the first-arriving engine company and battalion chief found a fire in the basement. But within minutes, fire was racing through the building, from the basement to the roof. It quickly jumped across the street and caught the St. Louis Housing Authority warehouse on fire, and then it spread to other warehouses on Locust Street and throughout the area. It became a firestorm! A firestorm is a fire that creates and sustains its own wind. Usually this is a phenomenon seen in large brush and wildland fires, and it is rare to see it in the middle of a city.

I volunteered for the Red Cross at the time, so I went to the scene to assist with the rehab of the firefighters. Traditionally, the Red Cross would have a truck on the street 24 hours a day to provide water, coffee, juice, and cookies for the firefighters at working fires. It was commonly known as the "cookie truck." On large fires such as this, they would also bring a canteen truck out to the scene, with sandwiches and other warm food.

I can remember watching in amazement as multiple, large, multi-story warehouse buildings burned, on both sides of the street, with fire coming out of every window. Firefighters were scrambling to move apparatus as the next building would catch on fire since they did not want to lose any engines or ladder trucks. The 5s did lose their engine, however, on the corner of 21st and Locust. It was hooked to a hydrant, and when the building took off, it was too hot and too dangerous to even try to unhook it and drive it away. I have seen several dramatic pictures of the engine burning sitting next to the building.

I have also seen other numerous pictures from that day of firefighters, whom I would eventually get to know and work with over the years, trying to deal with the conflagration. There is one dramatic picture of Jerry Diefenbach standing up, trying to drive Hook and Ladder 2 backwards in an attempt to get it away from a building that had just ignited. Jerry would eventually become a battalion chief.

There are other dramatic photographs of firefighters getting embers inside their coats, and other firefighters trying to pull the coat off and wet them down. Other spectacular pictures of the fire by J. B. Forbes of the *St. Louis Post Dispatch* shows the intensity of the fire, as water streams off fire engines just dissipated in the heat of the fire and had no effect. I got to know Jim pretty well, and at some point in my career, he shared his pictures with me. I still have them in my collection.

Charles Kamprad, who was fire chief at the time, debated actually dynamiting buildings to create natural barriers to stop the inferno from taking out all of the downtown area. Eventually every piece of fire apparatus in the city of St. Louis was there, as fires broke out on rooftops on other buildings two or three blocks away because of flying embers. The traffic helicopter for one of the local radio stations reported he could feel the heat of the fire at 1,700 feet, and the plume of smoke could be seen 30 miles away.

Eventually the fire burned itself out when it ran out of fuel and it hit natural fire breaks like vacant lots. When it was all over, six large warehouses had been destroyed, and numerous other buildings had been damaged. To add insult to injury, I was helping at the Red Cross canteen to dispense food and water to firefighters later on that evening when *another* four-alarm fire broke out at a furniture company at the intersection of East Grand and West Florissant. Tired firefighters who had left the scene as the fire died down now were pressed into service at another fire on the north side of the city.

Ironically, movie producers came to town a few years later and liked the area around 21st and Locust so much, with its boarded-up, damaged warehouses that they decided to shoot parts of a movie there. To illustrate what New York City might look like if had been abandoned and turned into a prison, the producers of *Escape from New York* filmed many scenes in the area of 21st and Locust. At 3:00 a.m., when I was working that particular shift, I would stand and watch Kirk Russell film a scene where he checks on the presidential plane that has crashed in the middle of New York City. The 20-second sequence was filmed about six times, with 20–30 minutes in between filming—each time done just a little bit differently. I remember thinking, *no wonder it takes months to film an hour-and-a-half movie.*

But, life in the fire service is not full of painful experiences, disasters, and things that you want to forget about. There are times that are fun, pleasurable, and full of joy. There are the pranks, and mealtimes with everyone in the fire station. I have had some of the best cooked food ever in some fire stations. And I have had some of the WORST cooked meals in some fire stations. When a certain firefighter was scheduled to cook, you knew to bring extra food, since you probably would not be eating much of his cooking. Other times you ate too much, since it was absolutely delicious. I have to give credit to the firefighters in Memphis. They know how to cook. Some of the best steaks I ever had came out of a Memphis fire station. Driver D. J. Daugherty, who cooked the steaks, turned them only once. He knew the right heat, and how long to keep the steaks on the grill initially, and when to turn them to the other side. He only turned them once, and they were perfectly cooked.

Some of the best chicken I ever ate came from the hands of Lieutenant Greg Moberly. He always kept the old grease and reused it. And the best popcorn I ever ate was in Memphis fire stations, with all the ingredients in the oil and the different seasonings that were put on the popcorn after it had been popped. Once in a while, Lieutenant Dan Harris and Lieutenant Billy Geyer from Engine 27 and Rescue 3 in Memphis would try to feed me lasagna with spinach hidden between the layers. I hate spinach—but the guys at the 27s were worth the visit. I ate many a fine meal in the Memphis and St. Louis fire stations. I wish I had room to list all of them.

What is entertaining from time to time is the pranks. Firefighters are notorious for pulling pranks on each other. Most vulnerable are the new rookies. As a chief, I could not be a part of pranks, but I saw and witnessed plenty during my 37-year career. If fact, even as a chief, I had a few pulled on me. I found it humorous, and it showed the guys were comfortable enough with me to do a little horseplay. Some of the pranks were innocent and good natured. Most were harmless; but they do cross the line if they have a racial or gender overtone, affects someone financially, or is intended to physically harm someone. Of course, you never know how someone is going to take a practical joke until it happens. It always seemed the firefighters who were best dishing it out were the worst at taking it when it happened to them.

Firehouse pranks come in a variety of groupings. The mechanically engineered pranks present a fair degree of difficulty. They usually require a large amount of advanced planning, and even precise measurements in some cases.

One prank that requires some mechanical engineering and advanced planning is the IV drip over the bed. This is usually used in bed halls where there is a false ceiling. An IV bag is placed in the ceiling over the unsuspecting victim's bed. Using extension tubing, the tubing is run to another bed where, if possible, the tubing can be hidden from plain view. The control for pinching the tubing on or off is near the bed of the prankster. One end of the IV tubing is plugged into an IV bag, and the other end is hooked up to a small needle. This small needle is then inserted through the false ceiling directly over the head of the victim. When everyone goes to bed, the prankster slowly unleashes one drop every minute or so onto the unsuspecting victim. The victim feels something dripping. Usually the victim gets up and looks at the ceiling, and lays back down when they don't see anything. Of course, the prankster has turned off the fluid so nothing drips. Many times the victim will have to use their phone to look at the ceiling, since they don't want to turn on the room lights and disturb the others who are sleeping. Usually everyone in the room knows ahead of time what is going to happen, and is only pretending to be asleep.

When the "victim" lies back down, the dripping begins again. Drip! Drip! Drip! Right into the face! In frustration, the victim gets up again to look. By this time, someone in the room cannot help themselves and begins to giggle. The plot has been revealed, and usually everyone else breaks out laughing, since they cannot contain themselves either.

So, what has happened to me in the past? Well, my phobia is snakes. I hate them! I know they say there are good snakes that eat the bad snakes and other rodents, but unfortunately they don't have a sign around their neck telling you which they are, and I don't have time to study all the different color markings, eye shapes, and shapes of the head. So I assume every snake is bad.

Firefighters smell fear. They can pick up on weakness. And once they learn your weakness, they exploit it. A fire station is no place to show weakness. I don't care how much something bothers you or scares you—never show it. Even if you have a medically documented phobia of something, no matter how painful it is, don't show it. My mistake was telling one firefighter in a conversation that I hated snakes. That tidbit of information was spread through all 56 fire stations, on all three shifts by the end of the week in Memphis.

One day I was scheduled to have dinner at a fire station. They knew what time I was coming. That is bad when they know when the "mark" is going to be arriving, and the path you are going to take, since you have done this routine over and over. They know where you are going to park and the path you are going to follow. My routine at this particular station was to park on the side of the station, and walk down a pathway in front that had a flowerbed around the front of the sidewalk and front door area where I came in. You probably know where this story is going by now.

Sure enough, I was minding my own business as I was walking up the walkway, and what came flying out of the flowerbed right in front of me was the biggest and blackest snake I had ever seen! It crawled across the sidewalk into the flowerbed on the other side. I jumped back and far as I could, even to the point of almost tripping over myself. I immediately heard laughing coming from inside the fire station. And I am not talking about ordinary laughs. It was deep-belly laughter from a bunch of firefighters looking out the window through the blinds. Immediately I knew I had been had! As it turned out, they had a rubber snake on a piece of fishing line that was intricately set up on a series of poles and pulleys to cause the rubber snake to run across the front of my feet as I walked up the sidewalk. I laughed with them when I got in the station.

On another occasion, I was invited for dinner. Knowing that I like pizza, the firefighters told me they were going to order a bunch of different pizzas, including my favorite—mushroom and sausage. So when I arrived at the fire station, it was business as usual. "How you doing, Chief?" "What's going on downtown, Chief?" The usual talk, and the usual little sidebar bantering as the guys were getting ready for dinner by setting the table, or while some others were watching television. Little did I suspect I was about to be the victim of a practical joke. I must admit, everyone kept a straight face, even though they knew what was about to happen. They were very cool, and kept it well hidden in their facial expressions. They were pros!

As I sat down to eat at the dinner table with some 10 firefighters, the four large pizza boxes were spread at random down the table. My rule is, I always let the firefighters get their food first, since they are subject to a call, so I want them eating before me. Strangely, and I should have picked up on it, nobody opened the mushroom and sausage pizza box. They all dug into the three other boxes of pizza. That should have been my clue; but I didn't pick up on it. After everyone got their pizza the lieutenant said, "Dig in, Chief; there's the mushroom and sausage right there," pointing to a box close to me.

Without hesitation I reached for the box and opened the lid. Out sprang the biggest snake I had ever seen, with its mouth wide open! I damn near fell backwards off my chair. Of course, the laughter erupted. Some guys were laughing so hard that they had to get up and walk it off. Of course, it was a rubber snake designed to spring into action when you open the lid of some container. "Okay! You got me!" I said. I laughed about it, too. A little practical joke helps to break up the day, and it also helps alleviate some of the stress firefighters feel from the things they have to see and do.

Some of the more famous practical jokes in the fire stations usually have to do with water. It's not uncommon for a guy to go to the cabinet to get a glass and when he opens up the cabinet, a pitcher of water falls out on him. Another famous one is to put a bag of flour on a mousetrap and tie it to someone's locker door in the locker room, or the locker next to their bunk. When the unsuspecting victim opens their locker door, the mousetrap snaps and pops the bag of flour, causing an explosion of flour into the victim's face. Ironically, everyone seems to be in the locker room when this happens. Give a firefighter enough idle time and they will come up with innovative and ingenious practical jokes!

Some of the more old and reliable practical jokes in the fire station are to take the slats out that support the mattress and box spring on the firefighter's bed, and just have the mattress and box spring rest on the edge of the frame. When the victim goes to lay down that night or sit on their bed during the day, they fall through with the mattress and box spring to the floor.

Every rookie firefighter who has seen YouTube should be aware of the recruit class picture. It usually encompasses all the new recruit firefighters standing for a group photo in front of the fire station in their brand-new uniforms or turnout gear for a group shot. The fire engines are neatly lined up in the background to top the picture off. Unbeknownst to the unsuspecting recruit firefighters is that a bunch of seasoned firefighters are on the roof of the fire station right above where the recruits are standing. In their possession on the roof are large buckets of water. As the recruits stand proudly for the picture, they are suddenly deluged with gallons upon gallons of water. Usually, the key to suspect it is coming is when someone has a video camera.

But the best practical joke I ever heard was pulled on a rookie when the firefighters in his station convinced him that their battalion chief needed a stool specimen from him because there was a suspected outbreak of Hepatitis in his rookie class. At first the rookie smelled the plot, but with insistence over a couple shifts, and also getting his other classmates to confirm for him that a stool specimen was needed, he complied. He was told to put the specimen in a sandwich baggie and put his name on it, and place it on the battalion chief's desk so he could send it downtown. The rookie complied, and I wish I would have seen the look on the chief's face when he came back from making his rounds to the other fire stations and he looked at the baggie sitting on his desk with the rookie's name on it.

Another humorous part of the job is those patients, bystanders, or family members who try to say a medical term but it comes out as something else. Some of the more funny ones I've heard over the years include: "I have a communications disease," "My groinacologist said...", She's having a grandma seizure," "He suffered a Cadillac arrest," and "He's having trouble breeding (breathing)." I've been guilty of it myself. During a television interview I accidentally said, "Firefighters also do mouth-to-mouth artificial insemination."

CHAPTER 4

✛

THOSE WHO TOUCH
OUR LIVES

There are fun times with firefighter and paramedics; but when the bell goes off, it's time to be serious. Lots of friendships develop among people you work with, and many become life-long friendships. Others, you get the chance to mentor and prepare them for their careers. Others have mentored me and prepared me in my career.

I have been blessed to work and make friends and acquaintances with thousands and thousands of people in the fire and EMS profession in different cities across the United States over my 37-year career. I have made some good friends along the way. One is a man named Ron Olshwanger. I knew Ron from his days volunteering at the Red Cross. While not a firefighter or a paramedic, he is one of the biggest supporters of firefighters and paramedics I have ever seen. For many years, he served as a member on a board of directors with a fire protection district in St. Louis County. He was also involved in other public safety activities throughout his life, including serving as a reserve police officer and a Red Cross coordinator for many years. Ron is also someone who loves photography—he combined this passion with the fire service by going to fires and taking pictures.

Ron became somewhat famous on December 30, 1988, when he snapped a picture at a fire scene on Boyle Avenue in St. Louis. I had just seen Ron and his son Steve at a multiple-alarm fire on the near south side that early morning when he left to go home, and heard a report of a fire on his scanner in a building on Boyle Avenue. When he pulled up, the mother was running from the house with her nightgown burned off. He grabbed his camera and stood in the street as firefighters rushed into the building to attack the fire and search for a little two-year-old girl who was missing.

Shortly thereafter, Firefighter Adam Long emerged from the building carrying the unconscious, blond-haired girl in his arms while trying to do mouth-to-mouth on her. She was lifeless, naked, blackened somewhat with soot, and was hanging like a ragdoll from Adam's arms. Ron raised his camera and snapped a picture of it. That split-second would etch both men in history, because Ron's picture would be published on the front page of the *St. Louis Post Dispatch* the following morning, and the following year he would win a Pulitzer Prize for Spot Photography from among the thousands and thousands of pictures that are submitted for consideration. Ron and Adam are both quality people with high characters. Ron and I became good friends over the years, and Adam and I worked in St. Louis for many years together. Adam even came to my father's funeral to pay his respects, which meant a lot to me.

The little two-year-old girl would eventually die some six days later at Children's Hospital. Ron and Adam also took the time to visit her in the hospital and hold her hand, even though she was unconscious and on a respirator. They also attended her funeral.

The picture is dramatic and speaks volume. It had a dramatic effect on others, and began a smoke detector campaign in St. Louis and other places for people to buy and hang smoke detectors in their residences. Ron told me that he and his, wife when they learned that he had won the Pulitzer Prize, celebrated by going and having dinner at White Castle. That was how unpretentious and humble Ron was. Incidentally, any prize money that Ron won, or any pictures he sold of the Pulitzer Prize-winning photograph, were donated to a smoke detector fund to buy smoke detectors for those who could not afford them. That is the type of man Ron is.

Adam would eventually be assigned to a staff position and become part of an effort to promote smoke detectors in homes. Ron told me later that the little girl probably saved more lives than we will ever know.

But tragedy also struck Ron some years later when his wife died of cancer. He was devastated. They had grown up next to each other, and played together as children. They dated in high school and eventually married. Ron took her death very hard.

Knowing that Ron liked to go to fires and take pictures, I invited Ron to ride with me some shifts. He eagerly accepted. When I got promoted and went to eight-hour shifts, I would go riding on Friday evenings sometimes and visit with paramedics, stop by fire stations and go on calls that sounded interesting. Ron also rode with me on many of those nights into the early morning hours. One night we went to 14 different shootings in an eight-hour period in St. Louis. Another night we went to eight different building fires in the same area where an arsonist had been working for weeks. Ron found riding with me very therapeutic, by getting his mind off his wife's death. Ron took many pictures at many scenes, but one of the most dramatic he would take would occur in the 4300 block of Aldine in north St. Louis one hot Friday summer evening.

A call went out for a shooting in the 4300 block of Aldine. The area at the time was a low socio-economic part of town, with lots of vacant homes and lots—along with gang and drug activity. We were not far away, and when we pulled up we had to park a little back from the scene because the narrow street was blocked with police cars. As we got out of the car, I grabbed my medical bag, and Ron grabbed his camera. We weaved in between two park cars to where we thought the shooting victim was by the way the people had congregated in front of one particular house.

What came into view to us was a grief-stricken lady, sitting on the sidewalk holding a young girl in her arms. The anguish, pain, and tears on her face looked like someone was sticking a thousand needles into her at the same time. The young girl she was holding in her arms looked like a young teenager who had been hit with a shotgun blast to the neck. The girl's shirt was soaked with blood, and the lady had blood all over her, also. The glazed look on the girl's eyes, with one eye half-open and the other fully opened, slumped in the lady's arms, meant she was already dead. One makes many assumptions when you see a scene like this. The lady is grieving uncontrollably. Yells of agony, and tears streaming down her face as she rocks back and forth, tell you this lady is probably the young girl's mother.

Before I could get to the lady, Ron stopped and snapped a picture. When I got to the lady, I tried to tell her to let go, because we needed to treat her daughter. She never heard me. She just kept calling out the girl's name, interspersed with screams and crying as she rocked back and forth in her sitting position on the sidewalk. Eventually, I was able to get her to let go of the girl, and some bystanders helped the mother away and comforted her. I checked the girl for a pulse. No pulse! She was dead! But that wasn't good enough for me. *Death is not going to win today!* I thought. This child is too young to not have a chance at life. I immediately reached into my medical bag and inserted an oral airway to keep her airway open. I also took out my bag-valve mask and started blowing oxygen into her lungs. Following the CPR standards, I began compressions on her chest, and then breathed into her lungs twice. Unfortunately and eventually, blood started coming out of her mouth and nose, and I assumed it was from being shot in the neck and compromising her trachea and/or esophagus. I tried to suction out the blood. I continued this ratio until the engine company and the ambulance crew arrived. The whole time I was doing CPR there was no reaction from her. If she had any chance, she needed an operating room; but I knew her chances were slim to none.

Once the ambulance arrived, I turned patient care over to the paramedics on the ambulance. They did their standard routine of intubation, EKG, IV, drugs, and continued CPR. They eventually loaded her in the ambulance and raced to the hospital. She was pronounced dead in the emergency room after they failed to get her heart started again. Death did win this day!

The next day Ron took his film to be developed, and just like the Pulitzer Prize-winning photograph, he had a dramatic image of this grieving mother holding her teenage daughter. This picture spoke volumes also of the human nature of grief, and the senseless loss of a young, innocent life. He took the picture to the *St. Louis Post Dispatch* again to see if they would publish it, and Ron told me later the editor felt he was looking at another Pulitzer Prize. The problem was—they would not publish it. They felt the picture was too graphic, and not suitable for printing in the paper. In order to win a Pulitzer Prize, the criteria requires that the picture be published in a newspaper, magazine, or news sites that publish at least once a week and have a certain number of circulation or readers. Since Ron's picture never got published, it would never have a chance to win a Pulitzer Prize. Just like Ron's picture of Adam saving the baby probably saved countless other lives with smoke detectors, I am sure this picture would have raised awareness of gun safety and gang violence. As it turns out, the young girl was 15 years old and was accidentally shot by a gang member when the shotgun he was carrying discharged after he pointed the weapon at the girl inadvertently—according to him.

Ron is not doing well health-wise these days, and his days of riding and taking photographs are over. But I still have fond memories of our friendship, and of all the hours we spent in the car over the years going from one scene to another, and just talking about life. I am good friends with his son, Steve, who is the fire chief in the Maryland Heights Fire Protection District in St. Louis County, and he always keeps me apprised of how Ron is doing. Once in a while the three of us get to go to lunch together.

Beside friendships, I have had some wonderful mentors over the years. The first mentor I ever had was a chief by the name of Rich Davis. Rich kind of adopted me when I walked through the doors as a young snot at age 18. Rich was already in his early 60s, and had been running fire and ambulance calls since the late 1930s. Rich had one of those memories that was like a steel trap. Once it was in his head, it would not escape. He could tell you what building or business was on every corner in St. Louis. He knew where every street was; where all 2,500+ fire alarm boxes were and their numbers; what the first alarm companies on those boxes were; and every significant fire St. Louis had had in the last 40 years. He was a large, imposing figure of a man who always looked like he had a scowl on his face and could be mean as heck. But in reality, he had a heart of gold, and would get emotional and cry at moving events like his retirement party. He was nothing but a big teddy bear. He loved his cigars, and it showed on his white shirt that constantly had ash and burn marks. On one of his birthdays we gave him a new white shirt with the burn holes already in it as a joke. He also loved his bourbon, but I never saw him drink on the job or be impaired. Once when he was in the hospital, I snuck him a small bottle of bourbon, for which he was deeply appreciative.

We would spend hours in his office, and he would pontificate of fire and EMS calls he had been on throughout the years. As an 18-year-old kid, I was mesmerized. And with his memory being a steel trap like it was, they were quite vivid and colorful stories. He told of the coldest he had ever been when he rode the side of Hook & Ladder 18 on the way to the multiple-alarm fire at the Casa Loma Ballroom in south St. Louis one cold, snowy, and wintry night in January 1940. Or his proudest moment, when the battalion chief asked him to go to the fire alarm box on the corner and ask for a second alarm for a building fire. He said the chief handed him his key, which was needed to open the inside of the box, and like a telegraph, he had to tap the message to the fire alarm office, since using portable radios was unheard of at the time.

Before radios, communication was handled by the fire stations and the field through a telegraph system back to the fire alarm office. I sat there for ten minutes and listened to him tap out the exact message like he had some 40 years earlier. I thought it would never end as he kept saying, "tap, tap, tap, (pause) tap, tap." He also claimed to have the record time for having someone pronounced dead in the city of St. Louis when he went to a call a couple blocks from the station. He said he was out the door in less than 20 seconds; drove there in less than a minute; went up the steps two at a time with the stretcher; loaded the guy on the stretcher; went down the steps two at a time with the stretcher; and had him to the hospital around the corner in under four minutes, where the doctor pronounced him dead as soon as they walked through the door. Rich said that when we went to call in service from the hospital, the dispatcher asked him if he was going to go on the call and Rich said, "Hell—go on the call? I'm at the hospital and the guy has already been pronounced dead." They were always colorful and lively stories.

I think Rich thought of me as the son he never had. Rich had three daughters that he thought the world of. But what I enjoyed the most was our long talks and the sage advice he gave me, along with the tricks of the trade. He imparted 40 years of wisdom on me in every talk we had. He shared with me his experiences of what worked and what didn't work. One thing he always taught me was to be a sponge and filter at the same time. Take in everything you can, but filter it, since the information you're getting might not be the best.

One of my most vivid memories of being on a scene with Rich was when an 18-wheeler tractor tanker loaded with 8,500 gallons of gasoline overturned near some refineries on the south side of St. Louis. The tanker did not catch fire, but there was a significant amount of gasoline leaking from different compartments, and the smell permeated the air. Firefighters had already diked where the gasoline was running to prevent it from running down sewers, and a nicely-sized pool of gasoline had accumulated around the truck. Rich and I were standing near the front of the truck when two firefighters decided to cut the battery cables to de-energize the truck of any power. They raised the hood as the truck sat on its side and exposed the engine compartment. Once they identified where the battery cables were, they took a bolt cutter and started to cut through one of the cables. They obviously did something wrong because with a loud pop, sparks flew everywhere, with what looked like a Fourth of July show in our nation's capital.

As a reaction, I immediately turned and ran as fast as I could. Rich never moved. When I got about 30 feet I turned around and looked, and none of the sparks hit the gasoline or ignited the fumes that were in the air. I walked back to Rich, who was still standing there with his hands in his pockets and I asked him why he never ran. He said, "It wouldn't have mattered. You would have never got far enough away before you would have been consumed by flames."

I am always appreciative for what Rich did for me as a young guy walking through the door. I'll never forget his kindness, compassion towards his employees, and his passion for the job. I stayed in touch with him quite a bit after his retirement. The last time I saw Rich was at his wife's funeral. His mental faculties seemed to have failed him, and he had periods of lucidness and periods of confusion. Rich died about three months later, and I will always be grateful for him sending me off in the right direction at the beginning of my career.

Another person I was able to pick the brain of on many occasions was the former fire chief of St. Louis, Neil Svetanics. Chief Svetanics was fire chief for about 13 years and was also like Rich, in that he loved the profession, and thought the world of his employees. I would especially love to sit and talk to him in his office after he just got finished managing a multiple-alarm fire. It was an opportunity to pick his brain on the tactics and strategy he'd used. He was a master strategist and tactician. I also learned from Chief Svetanics how to be progressive, and market your department. Chief Svetanics was a very progressive chief who was constantly looking at his fire department and trying to find ways to do things better. He once told me that you should always be looking where you can tweak things to make it better. He was a master at marketing the image of the St. Louis Fire Department. He had an excellent relationship with the media, and if there was ever a hiccup in the operation, it was smoothed over because of the relationship and rapport he had with news reporters.

Chief Svetanics also knew the art of politics. He came from a political family, and many times he had a political strategy with a planned four- or five-step process to achieve his goals. I saw him stand up to politicians who wanted to lessen the ability of the fire department several times. During a budget meeting with some aldermanic committee members one day, the chair asked Chief Svetanics how many fire stations he could close to save money. Chief Svetanics told the committee he could close all of them. "Just tell me who wants to give up the first fire station in their aldermanic ward, and I'll start with that one," he said. The entire group of aldermen and alderwomen looked down at their papers and went on to the next agenda item. Nobody ever brought up the subject again while he was fire chief.

I learned a lot from Chief Svetanics. He finished a 50-year career in 2014 by retiring from St. Louis, and then taking a job as fire chief for the Lemay Fire Protection District—a neighboring fire department to St. Louis city. He leaves behind quite a legacy.

Another person I have tremendous respect for is Chief Richard Arwood. As fire chief in Memphis, he hired me as a deputy fire chief in 2005, and gave me the opportunity to turn around a challenged and troubled EMS system. He always exerted the right type of leadership at the right time. A very intellectual and highly cerebral thinker, Chief Arwood was another leader who supported and believed in those who had lower rank than he. I saw him stand firm on several occasions when there were attempts by the politicians to cut the fire department budget. He argued that it would compromise public safety, and he could not close his eyes to jeopardizing firefighter safety and the fire suppression capability.

Chief Arwood gave me the freedom to turn his EMS system around. But he also had trust in me that I knew when I was crossing the line, and would have to come to him for guidance or permission. We had a great working relationship, and I tremendously missed his leadership when he retired. One of the things I most respected him for was that he did not have an ego, and he did not put himself before the organization. He always considered his firefighters first before making any decision—even if it was to his detriment. Unfortunately, I have known a few fire chiefs who have no ethical standards. They let their egos get in the way of their thinking, and they are clueless on how to lead.

The common thread among Chiefs Davis, Svetanics, and Arwood was that they believed in the people underneath them and they supported them. As a result, they were all successful and respected. They did not throw their employees or others under the bus, as I have seen others I have worked for do. I did not see them abuse their power. The life lesson I have taken away from these three mentors is once you stop supporting your people, you allow those with other ambitions and agendas to come through the door and disrupt the organization. Unfortunately, the Peter Principle is alive and well with several chief fire officers that I have worked for over the years. They know nothing about leadership, and I could write an entire book on what they did wrong, since they set an excellent example of what NOT to do! In their cases, they left the organization worse than they found it.

One other non-firefighting/EMS person I came to respect immensely was the former Chief of Police of St. Louis and then Mayor of St. Louis from 1997–2001. Clarence Harmon was a real class act. I came to know Clarence when he was just a lieutenant in the police department, and then he rose through the ranks at tremendous speed. Decision-makers could see the talent he brought to the table. What I respected about Clarence most, besides his intelligence, was the fact that he was not political. He would do the right thing for the right reason, regardless of who was putting influence on him. As a candidate for mayor, he personally inspected each donation check to make sure it was not from someone who would pose a conflict of interest down the line, or from someone who had a business deal going in the city and was asking for a favor. If they did, he returned the check. He would not take it. I will always have tremendous respect for the man. In an appalling show of disrespect, the mayor who replaced him, during his inaugural speech in city hall, never thanked Clarence for his years of service to the community as a police officer and then mayor, even though Clarence sat on the podium, not far from him. Even though they were competitors in the democratic primary, it would have been the respectful and professional thing to do. It taught me about being gracious and humble in victory.

Another friendship I developed was with a firefighter in St. Louis. That came about when our lives would become intertwined in the most bizarre and unfortunate of circumstances.

I was only on the job about two weeks in 1977 when we got dispatched to a report of a fire in Roosevelt High School on the south side of St. Louis. School was out for the summer when this call occurred, so we knew there was a good chance that no students were on the premises.

Roosevelt High School was built in 1925 and is a large, old, four-story brick structure that served as a high school in the St. Louis school system. The land was actually a cemetery at one time for bodies that were unclaimed, and they had to remove all the bodies in order to build the high school. According to legend, they did not find all the bodies, and during construction of the high school, workers would commonly find bones, jewelry, and parts of coffins. Dogs from the neighborhood were also showing up at home with strange-looking bones.

Behind the school is a large football field, and there is a thoroughfare for driving and parking between the school and the football field. Everybody responded around to the rear of the school where the thoroughfare was. I can't remember how long it took us to get there, but I do know that when we showed up, the 14s pumper had a single booster line off through a door in the rear of the building.

I was immediately ushered through the door where the booster line was laid. When I walked through the door, the first thing I saw was a human body grossly burnt just inside the door. Across the room were three more badly burned bodies. There was no more clothing on the people, and their belt buckles were melted into their skin. They had no more hair on their body or head, and you could see the veins in their scalps, almost as if they had an alien head. The one person I was looking at directly beneath my feet had their eyes closed and was not moving. What was unusual was that the bodies did not appear as those that burn long. Instead of the black and blistering you normally see on a body that has been exposed to heat too long, these people had blisters and skin sloughing, but their skin was a white color.

Firefighters were trying to attend to all four victims as best they could. When I looked around, it looked like we were in the cafeteria. The cafeteria looked like an explosion had occurred, with tables and chairs strewn about and ceiling tiles broken and lying on the ground after falling. The walls looked like they took a blast of heat also. I was trying to get my head around everything since it was a report of a fire, but if there was a fire, there really was no evidence of it, and the 14s only had a booster line off into the building. So there must have been a small amount of fire.

But here's where I really screwed up. One of the worst things I ever did in my career. When I looked at how grossly burned all four bodies were, I said, "These guys are dead." I said it because I thought they were already dead. The person lying on the ground closest to me, in a calm and matter-of-fact voice, said, "No we're not!" I am sure my jaw hit the floor. I could not believe the guy was still alive with how badly burned he was. One hundred percent of his body was burned, and he was lying there talking to me as if we were having an ordinary conversation about a baseball game. I stood there for a second, trying to gather my composure after what I had just said and what I'd just witnessed. That was about as dim-witted a comment as I could have made.

Throughout my entire career, I never again declared someone dead or made another stupid comment like that on an emergency scene without checking out the patient first. I definitely learned my lesson on this call. It has stuck with me for 37 years, and I do not hesitate to share this story with rookies when I get the chance.

Being the rookie myself, I was assigned the most serious patient. We loaded him on the stretcher and wheeled him to the ambulance. I was put in back with the patient, and we were on our way to Barnes Hospital where there was a burn unit. At this point in my career, I was not a paramedic, and I was not even an EMT. The most I had was an advanced first aid card from the fire academy. I had never been taught how to administer oxygen, so all I could really do is sit in the back of the ambulance with the patient as we raced to Barnes Hospital some five miles away.

On the way to the hospital, the patient and I began having a conversation. The first thing he asked me is how badly he was burned. I had to be honest with him and told 100 percent. His next comment back to me was, "Well, I'm dead." I tried to reassure him and tell him everything was going to be all right, but I knew he could see the look in my eye, and I could see the look in his eye. We both knew he was going to die. I asked him his name. He told me his name was Bill Lemmon,[4] and he was a St. Louis city firefighter.

Again, my jaw darn near hit the ground. I repeated back to him, "You're a city firefighter?" He confirmed again that he was, and told me the other three guys in the school were also city firefighters. *Oh no!* I thought. *This is horrible.* I didn't know him since I had only been employed for about two weeks.

His arms were involuntarily starting to contract and draw up in front of him and his hands were starting to make a fist. He was trying to stop it, but he said there was nothing he could do. Later in my career, I found out this is called the "Pugilist Posture" and it is caused by the shrinkage of body tissues and muscle due to dehydration caused by heating.

Once we got him to the hospital, we dropped him off in the emergency room, and doctors and nurses went to work on him.

As it turned out, these four off-duty firefighters were working secondary jobs stripping and cleaning the cafeteria floor at Roosevelt High School. The solvent they were using apparently was not well ventilated, and it reached a point where the solvent and the air combined to put it in an explosive range. One of the firefighters flipped the switch on the buffer, and there was a massive explosion that was estimated to be 2,500 degrees Fahrenheit. It was a flash explosion. Almost as soon as it happened, it blew itself out. But it did the damage to these four firefighters. Bill Lemmon, whom I took to the hospital, died some eight hours later. Killed instantly at the explosion was Firefighter LaVerie Sutton.[5] His brother, Captain Leon Sutton[6] died about a week later, and Firefighter Robert Marshall[7] died about three months later.

Ironically, many years later, a recruit class came through the St. Louis Fire Department, and the class was named in honor of Bill Lemmon. His son, Dan Lemmon, was in the class. One day I approached Dan and told him who I was, and that I had taken his father to the hospital. Dan, who was young at the time of the incident, told me that he and his family went to the hospital and he briefly saw his dad in the emergency room, and told him how much he loved him. Dan said he was crying so hard that he had to leave the room. That was the last time he saw his father. We immediately bonded, and remain good friends today. Dan is now a captain in the St. Louis Fire Department, and I tell him all the time how proud his father would be of him.

Throughout my career, I have had the opportunity to work with many excellent and professional police officers also. Like firefighters and EMS people, they are also dedicated people, and they get lumped in with the few bad cops who sometimes make the news. I had the opportunity to work with and got to know many police officers over the years—especially early in my career, when I worked on the streets and virtually every call I went on, a police officer was also dispatched. As a result of working with and seeing them almost every shift, I got to know many St. Louis police officers.

It was not uncommon for me to go to the police gym in St. Louis and play racquetball with many of them several days a week. I wish I had a nickel for every racquetball game I played with Major George Hydar. One funny story came out those working relationships and racquetball games. One St. Louis police officer I came to know and played racquetball with was a traffic officer named Dave. Dave was a tall figure of a man, who was probably close to 6'6".

One day, I made a left turn onto a street and there was Dave, sitting next to his police motorcycle. He was waiting for people who made an illegal left turn against the sign. Quite frankly, I did not see the sign that said, "No left turn between the hours of 4 p.m. and 6 p.m." Dave pulled me over in my unmarked staff vehicle. He immediately saw it was me and giggled. I explained that I did not see the sign. He let me go, and told me he would see me on the racquetball court later that evening. About six months later, I was racing down a street on the south side of St. Louis because I was late for a meeting. It was a street that had a grassy median in the middle, with periodic clumps of bushes. Dave was running radar that day and stepped out from behind a bush to wave me over for speeding. When he saw it was me, we both laughed, and he said that we've got to quit meeting like this. He did not give me a ticket.

About another three months later, I was traveling westbound on Interstate 44 en route to my office after attending a meeting at city hall. My radio cracked with a "police officer in need of aid" at Hampton and West Park. That address was just a few blocks off my next exit ramp, so I decided go by and see if there was something I could do if an officer was injured. It only took me a few minutes to arrive, but when I pulled up at the intersection I saw a police motorcycle laying on its side, and a police officer lying in the street with people surrounding him. My first impression was that there was an auto accident between the car and the police motorcycle, and it looked like the car made a left turn in front of the motorcycle. I exited my car and walked up to the injured officer. I found Dave lying on the ground, holding his shoulder. I stood over him and looked down. Dave saw me and said through his grimacing, "Gary, I think my shoulder is broken." Dave looked like he was in a considerable amount of pain.

To break the ice and maybe get a little smile out of him I said, "Aren't you glad you didn't give me those tickets?" He broke out laughing but it hurt so bad that he stopped.

The paramedics who responded and I took extraordinary care of Dave that day. Dave and I laughed about that moment for years later. Those of us who work in fire and EMS see police officers as one of us. We're all brothers and sisters working in the public safety arena.

I could write an entire book all by itself on all the wonderful people that I know who work and have worked in fire, EMS, and law enforcement. There are so many! I have been blessed to have so many of these wonderful people cross my path in life. I probably learned something from every one of them. The people who work in fire, EMS, and law enforcement are some of the best people in the world.

Whenever I think of all these wonderful people, I think of a quote I once read:

"You can easily judge the character of a person by how they treat those who can do nothing for them."

-Malcolm S. Forbes.

CHAPTER 5

✛

BIG FIRES NEED BIG WATER

There is a saying in the fire service. Big fires need big water! As simple as it sounds, in essence it means if you've got a big fire, you're going to need lots of water.

I have been to some horrific fires in my career, and I have been to thousands of ordinary house fires. However, one of the hottest and largest fires I have ever been to occurred in the early morning hours of October 6, 2006, in downtown Memphis. The fire started in the First United Methodist Church on the corner of 2nd and Poplar, about two thirty in the morning. The church was built in 1893, and was probably loaded with old wood beam supports. I lived in a condominium in downtown Memphis at the time that was only about two blocks from the fire.

It was a crisp fall night and I'd left my windows cracked just enough to let the cool air in to create a nice sleeping atmosphere. With the windows slightly cracked, I was awakened by sirens. I heard the 5's engine rolling down Front Street, just a half-block from my building. No big deal. I heard sirens all the time, with all the automatic alarms that go off in the downtown buildings at all hours of the day and night. So I attempted to roll back over and go to sleep. I must have dozed back off since I was next awakened by my pager going off. I picked up the pager and squinted at the alphanumeric display and it said, "Second Alarm—2nd and Poplar." As a member of the senior command staff with the Memphis Fire Department, it was not uncommon to get pager notifications when there was a working fire in the city, an employee got injured, four or more ambulances were dispatched to a scene, etc.

After seeing it was a second alarm downtown, I was immediately jarred awake and to my senses. As soon as I sat up in bed, I could smell it. With my windows cracked, the all too familiar smell of burning wood was oozing its way into my condominium. The smell is distinct. It is bitter to your nostrils, and seems to tell your brain that there is an abomination to the air. It chokes you with how pungent it can be.

I immediately got dressed and got to my car. I picked up the radio to tell the dispatcher that I was responding, and almost before I could put the microphone back in its cradle, I had to tell the dispatcher I'd arrived on the scene.

When I pulled up, a quick size-up told me this was going to be ugly. I have seen too many scenes like this to know it is not going to have a good ending. The Memphis downtown streets are well-lit, so everything was plainly visible to me. Heavy, thick, black and gray molasses-looking smoke was pushing out of the basement windows on the Poplar Street side of the building. The more it pushed out with force, the more you could tell how active and growing the fire was, since it is generating a byproduct (smoke). And, since there is only so much space in a container (the church), the smoke is going to push out and escape to make room for the smoke being generated behind it. It was clear that there was an active and large fire in the basement of the church.

I stepped out of my car while still gazing at the building to get a good size-up. The church was virtually all stone, with a steeple on the front that rises over 100 feet off the ground. The steeple and the bell tower sat on the corner of the building, right at the intersection of 2nd and Poplar. The building itself was a large, imposing structure rising about 60 feet off the ground, with a slanted slate roof that rose to a peak in the center of the building. There were other archways and other entrances on the side of the building besides the main entrance that sat on 2nd Street. Directly next to the church on the north side was a four-story school building, probably no more than eight feet away.

As I walked around to the rear of my car and opened the trunk to get my turnout gear and helmet on, I noticed the American flag on the corner.

There was a pretty good stiff breeze blowing—another warning sign that it wasn't going to be a good night.

I walked to the front of the church and saw heavy, black smoke pushing from the front door of the church also. I stepped briefly inside the church to see if I could get a feel for any heat or see anything. I was getting a fair amount of heat at the front doors, even though the fire looked like it was mainly in the basement and to the rear of the structure. Another bad sign! If you're getting thermal heating at the front of the structure that significant, and the fire is in the basement and the rear, the BTUs burning must be tremendous.

I reported to the rear of the incident commander's vehicle, which was east and south of the church building. The incident commander was Division Chief Ron Mitchell. Of course, he had his hands full just trying to manage all the radio traffic and resources. I asked, "What do you need, Ron?" He told me he needed someone to take the rear of the building and manage things from there because, like me, he knew we were going to lose the church, but we also had to think about the school building.

I immediately proceeded to the rear of the building. In incident management lingo, it is called the Charlie Division. Directly across from the church was another two-story building. I had no idea what was in the two-story building, I just knew we needed to keep the fire out of there, also. On the way to the Charlie Division, I bumped into Chief Don Kuhn, who served as the operations chief on the senior command staff with me. Don and I are good friends, and one of our favorite things to do is get lunch together at some Chinese all-you-can-eat buffet a couple times a week.

I told Don that I was going to be taking the Charlie Division, and we both took a quick look at the exposure building to the north. We couldn't see over a high wooden fence in the rear alley between the two buildings, so we stood on some dumpsters to peer over the fence to get a feel of how much separation we had. There wasn't much—probably about 8–10 feet, and an elevated passageway connecting the church and the school. I told Don I was going to send a company into the school to see if there were fire doors on the passage and, if so, to make sure they were closed.

Don had a million things running through his mind, and he told me to do what I had to do to keep the fire out of the school building. By this point, an evacuation of the church building had been ordered, and all firefighters were out and accounted for. Now it was time to set up defensive operations. I called the incident commander on the radio and told him I needed two truck companies and three engine companies to report to me in the rear of the building. We were going to set up a defensive operation to keep the fire from spreading. One of the tactics that Chief Svetanics always taught me was to stay one alarm ahead of the fire. He said you've got to think what the fire is going to be like, and what it is going to look like in the next ten minutes, and be prepared for it. He said if you try to play catch-up, it's too late.

We didn't see any flames at this point—just heavy and brackish, chunky smoke pouring from all parts of the building. It would be just a matter of time before the fire vented itself and we'd have visible flames all over the place.

The two ladder companies and the three engine companies that I'd requested reported to me in the rear of the building. I huddled the lieutenants from all the companies, similar to a football huddle, and told them what the game plan was. I sent Truck 6 into the school to check for fire extension, and to see if there were burn doors on the tunnel way between the school and church, and to make sure they were closed. The ladder companies needed to get set up, and the engine companies needed to find a water source so they could feed water to the ladder companies, which would eventually have their ladders elevated, throwing water onto the fire. Eventually, the engine company would report to me that there was no fire in the school building, and the burn doors were closed. I had them report back to me so that we could account for them once they exited the building.

One of the ladder companies sent to me was a rescue company with a snorkel-like basket, which made a raise in the alley and started flowing water. Soon after, the fire finally broke through what seemed like every window in the church simultaneously. It was like someone flipped a switch and the place just ignited. And did it! Flames flew out of every window, and the flicker of the flames in the windows of the other office buildings around the area made it seem like all of downtown Memphis was on fire.

The alley in the rear of the building was only about 30 feet across, so we did not have much room to navigate. I can remember feeling an ungodly amount of heat. It was some of the worst heat I have ever felt at a fire. It was almost as if someone opened the gates of Hell and let all the heat out. Firefighters had to rush to lower the basket on the rescue/snorkel since the heat was too unbearable. Other firefighters scrambled to lower the basket on the rescue company, but it jammed, and the two firefighters in the basket took the brunt of the heat. But they were eventually able to lower the basket to the ground and the two firefighters escaped the blistering temperature.

I had Truck 4 set up their ladder company on the north side of the school building, so that they could make a raise over the top of the school building and shoot water down into the church. This advantage also allowed them to deal with any embers that landed on the roof of the school or the building across the alley from the church.

We moved the rescue company with its snorkel basket further down the alley so that it was not so close to the church, with the tremendous amount of heat coming from the building. After it was moved, we still had a good vantage point to put water on the church, protect the school, and also protect the building across the alley.

As all big fires do, eventually they will go out. They either get put out by the water being put on them, or they lose the fuel that is feeding the fire. The truth be known, usually they lose their fuel and go out, since it would take a tremendous amount of water at the same time to put out a fire of this magnitude.

As I stood in the rear of the building, with not much to do except monitor our progress with the fire since everything was in position, I overheard a transmission on my portable radio say, "There is a fire in the building in the Charlie Division now." What? I turned around to look at the two-story building we were protecting across the alley to see if I could see any fire. I scanned the length of the building and I didn't see anything. I asked some firefighters standing near me, who also heard the transmission, if they saw anything. They reported nothing, either. I radioed Lieutenant Rike on top of Truck 4's ladder to see if he saw anything, and he reported nothing. But he did report that he could see fires in buildings about three blocks away.

Again, things weren't good. Probably embers from the church fire blew across town and started catching other buildings on fire in the strong wind. I didn't know that other buildings were on fire in the downtown area since

I was on a radio talk group dedicated to the church fire. Unbeknownst to me, three other buildings in downtown Memphis had caught fire, including a 22-story office building. There were three alarms' worth of equipment and firefighters over at the other buildings fighting those fires. It was determined open windows in one building, and old wooden beams in the other buildings helped catch them on fire.

Embers were seen flying all through the downtown area at the height of the church fire. Chief Kuhn had to set up roving patrols of fire companies in the downtown area to check for hotspots or embers that had landed. In some cases, they found dumpsters on fire and a car about to catch fire.

In all, three alarms were used for the church fire, and three alarms were used for the other building fires. After the church fire died down and all there was left to do was throw water on the collapsed ruins, I went over to the other building fires. They were still blazing pretty well, but it looked like there was no danger of it spreading.

As the 7:00 a.m. hour approached, Chief Kuhn turned to me and said that he just got a call that his daughter was about to have a baby and he needed to get out of there. I told him, "Take off, Grandpa, we got this." And away Don went to rush to the hospital where his daughter was in labor.

Altogether, we lost two buildings, and two others sustained moderate to severe damage in downtown Memphis that night. But no firefighters were killed, and that was the most important part of any operation. They can rebuild the buildings or fix them back up, but we cannot replace a firefighter's life.

Another large fire I was involved in occurred in October of 1998 in St. Louis. I was the chief paramedic for the St. Louis Fire Department at the time, and I heard a report of a fire go out over the fire radio; it was on the 22nd floor of the Council Plaza Towers. I was sitting in my office some five miles away. No need to jump up. It could be anything. Let the first engine company get there and report what it is. As Engine 29 was en route; they reported seeing heavy smoke coming from the upper floors of the Council Towers. The Council Towers was a large public housing complex built for the elderly back in the 1960s. There are two buildings. One is 27 stories tall, and the other is 16 stories tall.

The first company on the scene reported heavy fire showing from the upper floors and they wanted a second alarm. Time to roll! This was not a good situation. A high-rise fire where hundreds of elderly people live is a worst-case scenario.

As I raced to the scene, I heard the radio traffic on the fire ground. Firefighters were scrambling up the stairs to get to the fire floor while also trying to evacuate elderly people from their apartments. I'd been to other fires like this in St. Louis, and it is a challenge. You have elderly people who can barely walk; those on oxygen; those with walkers; and some even in wheelchairs. It is a nightmare trying to evacuate these types of people, and it takes extra manpower to do so. As I continued to the scene, I heard Chief Svetanics arrive at the scene and ask for a third alarm. Firefighters who made it to the 20th floor reported heavy smoke conditions, with zero visibility in the hallway.

Eventually, I would arrive on the scene. As in many other scenes like this, it is chaos until you can get it all straightened out, and everyone heading in the same direction. Being in charge of all the paramedics, I had whatever resources I had on the scene bring their equipment, and report to me in the lobby. My strategic plan was to set up a triage/treatment area in the lobby. Residents were brought down from two different stairways on either side of the lobby. Firefighters kept smoke out of the stairways by using large ventilation fans to pressurize them. Some residents came down the elevator. Regardless of whether they came down the stairs or the elevators, they would be triaged and, if not hurt, moved to an assembly area. And if they were injured, we would move them to an established treatment area. The lobby was also an excellent location to shelter residents in place and treat the wounded, since there was danger from falling glass some 20 stories above if they were to walk outside.

In the meantime, extra alarms were put in that would eventually reach to eight alarms—bringing most of the fire equipment from the city, and having the county fire departments come in and staff our fire stations with their apparatus.

As we were in the lobby, I could hear explosions going off some 20 stories above. I later found out these were oxygen bottles that were in the apartment that was on fire. As patients filtered to us, and more firefighters responded to the scene to control the blaze on the 22nd floor, the elevator doors suddenly opened. I saw firefighters dragging a firefighter out who was obviously unconscious. It was Mike LeBrun.[8] I knew Mike from the 17s, where he had been for many years. One look at Mike told me that his condition was critical, since he was unconscious and black soot covered his face. Paramedics and my medical director, who had been on the scene, went into immediate action. It seems to go to a new level when it's one of your own. As the paramedics began working on Mike, I could see he was not breathing. *Jesus! Not Mike,* I thought to myself. Mike was a pretty good and friendly guy. I knew his mother-in-law from the church I went to. Eventually they loaded Mike on the stretcher after he had been intubated. He still was not breathing. As they moved swiftly to the ambulance, I saw a resident drop to her knees in prayer.

Mike paid a terrible price for his unselfishness to save others. He did survive, but he suffered a permanent disability to his lungs, which in effect retired him for the rest of his career.

All total, some ten residents were transported to the hospital—of which, two were in critical condition. Three firefighters were transported to the hospital, with Mike being the most serious.

It always seemed like St. Louis had three or four large fires every year, and I expected the same when I went to Memphis. But that did not happen to be the case. While the St. Louis Fire Department runs a lot of house fires, like Memphis does, for some reason, the big building fires never really happened in Memphis.

But I did run into my share of fires in Memphis. The one-story frames were Memphis' bread and butter calls. The firefighters in Memphis handled them every day, but that did not mean they couldn't be a challenge sometimes. Sometimes there were exposure problems. Other times there were water supply problems. But Memphis has some big homes, especially in the mid-town and east sections of the city. Those fires also posed a challenge, but again, they were professionally handled, and extinguished in a timely manner.

There were some more notable moments during my career with fires in Memphis. One of the ones that bothered me the most was a single-story frame home fire on the south side of the downtown area. It was late at night, around 10:00 p.m. When the first engine company pulled up, they reported the house fully involved in flames. The call was also put out as someone trapped in the house. After the first firefighters arrived, they advanced the hand-line to the building and began to attack the fire, since it was their goal to get inside the structure because someone was reportedly trapped inside. A lot of the front yard was on fire as a result of the radiant heat coming off the building. The grass was on fire as were some other items, including a chair. What the firefighters did not see when they advanced the hose-line to the house in the darkness was the burning body laying in the front yard, among the grass and other items. It was a 95-year-old lady who witnesses reported coming out of the house fully involved and on fire herself, with her walker. She would eventually collapse in the front yard.

That call bothered me greatly. Here is a 95-year-old lady who has lived a long life, and she dies in this fashion. That was not right! Someone of her age, who has survived all these years, is entitled to die comfortably and warmly in her bed, peacefully, and surrounded by her family. It does not seem fair that she would die in such a horrendous fashion.

I made it to the scene just as they were extinguishing her. There was nothing we could do for her other than pronounce her dead and await the medical examiner to respond to the scene.

Again, there is not much said at these scenes. Most firefighters went about their business that night, taking care of things while deep in thought.

The other bread and butter fire calls in Memphis are apartment buildings. Memphis is littered with apartment complexes that are usually two-story structures. There is usually a whole complex of buildings on one piece of property that is managed by and owned by an investment company. Most of the apartment buildings have a total of 16 apartments in them—eight on one side and eight on the other, with four being up and four being down on each side. I wish I had a nickel for every apartment fire I went on while I worked in Memphis. I might be able to pay off my house today.

Most of the apartment structures were wooden, with light truss construction for the roof assembly. Most of these had common roofs, so once the fire got up in the roof area, it would spread across the entire apartment building unless something was done to cut it off.

The most common method for cutting off the fire was to go to the apartment on either side of the apartment that was on fire, and have companies pull the ceiling down with their pike poles. Once the ceiling was down, hose-lines could be used to extinguish any fire that was spreading out of the apartment into the attic area. Once this was contained, you could attack the main body of the fire in the apartment and extinguish the flames. Although three apartments would usually be damaged, at least you would not lose the entire apartment building.

I have so many memories of so many different fires that it is difficult to include all of them in this book. Some of the more vivid ones in my memory include a five-alarm fire at the Crown C Supply Company on Manchester Road in St. Louis in 1988. I heard the first alarm go out. After a first alarm, you listen to see what the first company reports, since many times there is no fire at all, or it's just a small fire. I listened and listened, and didn't hear anything. I thought, there was no way it was taking them that long to get there.

The next voice I heard was Jerry Eveland, who was the battalion chief. He said, "805 to Fire Alarm; give me a second, third, and fourth alarm." Holy cow! I'd never heard that one before. He wanted three additional alarms all at the same time. Traditionally, the way multiple-alarm fires are asked for is one at a time, and usually there is an interval between each alarm before it is asked so that you have time to manage all your resources. The only other time I heard that was back in the late 1970s when St. Louis had a grain elevator burning at the foot of Chouteau Street, and the battalion chief asked for all five alarms back-to-back—but not in the same sentence.

Another memory I have that was unusual was the report of heavy smoke coming from a building at Forest Park and Boyle in the Central West End of St. Louis. The first arriving engine company reported heavy smoke coming from all sections of the building. I immediately started heading in that direction. The battalion chief pulled up on the scene and after about three minutes, he asked for a second alarm.

When I pulled up, it was a large, two-story brick commercial building that ran the length of the block from Forest Park Avenue all the way over to Laclede Avenue. I could see what looked like white smoke also pushing out of whatever crevice it could find. I parked my car out of the way to allow the second alarm companies to get in, and walked up to the battalion chief, who was standing on the sidewalk surveying the building. He said to me, "Gary, something just does not look right." It did look bad—but it did look different than most working fires. White smoke was pushing out of any opening it could find on both floors. By why was it white? Usually it doesn't turn white until some water is put on the fire. Were sprinklers going off in the building and were we seeing steam conversion from the fire? Our answer soon came. The captain of Engine 28 came out of the building and reported that they'd found a huge, broken steam pipe. There was no fire. With a sheepish grin between laughing and embarrassment, the battalion chief had to get on the radio and report there was no fire and to "strike out the second alarm."

There were many other large fires throughout the years, including the vacant Gateway Hotel fire in downtown St. Louis on February 12, 1987. I was on my way home when I heard the radio report. Chief Svetanics was just leaving city hall and reported heavy smoke conditions in the downtown area.

The Gateway Hotel was a vacant 580 room, 20-plus-story hotel that sat on the corner of 9th and Washington in downtown St. Louis. I ate some dinner one time there in the cafeteria and got severe food poisoning. I never went back.

When I got there, heavy smoke conditions were belching from a large vent on a roof area about three stories up. The fire was deep somewhere in the building and there was difficulty finding it. The fight went on for over five hours into the late evening. The main fire was in the sub-basement but an arsonist in the building kept lighting fires and forced firefighters to run one hot spot to another. All total, there were separate fires on 12 of the 20 floors of the hotel.

Eventually the main fire was extinguished, and just about the time the smoke conditions subsided substantially, fire was seen on the top floor of the hotel, which was the ballroom. At one point, Chief Svetanics was contemplating pulling all the firefighters from the building, since he couldn't say if another fire was going to break out somewhere else, and he didn't want any firefighters getting trapped above another fire.

Five firefighters would be sent to the hospital that day, including a friend of mine who almost died in the sub-basement when he ran out of air in his tank.

Other fires are less dramatic, but to the person involved, it is the entire world that particular day to that person. Such was the case one winter in St. Louis when an elderly lady kept screaming that her dog was inside the house that was on fire. She was elderly, and didn't care about anything else. To her, that dog was her companion and best friend, and that was her entire world to her.

Firefighters successfully put out the fire, and they found the dog in a back bedroom under the bed. When they brought the dog out, it was not burned but it had breathed a tremendous amount of smoke and was unconscious. It was not a purebred dog, and it didn't look like an expensive dog. It was just a mutt, mixed-breed, brown and white dog of about 30 pounds that she had either befriended on the street or picked up at the pound. But it didn't matter what the dog was, it was the entire world to her.

We immediately grabbed a portable oxygen tank with a resuscitation mask on it where you can press a button and push air into someone's lungs. We put the mask over the dog's face and kept pushing fresh oxygen into his lungs. Eventually, after about seven minutes, the dog started responding and started to wake up. The entire time the elderly lady was standing over our shoulder, crying, calling out the dog's name. She kept saying, "Bella, please wake up, please!" When she could see the dog was responding, she started crying even harder—I am assuming from stress relief. When the dog opened her eyes and started wagging her tail when she saw her owner, I knew we'd done something pretty extraordinary that day.

Knowing that the dog could develop some complications down the line from breathing in the junk that is in the smoke of a fire, I offered to drive her to her veterinarian, since the dog might develop a lung infection or something else. After we had some neighbors agree to secure and watch her property after the firefighters left, I drove her to the veterinarian with the dog on her lap. It was a good feeling to see her sitting there, stroking the dog's head and just loving on it.

Other times I was left shaking my head on fire calls. One such call occurred in Memphis in 2009, when a mother left her two- and three-year-old sons at home alone while she and her aunt left to go drop off a friend. I made it to the scene and both boys had already died in the fire. Neighbors who tried to rescue the boys said it was heartbreaking to hear them crying and screaming in the house and they could not get to them. It was equally hard on the firefighters, since the boys would sometimes come into the fire station just a half-block away to get candy out of the machine.

But beyond the disturbing fact of leaving the boys home alone was the interview that the aunt gave to a local television station while still on the scene. First, the aunt said she had no regrets leaving the children home alone, and then she closed the interview by saying that she really needed to get into the house and see if her purse burned up because her food stamps were in the purse. This interview can be found on YouTube, and has been widely distributed on Facebook.

It's sad that some children are disadvantaged with their upbringing, and if these two children had not been left home alone, they would probably still be alive today.

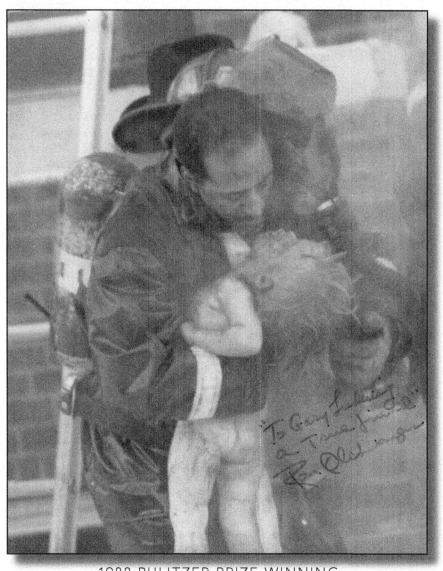

1988 PULITZER PRIZE WINNING
PHOTOGRAPH SHOT BY RON OLSHWANGER
WITH FIREFIGHTER ADAM LONG.

THE AUTHOR MEETING PRESIDENT BILL CLINTON.

THE AUTHOR AT BOTTOM CENTER AT
SCENE OF MULTI-ALARM FIRE.

THE AUTHOR IN WHITE SHIRT ASSISTED BY
CAPTAIN VINCE WRIGHT AFTER DISLOCATING
SHOULDER ON VERTICAL RESCUE CALL.

LIGHTHEARTED MOMENTS ON
BEALE STREET IN MEMPHIS.

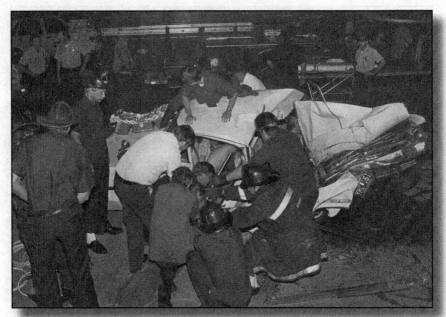

THE AUTHOR, CENTER OF PICTURE IN WHITE
SHIRT, REMOVING VICTIMS FROM CAR ACCIDENT.

THE AUTHOR IN WHITE SHIRT OPERATING
AT AUTO ACCIDENT SCENE.

THE AUTHOR OPERATING AT THE GREAT
FLOOD OF 93' IN ST. LOUIS.

THE AUTHOR WITH A GROUP OF FIREFIGHTER/
PARAMEDICS IN TRAINING.

THE AUTHOR WITH CAPTAIN DAN LEMMON.

CHAPTER 6

✛

THE FOURS, FIVES, AND SIXES

The number of deaths I have had to deal with over the years is a number I will never know. From homicide scenes, car accidents, accidental deaths, suicides, and natural deaths, the number is well over several thousand. Usually these deaths were single deaths, but multiple deaths also happen. These are a lot to deal with, and something I do not look forward to. It's one thing to have one or two deaths at one event, but the numbers four, five, and six have haunted me. Eight times during my career I have been on scenes where we had four, five, or six people dead. Those scenes total 46 people that were patients, of which 39 died! That is 39 people who met untimely demises, and did not die from natural causes. These were people who did not die peacefully in their beds, surrounded by their families, like so many times you hear about when a famous person dies. These eight events included three fires, two cases of carbon monoxide, one auto accident, and two different shooting scenes.

One of the first times I experienced this was December 16, 1981, in a building I was very familiar with: St. Francis de Sales Catholic Church in south St. Louis. St. Francis de Sales, also known as "de Sales," is a large Catholic church modeled after a cathedral in Germany. From the moment you enter this church, the darkness and coolness of the old stone architecture, the hushed silence, and the soaring vaulted ceiling makes you feel small, and gives you the sense of becoming diminished before the presence of something greater than yourself. It is the second largest church structure in the Archdiocese of St. Louis after the cathedral-basilica. The church is popularly known as the "Cathedral of South St. Louis." The steeple rises to over 300 feet, and it is topped by an 18-foot gold-leaf cross. German immigrants who settled in south St. Louis in the late 1860s started the parish, and brought the blueprints of a cathedral with them from Germany. It is a large, gothic structure that can easily seat 1,200 people. The wood carvings of the back alter, the communion rail, the pulpit, and statues are beyond description, and show the detail the German wood carvers from the 1800s used.

But beyond the structure, there are emotional ties to the building for me. My mother went to kindergarten in the 1920s at St. Francis de Sales, and was married to my father there. I was baptized in the church, and all my children have been baptized there. I went to grade school there, sang in the choir, and served as an altar boy. Almost all of my family, including my mother, have been buried from de Sales, and I played the organ for Mass there for 36 years. This is not just a building of wood, bricks, and mortar—it is an edifice of reminiscences, celebrations, and moments of sorrow.

That is why the address of 2653 Ohio was familiar to me one particular night. I actually was visiting the dispatchers in the communications center late one night when a 9-1-1 call came from a wife who went looking for her husband when he did not return home after playing cards in the basement of de Sales. It was a traditional gathering every Wednesday night for a group of elderly gentlemen to meet for a game of pinochle after taking food orders for the St. Vincent de Paul Society—an organization that helps the poor. They would always gather in a small room in the church basement that had a single gas-burning heater, a table, and some chairs. The men would always have some libations to also warm the spirit. But this night, none of the men returned home at the expected time, so the wife of one of the gentlemen went looking for her husband around 11:00 p.m. When she opened the door of the small room in the church basement, she found all six men spread out throughout the room—all unresponsive.

As I listened to the dispatcher screen the call and heard the details, I knew I needed to start heading that way. At this point in my career I was a paramedic-captain, responsible for my half of the city on a given shift. Leaving the communications center, I moved to get to my car at a rapid pace that quickly turned into a good gallop. I stepped into December's cold winter evening and was immediately caught up in the brisk wind as it whipped through the buildings in downtown St. Louis. I knew that what I was en route to was not going to be pleasant, but I had no idea what would have caused six men to be unconscious. Carbon monoxide was on my mind, since it was wintertime. This many people all down at the same time made me very suspicious of carbon monoxide.

Before I arrived, the first ambulance was on the scene and I heard the radio crack, "Medic 3 to dispatch, I need at least five more ambulances. I got six men down." I stepped a little harder on the accelerator since I was guessing it was people I probably knew.

That is one of the worst parts of this job. Sometimes you go on calls where you know the people involved. I have even heard of stories where firefighters or paramedics responded on auto accidents, and when they pulled up they recognized the car. Sure enough, it was a loved one, dead inside the vehicle. This especially happens in rural areas, where volunteers respond on every call in their community. Eventually, the odds are, you're going to roll up on a loved one, or someone you know personally. The smaller the community, the better the probability. I have been on calls of people I knew, but I have never rolled up to find a loved one, and I hope it never happens.

When I arrived, I tried to park my car so it did not block any emergency apparatus that had to get in or out. There is nothing more aggravating than trying to leave a scene in your ambulance with a patient and being blocked in by a police car or a fire engine, and the driver cannot be found anywhere. This happened in the Columbine High School shootings in Littleton, Colorado in the 1990s. Some police officers parked their police cars, locked the cars, and took the keys with them. Some ambulances with critical patients were delayed leaving the scene because they were blocked in. Others had trouble accessing the high school. Those driving ambulances also have a responsibility to try and park where they might not get blocked in, and try to anticipate other emergency apparatus that may be coming in behind them.

I parked on Iowa Street, which is on the west end of the square block complex of the church, rectory, two school buildings, three large playgrounds/parking lots, a convent, and a gym. I know the complex well, and I know all the entrances to the church basement where the men were located. I stepped from the car; the cold wind was even more wicked than it was downtown as it whipped through the complex of buildings around the church. Several ambulances and some police cars were already on the scene, and there was a hint of snow flurries in the air. I could see activity around a doorway in what is typically known as the upper school yard that is on the north side of the church. Some people were milling around, but the brunt of the activity was going on down in the room in the church basement. As I made my way through the crowd that was lingering, I came face-to-face with the pastor of the church, Monsignor Robert Krawinkel. He actually had a tear running down his face. I didn't know if it was from the cold wind or the sorrow that he was feeling. He is a kind man, and an excellent priest.

He told me, "Gary, I'm trying to stay out of the way but please, please see what you can do." I assured him I would do everything I could. I headed down the stairs as I have many times before over the years for either a breakfast after Mass, or a wedding reception at the church.

As I reached the basement, I saw the door leading into the room where all the activity was going on. The church basement is one large, expansive hall, with a variety of rooms ringing the large room. A stage is at one end, and the kitchen is at the other end. As I entered the smaller room off the main hall, I could see fully what I anticipated. Six men in varying levels of unconsciousness were lying around the room. Some of the faces were very familiar to me, as these were some of the older men from the parish. Several police officers were also there, writing information in their small, wire-bound notebooks in preparation for future reports. The four paramedics who were already there had divided themselves among four of the six victims. All were feverishly working on the men to get them breathing again. Some were doing CPR on their patients. The first paramedic there had to make a decision—a decision sometimes that determines who lives and who dies. This process is called triage. Under triage principles, you sort the victims into different categories, with red being the most critical or severe. The three other categories are yellow for non-life threatening, green for minor or walking wounded, and black for those who are dead. Unfortunately, in this case, all of these men were red, since they were critical. As a paramedic you must use your experience, skills, and training to make a determination as to who you think has the best chance of surviving, and you make a choice to medically work on them first. I've had to make that decision many times over the years when there were multiple critical victims and not enough resources. You think about it later. Did I make the right decision? You basically have to decide who lives and who dies. But you cannot dwell on it. It is a decision you made, and you have to live with your decision. You cannot go back and change it.

I took a quick assessment of the room and my first concern was safety. I asked one of the paramedics, "What the hell happened?"

The paramedic, whose name is Greg, said, "We have no idea. But we suspect carbon monoxide."

Another paramedic, named Elaine, said, "Check the heater out," as she continued to do chest compressions. I was also thinking the same thing. All of the men had a ruddy, red complexion—a sign of carbon monoxide poisoning. There was a gas space heater burning in the room, and the vent fan was not running. The byproduct of combustion is carbon monoxide. Carbon monoxide is odorless, tasteless, and colorless. As it is absorbed into the body, it prevents oxygen from binding to hemoglobin. The end result is that oxygen cannot be delivered to major organs, such as the brain. That is why people who suffer from carbon monoxide poisoning initially have headaches during the early stages. Eventually you lose the ability to make decisions, become disorientated, fall asleep, and die.

Typically, carbon monoxide is pumped to the outside through a flue or some other vent. If the flue or vent becomes blocked, from a bird's nest, or a brick that comes loose and falls into the vent, it can cause carbon monoxide to back up into a building. That is why I have a carbon monoxide detector in my home. I have a gas furnace.

Realizing we were going to need more manpower to get six men who were all critical up the stairs, and that we also needed to check for carbon monoxide, I called on my portable radio for a rescue assignment. This would bring an engine, a ladder company, a rescue squad, and a battalion chief. We were going to need the extra help moving these men. The rescue squad has six firefighters assigned to it, and has special equipment for measuring the amount of carbon monoxide in the room. In the meantime, we shut down the heater, since it was probably the main culprit.

Eventually all six ambulances arrived on the scene, along with the rescue assignment. My job mainly at this point was not to touch any patients, but to supervise the paramedics, assign patients to paramedics, watch for safety issues, and try to support the operations with any other needs. Basically, I needed to coordinate all the medical activity. I also needed to tell the paramedics which hospitals to take their patients to. You don't want to overload one hospital with six critical patients. Even the larger emergency rooms would be swamped, and would not have the necessary resources. They might even have some critical patients from other scenes already in the emergency room, and that would really compromise patient care if they got overloaded even more. I needed to look at the patients, assess what I could from their conditions, and even though every one of them was critical, I needed to determine who was the *most* critical, and send those two patients to the closest level one trauma center. The other four patients would be sent to other hospitals that could handle their critical condition. I sent all six patients to three different hospitals that night. Each hospital got two patients.

The choice of sending these patients to different emergency rooms is not too difficult a decision for me, since there were at least eight hospitals within five miles of where we were. St. Louis, at the time of this incident, was blessed to have 17 hospitals within its 63-square-mile boundary. Three of those hospitals were level one trauma centers and two were children's hospitals.

The paramedics had done a fantastic job. By the time we got ready to start moving the patients, five of them were breathing again and had a pulse. There was one patient still in cardiac arrest, and I knew him. His name was Joe Pruente,[9] age 82. He was a tall man with white hair and little wire-rimmed glasses that almost look like bifocals. He was a stalwart of the church. He was the first one every morning, who came early enough to open the church for Mass, which is at 6:00 a.m. on weekdays and 7:30 a.m. on Sundays. He also served as an usher at each one of those Masses. When he was not opening the church and serving as an usher, he walked the neighborhoods surrounding the church, going door-to-door in an effort to sell raffle tickets to raise money for the church. Unfortunately,

Mr. Pruente would not survive this night. He would succumb to carbon monoxide poisoning in the church he so loved. He would also be buried from the church, and I would play the organ at his funeral Mass.

Unfortunately, carbon monoxide is a killer. This colorless and odorless gas is responsible for taking many lives prematurely.

Such was the case on Sunday, April 29, 2001, when we got a call for five men found down in a garage in the rear of the 4000 block of Tholozan Avenue in south St. Louis. I was just coming in service from a fire at Taylor and Delmar in a commercial building when I heard the call go out over my radio. I decided to head that way, since it was unusual to hear a call with that many people down, especially in a garage.

When I arrived, the area had already been barricaded and taped off to keep bystanders from getting near the scene in the rear alley. Many of the streets in St. Louis have an alley that runs behind the homes. The garage is accessed through the alley, and usually the garage is detached from the home with a small yard. Some homes do not have a detached garage and there is just a fence that runs along the back of the property, which exposes the backyard. Before they were converted to gas furnaces, many of the older homes still have ash pits in the alley where people would dump their ashes from coal- burning furnaces that were in the basements of their home.

This particular property had a detached garage and a small walkway from the backyard that ran alongside the garage to the alley. When I walked up there were many emotional and screaming Vietnamese people who were comforting each other, and crying out in their Vietnamese language. Some were on their knees, with their hands folded in prayer. It was a very emotional and chaotic scene, but the police officers were able to successfully keep a large enough perimeter so that the scene remained intact.

Inside the garage, in a Nissan Maxima, were five dead Vietnamese men: one age 19, three age 20, and one age 21. When I looked in the car, it looked very much like they were all sleeping. In fact, the one young man's father who lived at the home where the garage was located had looked inside the car at 11:00 a.m. that Sunday morning and also thought his son, with his four other friends, were sleeping. Two hours later he became concerned that they were sleeping too late into the day, and that is when he discovered that they were all dead. Four of the men were in the backseat, and the fifth young man was in the front passenger seat. It looked like the young man who was sitting in the front seat had tried numerous times to light a cigarette, since I saw numerous burned matches laying on him and about the car floor. It almost looked like the match would burn down, he would blow it out, and light another match. He must have had an altered mental status and could not coordinate the lighting of the cigarette.

The father heard the garage door open late Saturday night and did not think much of it. After all, his son and his four friends had gone to a talent show at a south side Catholic church to observe the anniversary of the end of the Vietnam War on April 30, 1975. After the talent show, the five men went bowling. Some accounts put the men alive at 1:30 in the morning, when one of them made a cellular phone call to a friend.

It was suspected that since they were coming home late, they decided to sleep in the car instead of bothering their families.

When the scene was investigated, it was determined that the ignition of the car was turned in the "on" position. Investigators attached jumper cables to the car battery, and it was also discovered that the air conditioner and the in-dash CD player were also on. The gasoline gauge showed that the tank was empty. Additionally, further investigation of the garage showed there were no broken glass windows, and the garage was pretty airtight. Everything pointed to carbon monoxide poisoning from a running automobile.

Later autopsy and toxicology reports showed some men had also used an illegal drug called Ecstasy. Ecstasy is a street drug that produces a feeling of euphoria. Apparently the effects of Ecstasy made them feel everything was good, and may have even altered their thinking about allowing the car to run in an enclosed garage. Nonetheless, the byproducts of combustion from the car engine filled the garage with carbon monoxide, and each of the young men simply drifted off to sleep, never to wake back up. Five young men, all in the prime of their life, who will never have a chance to experience so many wonderful things that life has to offer.

It happened every winter in St. Louis—we would find people dead from carbon monoxide. I cannot remember a winter in 25 years that it did not happen. Usually the culprit was old brick homes with older brick chimneys that the mortar would crumble, and a brick or two would fall into the chimney and block the flue. The blocked flue would result in the buildup of carbon monoxide in the home. The people in the home would not realize it, since carbon monoxide is colorless and odorless. Usually the first hint that something was wrong was that people would feel bad, think they had the flu, and complain of headaches. The first clue was everybody in the home was sick. In many cases, disaster would be averted when somebody stayed home and somebody went to work, where they would breathe fresh air and come home and find those that remained home were sicker, either by having an altered mental status or they were unconscious.

The rescue squads in St. Louis and Memphis carry devices that measure the atmosphere. The devices can tell us how many parts per million (ppm) of carbon monoxide is in the air. There is always going to be about .5–5 ppm of carbon monoxide in a normal home. When carbon monoxide reaches about 70 ppm, people usually start experiencing headaches, fatigue, and nausea. Usually when we find a home with carbon monoxide at 150 ppm and above, we can expect to find people unconscious, disorientated, and possibly even dead, depending upon how long they have been exposed.

I have been on many other calls in my career, especially during the wintertime, where we found one or more dead persons in a home from carbon monoxide. Carbon monoxide is a definite killer, and that is the reason why I keep a carbon monoxide detector in my home. There has, and rightfully so, been an emphasis on smoke detectors. I think there should also be an equal importance on carbon monoxide detectors for homes that have fireplaces, gas stoves, and gas furnaces.

During my career, I've also had two different events where six people died, and one where four died—all from fire. Unfortunately, all 16 of these deaths were children. Sweet, innocent children who will never know what it's like to grow up, experience high school, their prom, their first date, driving a car, getting married, having and loving their own children, watching their children grow, and maybe even experiencing grandchildren. Their lives were snuffed out in violent ways, and you can only pray that they were unconscious from the smoke before their bodies felt the heat of the fire. Burning must be horrific! Why else would people jump from high buildings like the World Trade Center to a certain death when fire is starting to burn them?

The date was April 19, 1999, and I was sitting in my office at the fire department's EMS administration building on the south side of St. Louis. As the chief paramedic, I always have the fire radio on in my office so I can hear what is happening in the city. As I was typing away on the computer, I heard the familiar pre-warning tones come across the fire radio before they dispatch any calls. It's amazing how you learn over the years to listen to the radio, but *not* listen to the radio at the same time. It's the same thing as if you were in a crowded room with a bunch of people talking, and all of a sudden you hear your name from across the room, among all the conversations and chatter. It's the same way listening to a fire radio. You're conditioned over the years to not really pay attention to all the gibberish, but when something important is being said, your ears perk up.

That was the case this day. The dispatcher started the radio announcement with a report of a first alarm for people trapped in a burning building at the intersection of Salisbury and Blair. I thought to myself, *Salisbury and Blair, that's strange; the 8's fire station is at that corner.* The way it was dispatched told me they'd received a phone call. If someone had run into the engine house, it would have been dispatched with different terminology. That made it even stranger. Why call 9-1-1 when you're already at the same intersection where the fire station is?

I thought to myself, *There must not be anything to it, otherwise someone would have run to the fire station; unless the person who is trapped in the house is the one who called. But it doesn't matter; the 8s are right there, and should report something back relatively quickly.* And did they! In less than a minute, the radio barked back, "Engine 8 on the scene, we have three-story brick, heavy smoke, we have a report of people trapped." The other thing that comes from listening to the fire radio over many years is that you learn to listen to the urgency in the voice of the person providing the status update. In this case, I could tell the captain on the 8's pumper sounded overwrought. They must have something.

I immediately rose from my chair and headed out the door. My car was parked right outside my office door, so it didn't take me long before I was driving urgently to the scene. I had to jump on Interstate 44 and head through the downtown area and then go west on Interstate 70 and get off at the Salisbury exit, which would put me about two blocks from the fire. I estimated it was going to take me about 12 minutes to get there.

On the radio, I could hear the urgency that was coming from the scene. It sounded like they were making a raise to the roof with a ladder to rescue some people. I was thinking hopefully those were the only people, and they could get them off the roof before they got harmed.

At the time of this fire, every fire engine in St. Louis was a quint. A quint is a piece of fire apparatus that can pump and flow water, but it also has a ladder attached that can be raised to make a rescue or ventilate a building. It also has a piped waterway with a nozzle at the tip so you can raise the ladder and flow water on a large fire. To make every piece of fire apparatus in St. Louis a quint was the brainchild of Fire Chief Neil Svetanics. I knew his idea had saved other lives already when a ladder could be raised to save someone from a burning building; I was hoping it would work today.

When I pull up, I always park my car out of the way, since there is nothing I carry that can be used to fight the fire. Parking my car in the wrong location just means it can get in the way of more critical apparatus that needs to get closer to the fire. I got out of my car and walked around the back to put on my turnout gear and helmet, but I couldn't take my eyes off the building and what looked like a frenzied effort to get inside.

My first observation was that firefighters had raised the ladders attached to some of the fire trucks, attempting to make entry to the third floor windows, while other firefighters had ground ladders up to other windows trying to get inside. Other firefighters were stretching hose-lines around the back of the building and were trying to advance on the fire. There was heavy brown and black smoke coming from every third floor window, from underneath the eaves, and through any crack the smoke could find in the roof or walls. There were some flames licking out from the side windows on the second floor toward the front of the building. My ability to read smoke from observing it for many years, and other conditions I was seeing, told me the fire was well advanced, and was heaviest in the front of the building.

I hooked up with Mike Pollihan, a seasoned battalion chief on the scene, and in between his many orders he was giving over the radio, he verbally told me he had a report of six children trapped inside. My heart sank! Six! Time to put the emotions aside; I needed to get some paramedics here. I immediately called for five ambulances and told them to stage about a block from the incident. I didn't know if there would be extra alarms or other resources coming, but I didn't want any of the ambulances blocked in if they arrived before the extra fire apparatus.

In the meantime, Chief Svetanics arrived on the scene and as I suspected, he struck a second alarm, which would bring five more quints, another rescue squad, and another battalion chief. Chief Svetanics had always taught me that you want to stay one alarm ahead of the fire. As he said, "You can always send them home, but it's difficult to catch up if the fire gets away from you and you have to wait for resources to show up." He has been correct in so many cases over the years.

As I was walking toward the building, I rounded a fire engine and saw two paramedics working on a lady on the curb next to the building. I walked up and it was obvious she had injuries from a fall, and she also had burns on her. I later learned that she had been hanging from the third floor window and fell to the ground when she could no longer hang on. They were getting ready to move her on a backboard to the stretcher and transport her to the hospital. With a plea of desperation in her voice and face, all she kept saying was, "Save my babies," as she reached her arms out to me. She was extremely emotional. The paramedics had all they could do to keep her calm. They placed her on the stretcher, belted her in, and wheeled her away from the scene toward their ambulance.

I walked around to the rear of the building and found myself in a courtyard off the alley. The fire conditions were the same; heavy, blackish-brown smoke, banked out and low off the ground. I could tell the smoke had pressure behind it and was pushing out of the building instead of just drifting from the building. The fire was well advanced, and I had been on enough fires to know that if anybody was in the building, there was a good chance they were already dead. No one can survive these heavy smoke conditions unless they have a breathing apparatus on.

I could see that firefighters had a hose-line up the rear stairs and were advancing on the fire. All we could do was wait to see what they found. In the meantime, on the other side of the building where I had originally come from, firefighters were being driven back by the flames that were now coming out of several windows. Unfortunately, they couldn't use hose-lines from this side of the building because of the firefighters advancing the hose-line up the stairs on the other side of the building. Firefighters fighting fire with hose-lines from opposite sides of the building means that all they would be doing is blowing the fire back on the other firefighters, along with steam. Opposing hose-lines during a fire operation is not a good thing!

After what seemed like an eternity, I looked up and saw Captain Mark Bradshaw coming down the stairs from the second floor with a lifeless body outstretched in front of him. It was a small child, I'm guessing around five years of age. I couldn't see any immediate burns, but the body was covered in dark soot from the smoke. Immediately behind him I saw another firefighter coming down the steps with another lifeless child in his arms. Oh God! Please help these children!

I immediately called for two ambulances from the staging area to come around the rear of the building where firefighters had begun administering mouth-to-mouth resuscitation and chest compressions on the two small children.

Two paramedic units rolled around to the back of the building and pulled into the alley, which was the best way to access the courtyard where we were located. All four paramedics jumped out with their equipment. The paramedics and the firefighters feverously attempted to resuscitate the two small children. Both appeared to be girls, and I didn't see any burns on their bodies. But they had heavy soot on them since they were obviously in the thick of the black and choking smoke.

In what seemed like a very short amount of time, a third firefighter came down the stairs, also carrying another small child. This child looks lifeless also as it dangled from his arms. The firefighter looked completely physically exhausted, but nothing was going to stop him from delivering the child to the courtyard at the bottom of the steps. I immediately called for a third ambulance in the staging area to come around to the rear of the building.

As I put my microphone away from my portable radio and looked at what was happening with both of the two original girls who came out of the building, there appeared to be herculean efforts to obtain some type of airway by the paramedics by the process of intubation, where a tube with a balloon on the end of it is inserted in the trachea and then the balloon is inflated to seal the airway. Both paramedics were on their knees, since the girls were lying on the brick courtyard floor where all the resuscitation attempts were going on.

It is tough trying to intubate patients who have suffered from smoke inhalation. When you look down the throat with a device called a laryngoscope, it's difficult to find landmarks because of all the black soot and all the other junk that can get into the mouth and throat. I could see that both paramedics were having difficulty intubating the girls. I told them both, "You've got 30 seconds to get that tube, or else you're bagging them. We've got to get them moving to the hospital." Without looking up, both paramedics continued their efforts. They'd both heard what I'd said.

Within seconds of my instructions, one paramedic pulled the laryngoscope blade from the child's mouth while leaving the tube in, a sign that he may have been successful! He attached a bag-valve mask to the end of the tube and began bagging, while watching to see if the chest rose and fell. Another paramedic listened to the lungs with a stethoscope for the movement of air. The danger of intubating is putting the tube in the esophagus. If you miss the trachea, which is the pathway to the lungs, the tube goes in the stomach. So when you pump oxygen through the tube into what you think is the lungs, you are actually pumping oxygen into the stomach, and the patient gets no air and eventually can suffer brain death.

As the paramedic with the stethoscope listened to both sides of the chest, he looked up at the paramedic who was bagging the patient and said, "You're in." The paramedic who was bagging now secured the airway with some tape so the tube cannot come up or move too far down into the lungs.

At this point there were probably about seven firefighters and four paramedics working on three small children in cardiac arrest in this bricked courtyard behind the fire building. Shortly thereafter I saw the third set of paramedics show up with their equipment. Their eyes met mine and all I had to do was point to which patient was theirs. No words needed to be exchanged. They knew what I meant.

The first set of paramedics were now ready to transport the first girl, who was now intubated and having chest compressions done by a firefighter. It is an extraordinary feat to have just gone through the physical and exhaustive effort to get into a burning building, perform a search, bring the child outside, and now perform what is normally a physically-taxing process of pumping on someone's chest. It can exhaust you, but the adrenalin and human drive keeps pushing you to do your job.

Some firefighters brought a stretcher from the ambulance, and I saw directly behind them in parade fashion the other two stretchers from the other two ambulances. The first stretcher was lined up next to the girl who was ready for transport. There was already a red plastic backboard on the stretcher, and it didn't take much effort to lift the tiny frame from the ground to the stretcher about one foot above. The only complication sometimes is the EKG cables that get hooked on something, or they're not long enough when stretched out with the patient being moved.

I glanced at the EKG monitor of the first girl and it showed flat line. I glanced at the second EKG monitor of the second girl who was brought out and it also showed flat line. These were not good signs, and I was afraid they had been down too long for any resuscitation efforts to be successful.

The stretcher was raised with the first child, and two paramedics and two firefighters wheeled her to the ambulance while breathing for her and compressing her chest. The second girl, who looked to be about 4 or 5, was also raised to the stretcher, and her little arms dangled down in a motionless fashion. She was also strapped to the stretcher as the paramedics continued to perform CPR on her. She also was wheeled away with a rush of urgency to the waiting ambulance. Other firefighters gathered up the medical equipment left on the ground and scurried to the ambulances where the two girls were fighting for their lives.

The third child was a male, and also didn't look like he was burned, but he was heavily covered in black soot and was also unconscious and not breathing. His body was also lifeless as it laid on the bricks of the courtyard, being attended by two paramedics and several firefighters. Again, heroic attempts of every possible and conceivable method were occurring, including using IVs, drugs, defibrillation, oxygen, and chest compressions in an attempt to save his life. Looking at the EKG monitor, I could tell this was not going to have a good outcome for him. I told the paramedic to start thinking of moving to the hospital.

As if on cue, one of the firefighters grabbed the stretcher and moved it next to the small boy to position him for an easy movement to the stretcher. Chief Pollihan told me there were six kids inside, and that was still in the back of my mind. I was thinking, *I've got three more kids coming out and I'm going to need more ambulances.* Just then Andy Weber came down the steps and I asked if we've got any more kids coming out. He said, "No, they're all burned up."

I said, "Please don't tell me that, Andy." Andy hung his head and wiped his nose and told me it was true in a solemn and low voice. Unfortunately, Andy would be killed himself in a motorcycle accident some four years later.

Now I knew this was going to be a terrible day. We had three dead kids upstairs in the third floor apartment, and I've got three en route to the hospital that would probably not make it. There is that dreaded number of six again.

After the fire was out, I headed up the stairs to the third floor and looked where the three remaining children were. It is interesting to me that the stairs that I was walking up, starting somewhat close to the top, were burned pretty well. I thought it was a bit unusual, but I didn't really think much of it. Usually you don't see fire traveling in a downward fashion, where it would burn steps leading down from a third floor apartment. As I stepped on the burnt wooden steps, I thought that these steps saw a tremendous amount of fire. They were charred black, and it was not just debris and other rubble that may have washed out of the apartment when enough water is applied on a fire and water starts running out the door when it has nowhere to go. These steps were burnt, and obviously saw a tremendous amount of fire.

The apartment was full of firefighters looking for hot spots, pulling ceiling and punching into plaster walls, looking for hidden fire or sparks that can be hit with some water to prevent rekindles. The apartment was pretty charred, and you can never really walk on a floor of a building that has been on fire. You're walking on charred debris and other rubble that is soaked with water. Water drips off ceilings and off walls from what once were rooms of furniture that has no more true sense of fashion of any type. Hose-lines wound their way through the apartment. You could pick out what was once a sofa because of the blackened springs and frame. A television console was evident against another wall as are broken tables, chairs, and other items that once decorated the apartment that can no longer have their original look.

I wound my way through a hallway, moving toward the front of the building, surveying the damage as I went. It was quite evident that the apartment reached some unreasonable levels of heat. As I made my way to a front portion of the apartment, I could see firefighters huddled near a doorway. Their actions pulled me to this room. As I looked in the room, I saw the reason for everyone's focus. Inside what appeared to be a bedroom were the bodies of three small children—all severely burned. The room that was on fire, from the evidence of the burned remnants, looks like it was a bedroom, with several beds that have nothing left but the blackened bed springs, a burned and blackened dresser, a nightstand, and what appears to look like the burned remains of children's toys. One of the firefighters said to me, "It is a damn shame. See how close they are to the window dormer? We were that close to getting to them," and he showed me a measurement of a couple inches with the fingers of two dirty gloved hands. I shook my head in disappointment that their efforts were not successful. I knew every human effort was made to reach them. The room they were in is on the same side of the building that I first saw when I pulled up. It's the same side of the window where the woman fell three stories to the sidewalk after hanging by her hands. It's the same side of the building that I saw ladders raised from fire apparatus to multiple windows, and firefighters were frantically trying to get into the apartment through the windows to make the rescue.

I asked one of the firefighters where the other children were found. He took me to another room and showed me a closet. I couldn't help but notice the smears of small hands on the blackened and sooted back wall of the closet. The three children who were brought outside were the ones that were found in this closet. In an obvious move to escape the fire, the children retreated to the closet and huddled there until the smoke became overwhelming and they died from breathing in the poisonous gases. Unfortunately, it looked like they tried to claw their way out through the back wall of the closet in desperation.

I told the firefighters we needed to leave the bodies in place so that they could be properly photographed and the scene documented as a part of the investigation. It doesn't matter whether criminal activity is suspected or not. Any fire deaths are considered a homicide until proven otherwise. All fire deaths needs to be investigated to determine what started the fire. Arson investigators would be able to tell where the fire started. They'd look for burn patterns, and once they determined where the fire started, they'd look for a point of origin. Are there burned wires? Is there still a candle lying there? Or does chemical testing show an accelerant was poured? Burn indicators are the effects of heat or partial burning that indicate a fire's rate of development, points of origin, temperature, duration, and time of occurrence, or the presence of flammable liquids. Arson investigators will interpret burn indicators as the principle means for determining the cause of a fire—especially arson. Once they are able to determine the point of origin, they'll also be able to tell the path of the fire, and look at demarcation lines of smoke on the walls to determine how low the smoke got in a room.

I headed back outside. I was going to check in with Chief Svetanics and give him an update on the three children we transported, and the three children found dead in the apartment. I let him know that the three children we transported to the hospital were in cardiac arrest, and their prognosis was not good. He told me to make sure the three dead children found in the apartment weren't being moved because we were looking at an arson case. I asked him what was pointing to arson so fast, and he told me that someone had a fight with the people who lived in the apartment right before the fire.

Over the course of the next hour, the arson investigators got into the apartment, started their investigation, and photographed everything in detail. As I was standing in the back of the building in the familiar bricked courtyard, where earlier we had worked on the three children who were removed from the building, I took a moment to speak to one of the investigators. He told me that it looked like the fire started on the back porch, and the steps had been poured with some type of accelerant. Now it was starting to make sense to me. No wonder when I walked up the back steps the first time, I noticed some of the back steps were burnt so badly and the back porch was so blackened.

Shortly after, I received bad news over my portable radio from one of my paramedic captains who was at the hospital. All three children we transported to the hospital were dead. The poor kids didn't make it. I walked back around the front of the building and let Chief Svetanics know that we had three dead children at the hospital. He hung his head and bit his lower lip ever so slightly, but he is a professional, and went right back to work commanding the fire scene. Killed this day would be three boys and three girls, ages 6 1/2 months, 2, 5, 6, 8, and 9.

The medical examiner was also on the scene, doing his medical/legal investigation. He would also photograph the scene with the three remaining children in the apartment, document his findings, conduct some tests on the bodies, and make arrangements for the bodies to be transported to the morgue. Normally he would make arrangements for a service with a plain gray van to transport the bodies to the morgue, where autopsies would be conducted because they are homicide victims. But this day, the service was tied up and busy. The medical investigator on the scene came to me and said, "Gary, we've got a problem; the livery service cannot get here for about four hours. Can your people take the bodies down to the morgue?"

"Sure," I said. "I don't see a problem." I really didn't want those kids laying up there in that burned apartment for hours. Even in death, people should be treated with dignity. I called for one of the remaining ambulances in the staging area to come to the back of the building and park in the alley. In coordination with Chief Pollihan, the arson investigators, and the medical examiner, we started to move the dead children from the apartment down to the ambulance. I remained in the bricked courtyard as they took a wire-meshed stokes basket up the stairs to the apartment. For what seemed about ten minutes, we waited in anticipation for the firefighters to bring the bodies down.

Eventually I saw some firefighters emerge on the third-story porch above us carrying a stokes basket with a white sheet thrown over it. They slowly wound their way down the wooden stairs and, because of the width of the stairs, one firefighter had to be on the front and one on the rear of the basket as they carried it down. Eventually they reached the bottom of the stairs in the courtyard, where other firefighters grabbed onto the basket and walked toward the waiting ambulance in the alley with its rear doors open.

As I approached, I told the firefighters to put the stokes basket up on the bench seat of the ambulance, since we would need room for the other children who would be brought down. One of the firefighters told me that all three children were already in the stokes basket. Aghast that all three children had fit into one basket, I looked at the disheveled white sheet that had several uneven surfaces, and I realized that the children were so small they all fit into one basket that would normally only hold one adult. My heart sank a little bit more. In some small way, to honor them and pay respect, I grabbed onto the basket and helped load them into the ambulance. The doors were closed, and the ambulance slowly pulled away to drive their bodies to the morgue.

As I walked back into the courtyard, I saw a firefighter standing off to the side. He had a pike pole at his side that has a metal hook and prodding tool on the end of it that he was using to brace himself to stand up. He had that stare on his face that I've seen so many times before among police officers, firefighters, and paramedics who have worked some horrific call. As I got closer to him, among the dirt and grime on his face were also tears that were streaming down from both eyes. He saw me coming and tried to gathers himself. I asked him, "You all right, man?"

"Yeah, I'm fine," he replied.

I know better! I said, "No, you're not." I told him to sit down.

As soon as he sat down on some stairs, he broke down crying. "I can't believe it! We almost had them!" I tried to comfort him as best I could, but I knew he needed to talk about it to get it out. Firefighters and paramedics are fathers and mothers also. The death of any person is difficult, but when it involves a child, in such a horrific way as this fire, firefighters and paramedics put themselves in the same role as the father or mother of the dead child, and wonder how they would deal with something this awful. It's something you try to put out of your head right away because sometimes the thought of losing one, or even all of your children, is something you don't even want to think about.

I later learned that the firefighters at the 8s had seen three people fighting earlier in the street that afternoon. The firefighters called the police. When the police arrived, a firefighter gave them a report of what he saw, and returned to the inside of the fire station. A few minutes later, a police officer was banging on the firehouse door, screaming about the fire across the street. That's about the same time the fire alarm office was dispatching the call after receiving a report from a citizen of the fire.

As it turns out, a man and woman beat up another man who apparently robbed the woman the month before. After beating him up, the man and woman drove off. The man who was beat up, who was later identified as Nevelyn "Wilbur" Stokes [10] went to the gas station and came back with some gasoline. He then allegedly poured the gasoline on the back stairs and porch leading up to the apartment. He claimed he did not know anybody was home when he lit the fire. Unfortunately for the children, the stairs were the only way in and out of the apartment. As the fire was drawn into the apartment by open windows in a chimney effect, the children had no place to escape.

After the fire was out, the on-scene investigation was done, and the scene was turned back over to the landlord, it was time to turn our focus to the firefighters and paramedics who had dealt with this horrific death of six small children.

Professional CISD counselors were brought in to meet with all the firefighters and paramedics that evening. Several counselors responded this particular evening, and we assembled all the personnel involved in the incident in the 8's fire station, 300 feet from the building where six children had just died hours earlier. Usually, the chiefs are separated from the line firefighters so that the firefighters don't feel intimidated, and firefighters can speak freely if they feel a chief made a wrong decision. That would be the case this night. The line firefighters met by themselves with the counselors, not because any chiefs made any bad decision, but because it was a matter of protocol.

About a week after the fire on Salisbury and Blair, I drove past the fire scene, and the front and the side of the building were inundated and smothered with flowers, teddy bears, and other items to memorialize the six children. They had obviously been placed there by people who knew the children, as well as complete strangers who probably had to look up on a map where the intersection of Salisbury and Blair was. But they all came together and left something behind to express their sorrow for their untimely and tragic death. Unfortunately, the firefighters in Fire Station 8 saw the large memorial every time they looked out the window, and it was a constant reminder of how close death is separated by life, and how death can come so fast and unpredictably.

Unfortunately, I would have another fire in my career where six children would die. Regrettably, I could always count on a child dying in a fire somewhere around Christmastime every year. This time it would be six.

It was early in the morning when I was getting ready for work as the EMS deputy chief in December 1988. I was getting ready to get into my car and drive to work. I usually tried to be in the office early, since I have always found that is the best time to get work done. The phone doesn't ring at all.

As I was putting on my coat and getting ready to head out the door, my pager went off to call the office right away. I figured I would call on my radio from my car. This was a time before cell phones were so abundant. I didn't have a cell phone at the time.

I got into my car and pulled out of the driveway when I was going to call the dispatch office over the radio to find out why they were paging me. I didn't have to call. I could hear all the chatter on the radio. They had a fire working somewhere, and it sounded like a frantic effort to get into the house. No doubt, judging by the frenzied pace of the voices on the radio, they had someone trapped. The dispatcher answered the radio when I called and they told me they had a report of numerous people trapped and hurt in a house fire at 4580 North Market in north St. Louis. I told the dispatcher to show me en route.

It took me about 15 minutes to get there. Fifteen minutes in the course of a fire can be an eternity. In the case of a small home, it's over before you even get there. An aggressive fire company that is first on the scene is going to take a hose-line into the building and put out the fire. Many of the St. Louis fire companies, as well as those in Memphis, are aggressive in their fire attack, and can generally knock down a fire down before it has a chance to get too advanced.

I parked as I traditionally did, in such a way as to not block any fire apparatus or ambulances that may still be coming into the scene or need to leave with a patient. The 4500 block of North Market is in the Ville neighborhood of St. Louis, and is a crime-ridden area of mostly one-story brick homes, with some scattered two-story brick homes. The one- and two-story homes are small, and the street is not exactly that wide.

I got out of my car and put on my helmet and turnout coat. It was cold, but not too bad. I would say in the low 40s. What made it feel cooler was that the sun was not up yet and everything was dark.

I walked up to the front of the building. The raised voices I heard on the radio had now dissipated. There were a couple of patients still there in the back of the ambulances. The battalion chief was standing in front of the building, commanding the scene. I walked up to him and he told me, "I got six dead kids inside." Six dead! *Merry Christmas,* I thought in a sarcastic tone.

There were firefighters still in the one-story brick building looking for hotspots. Steam from the burned-out shell of the building and some remnant smoke still came from most windows and doors in the cool morning air. I asked the battalion chief, "You're sure they're dead?"

He looked at me like, *Did I not just tell you they are dead?* as he said, "Yup." It was a stupid question to ask, but I guess deep in my mind I was looking for some hint that this wasn't real. But deep in my heart, this is as real as it gets.

I told the battalion chief that I was going inside to take a look. As I walked up the steps and side-stepped the overlapping hose lines running from the engines up the sidewalk and into the front door of the house, I ran into a firefighter I had known for many years on the 10's pumper. The 10s were the first company in, and he told me when they pulled up the house was fully involved, and there was a bunch of family and other neighbors in the front screaming that there were kids inside. He told me the flames were blowing out of the house. The damned shame of it is the 10's engine house is maybe only about five or six blocks from the house that was on fire. But it goes to show how fast fire can grow before someone gets there.

I walked through the front door, and the building had a good number of firefighters in it looking for hot spots. What they were not doing was overhauling the building. Overhauling is not the sexy side of firefighting. Overhauling is when firefighters break into walls, ceilings, and void spaces, looking for the extension of the fire. It is also a time when they will throw debris out the window. If you have six fire deaths like this house did, you do not want to completely overhaul, since there will be an investigation conducted inside the building. You want to leave the building intact as much as possible. If you throw debris out the window, you could be throwing out some piece of evidence. They may find the piece of evidence outside the window later, but determining what part of the house it was in can ruin any investigation.

As I made my way through the front hallway of the home, I could see the heat remnants on the walls, and I had no doubt from the blackened and heat-wrinkled walls that it was hot in the house. I asked one of the firefighters where the bodies were. Almost like a tour guide, he walked me to the front bedroom, where I saw two small children on the floor, and one small child on the burned mattress that had nothing but springs left. All were burned severely. There was no need to check them for life. Their chests were not rising and falling, and their burns were incompatible with life. I asked the firefighter, "Where are the others?" Again, flashlight in hand, he walked me down a hall into a back bedroom, where I saw three more small children laying on another burned mattress that only had springs left. They were severely burned also, and there was no possible way they could have survived their injuries.

I'd seen enough. Nothing I could do here. I made my way out toward the front of the building and checked with one of my paramedic-captains who was managing the patients on the scene. He told me he had three ambulances there and they had transported three adults to Barnes Hospital. He told me one patient had severe burns. Barnes Hospital is the only hospital in the city of St. Louis that has a burn center. The paramedic-captain told me they also examined one adult and four children who escaped from the building but had no injuries. He told me he had another ambulance en route to stand by in case someone else got injured.

As I looked around, many members of the neighborhood had gathered behind the yellow police line. Word had spread through the crowd, and you see the look of horror on people's faces, since many knew some or all of the small kids. In the dark of the early morning, I could see tears running down the faces of some of the people in the crowd. The paramedic-captain told me that one of the neighbors said she could hear the kids screaming in the house before the first engine company got there.

I later learned that the investigation determined a 13-year-old boy who lived in the house poured gasoline into the kerosene heater instead of kerosene heating oil. A gasoline can was found near the kerosene heater. Apparently the kerosene heater ran out, and the house or the room probably started getting cool. Thinking he was doing the right thing, the 13-year-old boy put gasoline in the kerosene heater to restart it. Putting gasoline in a kerosene heater is like putting a bomb in a house. No wonder the house burned as fast as it did. Witnesses also said they saw the 13-year-old boy outside the house at one point, but he must have run back in to save the others.

It was not a good Christmas in the Ville neighborhood. Firefighters later blanketed the neighborhood with smoke detectors as part of a campaign and effort to get more smoke detectors into homes, and possibly prevent any more fire deaths in that area.

The Salisbury and the North Market fires took the lives of twelve children—six children at each fire. Still, I had one more fire that resulted in multiple children dying.

It was March 1994, and Fire Alarm put out a first alarm for a fire in the 5900 block of Theodosia, with a report of children inside. I was coming from my office on the south side of St. Louis on Hampton Avenue and had to cut through the large park in St. Louis known as Forest Park to get to the north side of town where the fire was. Forest Park is supposedly the largest park in any city in the United States, and divides the western part of the city from the south and north. Forest Park houses the zoo, lakes, the open air theater, the art museum, the planetarium, ice skating rinks, ball diamonds, two golf courses, the history museum, tennis courts, and miles upon miles of walking and running trails. My wife and I got married in the rose garden at the Jewel Box in Forest Park. The Jewel Box is a large indoor, climate-controlled building for flowers.

As a deputy chief, I put myself on the call and headed in that direction. The first arriving engine company reported heavy smoke and fire showing from a two-story, four-family brick. Shortly thereafter, the first engine was calling for at least two ambulances. That is usually about the time you step on the accelerator a little harder. It took me less than 10 minutes to get there, but when I did, I could see firefighters and paramedics working on two small bodies in the front yard on the grass. The telltale sign of where the fire was licking on the building was apparent above the front window, where the bricks above the large broken-out front window were stained black. Evidence that heavy smoke and fire came out the front window and discolored the red bricks to a black color is an indication there was heavy fire at least in the front of the house, and was pushing out the front window.

Almost like two separate football huddles, a group of firefighters and paramedics were bent over two small, lifeless bodies in the front yard. I could see that both children were receiving CPR while firefighters attempted to push air into their lungs with a bag-valve mask. There is not much you can do on the ground in front of a house that apparently still has some small fires going on, from the color of the smoke I was seeing. The paramedic-captain, who had overall control of the medical scene, ordered the two patients to be loaded onto stretchers and rushed to the hospital. Shortly thereafter, like synchronized swimmers, the firefighters and paramedics worked in coordinated fashion to load both small children onto stretchers and moved them to ambulances, where they would be transported to Children's Hospital about two miles away. Both children would die the next morning, as did two other children in the back bedroom of the apartment that were so badly burned there was no chance of even trying to resuscitate them.

The tragedy with this fire was that no adult was home. However, it wasn't long after the two children were transported to the hospital that we saw a woman running up the street to the scene. You can always identify the family members who show up at the scene after we have arrived. The look on their faces and the panic they put on display is clear evidence to me that they are family. I've seen them even drive through police lines in an effort to get to the home as soon as they can. In this case as I suspected, it was the mother.

This mother left the house after arguing with the father of three of the four children, who had also left. She walked half a block away to use a pay phone to call her mother. After the phone call, she then met up with the father again and continued the argument. She was walking home when she heard the fire truck sirens.

When I saw her, she was just arriving at the apartment building and doing everything she could to get into the building. We finally had to put her in the back of an ambulance, and the news was broken to her that two of her children were dead, and the other two were transported to Children's Hospital in critical condition.

I cannot begin to describe the emotions some parents release when they find out they have lost all their children. Losing a child is something that no parent should go through, even with one child, let alone four.

Losing children is a nightmare no parent ever wants to deal with. The thought of burying one of your children is incomprehensible. The parents of these 16 children from three different fires that I described know that pain.

More parents would feel this pain on another call that I responded to on May 30, 1981, at South Broadway and Interstate 55 in south St. Louis.

I was only about six blocks from the call when an auto accident with people trapped in the car was dispatched about 3:00 a.m. at Interstate 55 and 4500 South Broadway. I was returning from a call, and was already on the street in my paramedic-captain vehicle.

As I proceeded to the scene, I got off on an exit ramp on Interstate 55 at 4500 South Broadway. I looked to my left and I could see all the commotion. There was a white car that had crashed head-on into the concrete bridge pillar that supported the interstate highway above it. Some police officers and some fire apparatus were already on the scene. I picked up the radio microphone and put myself on the scene. I walked up to the car, stepped back, and tried to make sense of what I was looking at. It looked like a car hit the concrete pillar head-on at a high rate of speed. Inside was a tangled mess of bodies. It was tough to discern, but it looked like there were three people in the front seat and three people in the back seat. The concrete pillar was virtually where the firewall of the car should normally be. The three people who were in the front seat were pinned because the front of the car and the engine were now in the front passenger seat. It was a rather large car, and I'd learn later that it was a 1963 Oldsmobile. The front doors of the car were folded together like an accordion. It was going to be a herculean task to get those in the front seat out. The smell of antifreeze, oil, gasoline, and death hung in the air in the quiet early summer morning.

I couldn't get close to the car because firefighters were already working to open the doors on both sides. They went after the rear doors first to rescue the people in the backseat. They were the easiest to get to since these were the least damaged car doors. I had one ambulance en route, so I called for two more, just to get help moving in our direction. From what I could see, no one in the car was moving, so calling for the extra ambulances might be a moot point if everyone was dead.

Firefighters finally got the rear door open on the passenger side. They accomplished this by using the Jaws of Life. The Jaws of Life is a hydraulic rescue tool that has two metal arms that come together at the tip, and was first used in the racing industry to free race car drivers from wrecked cars. The tip of the two arms is rammed into whatever opening you can find between two objects, and then hydraulic pressure spreads the two arms apart. Whatever objects are butted up against the arms are spread apart. If you put the tip of these two arms into a crack of where a car door meets the frame, you could pop the door open.

All they needed was to get one door popped, and we could at least get to the people in the backseat. Once the door was popped, it can only open so far because of the twisted frame and metal of the car where the door is attached to the car. That's all the firefighters need. Three firefighters grabbed the door and, in a scene similar to football players hitting a tackling dummy and pushing it, they bent the car door far enough back so that it didn't even look like a normal car door would look if it was opened. It was bent past its normal point, and bent back more forward than it is intended to be. This gives us excellent access to the three victims in the back seat.

I moved forward to start the process of removing the victims from the car. Ralph Break of Rescue Squad 1 assisted me with the closest male, who was next to the open door. I checked him. He was unconscious, barely breathing, but he was still alive. His face was covered in blood, and he had obvious fractures and a head injury. We placed a cervical collar around his neck and positioned a backboard so that, as we lifted him out of the car, he could be slid directly onto it. A stretcher was positioned close by, ready to accept the patient after we removed him from the car. There was only time to get a quick airway. There was no time to do any other procedures. He was in critical condition, and we needed to get him into the back of the ambulance where he could be treated in a more optimal setting.

After we got the first person out, I climbed into the backseat to find two more people tangled together. I checked the closest person to me. There was no pulse, and she had massive injuries; she was dead. I looked to the front of the car and it looked like at least three people pinned between the front seat and the firewall of the car that was now almost pushed up to the front seat. There was no movement from anyone in the front seat, either. One person clearly had a broken neck, as their head was twisted in an abnormal direction.

I checked the final person farthest away from me in the backseat. It looked like they were breathing. I checked for a carotid pulse. I thought I felt one, but it was weak. I yelled to Ralph, who was right behind me. "This one's alive!" Ralph called for another cervical collar and backboard. I was reading Ralph's mind, and he was reading mine. We'd worked many calls together before, and came on the job about the same time. This was not the first car the both of us had crawled into to pull people out, and it would certainly not be the last. Ralph would eventually rise to become a deputy fire chief at the same time I achieved my final rank as chief paramedic.

We were both thinking, *immobilize this patient as best we can so we do not do any more damage to them if they have a neck or back injury.* That's exactly what we did. Ralph handed me the cervical collar, and I got it around the person's neck as best I could, with the goal of trying to stabilize the neck. If the neck was broken, I did not want to paralyze or even kill the person because I handled them wrong. The phrenic nerves run through the cervical column, and mainly carry messages from the brain to your lungs to breathe. Pinching or cutting it with a jagged piece of the cervical vertebrae that is fractured can be disastrous.

It was going to be tough getting this person out of the car. I was actually kneeling on top of a dead person who was sitting in the middle of the backseat to reach the person I was trying to help. The only way we'd be able to get him out would to drag him over the dead person and take him out the passenger side door in the rear seat. It took a formidable effort to get the passenger side door open, and I doubted we should waste time trying to pop open the driver side door of the back seat. There was no time. Out of six kids in the car, I only had two who were alive. Both were unconscious and in critical condition. We'd gotten one out, and I needed to get the second one out. I didn't want him dying in the backseat because we delayed extricating him from the car.

I pivoted the patient who I'd just put a cervical collar on and tried to turn him so I could start getting out of the way, and a backboard could be slid into the backseat. The person must be put on the backboard and taken out of the car to try and prevent any further damage if they also have a broken back. Ralph, who was also partially in the car through the rear passenger side door, was trying to help me as best he could. I was also getting assistance from hands that were reaching through the broken window of the rear door on the driver's side. He was a young male teenager, and not that big of frame, so turning him and getting him on a backboard was not going to be a challenge.

That was exactly what we did. Ralph and I continued to read each other's mind. We got him turned so that we could lay him flat on the backboard. In order to do so, I had to partially stand up and put my back against the roof of the car, while putting most of my butt into the front seat of the car. The backboard came in through the rear door on the passenger side, and one portion of the backboard actually had to rest on the legs of the kid who was dead in the middle of the back seat. I could see that this person also had a broken femur, and the backboard was going to have to rest on the broken bone, but it didn't matter. He wouldn't feel it.

As the backboard was resting on the legs of the dead person in the backseat, we slowly lowered the young man to the backboard. After he was on the backboard, Ralph and I each grabbed him under an armpit and slid him further up on the board. After he was fully on the board, the firefighters outside the car slowly pulled the backboard out, almost in assembly line fashion: they lined up on either side until eventually the backboard was between four firefighters, two on each side. The stretcher was already positioned close enough—almost an extension of the firefighters. They moved the backboard with the fragile and unconscious young teenager to the stretcher, where the paramedics took over. They hurriedly snapped the three belts together that would hold the patient to the stretcher and speedily wheeled the stretcher to the waiting ambulance. When I climbed out of the car, I needed to focus on the four remaining kids. I knew the young man in the backseat was dead so, in reality, we needed to start cutting the car apart to get the remaining three kids out of the front seat. They all looked dead from my vantage point, but I couldn't assume that.

In order to get these three kids out, the rescue squad was going to have to virtually take off the two front doors and use various rescue tools to pull the dashboard off the three kids. One of their main tools is to use a Come-a-Long rescue tool to pull the steering wheel back, and the dashboard with it. As the firefighters from Rescue Squad 1 hooked up the extrication tools, all we could do is stand back and wait for them to do their job.

I saw Lieutenant Art Hammer standing there from the St. Louis Police Department. Lt. Hammer was usually a pretty calm and cool police officer on scenes where I have seen him before. This night he looked a little shaken. I made some comment to him that I didn't think the two we took out of the car were going to make it. With his hands on his hips, he muttered something with the word "bullshit" in it. Not knowing what he said, and with no time to chitchat, I moved to the other side of the car to see how the extrication was going. The firefighters were making progress. They got the doors peeled back, and the crew of Rescue Squad 1 was preparing to hook the chains to the steering wheel so they could pull it off the kid who was pinned behind it.

As I continued to stand there, trying to take in everything around me, I saw another familiar face in the crowd. It was Earl Morris. Earl is a freelance photographer who roams the city streets at night, going from one fire to another, or whatever else is happening at the time. He typically sold his pictures to the local newspaper, or whoever wanted to buy them from the media. Earl made copies of his pictures for me, as he had done with many other scenes that we have been at.

The crew of Rescue Squad 1 was making fantastic progress pulling the dashboard back. The car groaned and creaked as the twisted metal was pulled in different directions. Normally we would put covers over the people in the car as the extrication was occurring to prevent any shards of glass from hitting them, or from other debris falling on them. There was no need to do that this early morning. They were all dead. There was nothing more we could do for them.

Once the dashboard was pulled back, the Jaws of Life were then used to push the seat back. The two arms of the Jaws were placed on the floorboard of the car, and one arm pushed against the bottom of the seat while the other arm pushed against the frame of the car.

The seat slowly moved backward, away from the front of the dashboard that had already been pulled the opposite way, exposing the three occupants of the front seat. We could easily access them now. As the firefighter stepped back with the Jaws from the driver side door of the car, I moved forward. I checked the young kid behind the wheel. I checked for a carotid pulse, and I told a nearby paramedic to run an EKG strip on him and the person in the back seat to make sure they were both dead. Another paramedic approached the car from the passenger front door and went through the same process of checking pulses on the other occupants of the car. The paramedic determined that the person sitting in the front passenger seat was dead. It was pretty obvious. They had a massive open head wound incompatible with life. The person in the middle was also dead from massive wounds and an obvious broken neck. All we could do was remove them from the car and lay them on the sidewalk for the medical examiner's office to transport them to the morgue. To provide a little bit of dignity, we covered them fully with white sheets, even though no civilians could get close to the scene.

At the end of this rescue, we had four dead on the scene, and two who were transported to trauma centers unconscious and in critical condition. The two who were transported died within several hours of arriving at the hospital. Their injuries were so massive that their chances of survival were not good. They eventually died also—for a total of six.

As the scene was winding down, I took another look in the car. I wanted to make sure we had not left any equipment behind, and wanted to make one final sweep. I did notice something significant. The speedometer was stuck on 75 miles per hour. This accident happened back when cars had speedometers that were not digital. It was a dial on the dashboard, and a needle would move across the dial to reflect the speed. In this case, it looked like the needle got stuck on 75 miles per hour when the car hit the concrete pillar. I always looked for beer cans or other alcohol in the car on these types of accidents. Interestingly, I noticed no alcohol in the car.

The next day in the paper I read that the six teenagers were all friends, and a 13-year-old boy was the one driving. Police reported the car had been stolen from the older teenage brother of the 13-year-old who was driving. The group was celebrating the graduation of one of the teenagers from the eighth grade.

Lt. Hammer and another police officer were patrolling that morning when they noticed the Oldsmobile parked near a street on South Broadway. Standing outside the car was a teenage boy. The officers wished to talk to the group because of the early morning hour. As the officers got out of their patrol car to talk, the teenager jumped in the car and sped off. The Oldsmobile then sped north on South Broadway. The police officers jumped in their car and went in pursuit of them. Shortly after the police began pursuit, the car ran a red light. The Oldsmobile did slow down, and the police officers pulled up alongside and motioned for the teenagers to pull over. As the police officers were motioning for them to pull over, the car attempted to cut them off and then sped up. The police officers then continued the chase, but shortly thereafter decided to cancel pursuing the car because the most serious violation was running a red light. Seconds after deciding not to pursue the car, the police officers heard a tremendous crash. They found the wrecked car about two blocks away under Interstate 55, some 10 blocks from where the pursuit began.

The local newspaper said it was the worst crash in recent memory in St. Louis, and no other crash had equaled the number of people killed.

I always regretted that we were not able to do anything for them. I am sure the four who died were killed instantly, from the injuries I saw. Unfortunately, I can only conjecture the horror they must have felt as they saw the concrete pillar coming at them. The ages of the teenagers in the car were 13, 15, 16, 17, and two 18-year olds. The 16- and 17- year-olds were also brother and sister.

***

The violence that one person can do against another person continues to defy my logic. I can understand, but not condone some violence, when emotions get involved with two people who know each other. But I cannot understand the violence that one person does against someone else they don't know—especially when it's cold-blooded. The Nazi films of World War II typify this when millions were systemically murdered without any regard for the fact that a human life was being taken, from people who didn't know each other, or where one person had done nothing to the other.

Such was the case on Friday night, September 5, 1987. I was the deputy chief on duty that night when I heard a shooting call go out at the National Food Store at 4331 Natural Bridge in north St. Louis. I was nowhere near the call, and was probably at least 10 minutes away. Unfortunately, to me, it was just another shooting call. Nothing to get excited about! I figured someone had called from the payphone in front of the National Food Store. Many times, these calls from payphones turn out to be false.

This particular National Food Store is just like any other one-story large-box food chain store, with many aisles of food, produce, and other products. There were the numerous checkout lanes in the front of the store, and off to the side was a service counter. Natural Bridge is a main thoroughfare in north St. Louis, and the front of the building butted up right next to the street with a sidewalk. The parking lot for the store was on the side.

Several minutes later, I heard an excited voice come on the radio and say they needed the police immediately to the National Food Store. That excited voice was paramedic Sheila Patton. She said she could see numerous people shot inside and they were unsure if the shooter was still in the store. She also said there were several employees on the roof, and they had thrown the keys to the store down to her.

It was around 10:30 p.m., and the store was closed for the night.

I flipped on the lights and siren and picked up the radio to announce that I was responding. This didn't sound like any typical shooting. While I was en route I heard Sheila call for three more ambulances, and report that police had arrived on the scene.

It took me less than the 10 minutes I estimate to get there and, by that time, the police had arrived on the scene and verified the shooters were gone. I parked my car to make sure I didn't block any emergency vehicles, and immediately walked into the store. What I saw is nothing like I have ever seen before. "Bloodbath" is exactly the term I would use. Most of the activity was centered just off the checkout lanes by the service counter. When I got near the service counter, we were literally slipping in all the blood that was on the floor. Imagine if there was something wet on your typical white tile supermarket floor, and you get the idea how slippery it was.

There were a total of seven people shot. Three were laying face down in front of the service counter. A young teenager who appeared to have tried to get up and run was lying on his back a short distance away, obviously dead. One person was still alive near the front of the counter, and another person was behind the counter, still alive. The security guard was near the checkout lanes and was still alive and conscious, but he was obviously in critical condition, since his color did not look good.

As I made my way toward the service counter area, some of the paramedics were trying to lift the person behind the counter over it and onto a backboard. Some paramedics stood on one side of the counter and tried to hand him over to other paramedics, who were waiting for the handoff. Unfortunately, during the transfer across the counter, a large display of cigarette lighters and other products got knocked down and spilled all over the crime scene. It didn't matter. They needed to get him to the hospital.

Behind me, another set of paramedics was loading the security guard onto a stretcher and attempting to start an IV. I can still see him reaching out with a panicked look on his face to one of the paramedics to hold his hand. Unfortunately, he would die later at the hospital.

The third person who was shot and still alive was about to be treated and transported by another paramedic crew coming in the door. Thankfully, he and the person behind the counter would survive. Unfortunately, a total of five would die this night—three lying face down in front of the service counter, a young kid who looked like he might have been a bagger, and the security guard.

Realizing we may have more victims throughout the store, I had a paramedic crew sweep the rest of the store with a police officer, to make sure we didn't have any more victims in any of the aisles or in the storeroom in the back. Thankfully, no more would be found.

After all had been transported, and no more victims were found in the store, I had a chance to take a breath and look around me. It was surreal! Lying in front of me were three unfortunate people, all face down, shot numerous times in the head and the back. A short distance away was the young boy who appeared to be a bagger. All had been murdered in a cold and calculating way. It was obvious they had been made to lie in front of the service counter and they were executed where they lay. All over the service counter area was blood. Blood was everywhere! What was evident to me was the numerous footprints in all the blood from all the paramedics and police officers who'd had to walk through the area to deal with the victims.

Later I learned that all who had been shot were employees of the store, and the store was closed. Apparently, the security guard let two suspects into the store thinking they were the cleaning crew coming in. In reality they were coming to rob the store. Another report indicated they may have posed as janitors to get into the store. According to witness accounts, one man shot all seven while another man stood watch by the front windows as a lookout. The two employees who had been on the roof when the original ambulance showed up had been in a different part of the store when the robbery and shooting started. They ran into the storeroom and up to the roof, where they called from the roof for a passerby to call police.

Late that night, at almost midnight, Captain Charles McCrary, commander of the Homicide Division, called me and wanted all the paramedics who were in the store to come down to the Homicide Division at police headquarters so that they could take impressions of the bottom of our shoes. There were so many shoe prints in the blood that the homicide detectives needed to sort out who were police, paramedics, and then maybe they might have the shoe prints of the suspects. Shoe prints in the blood can be critically important later during a criminal trial if the prosecution can place a suspect at the scene at the time of the murder through their shoes.

During the trial for the National Food Store murders it was disclosed that ten employees were in the store at the time of the robbery and murders. The gunmen supposedly got into the store when the security guard went to let an employee out through the locked front door. One of the gunmen entered the manager's office and demanded the money from the safe. The gunman hit the manager in the head with the gun and punched another employee in the face when they had difficulty getting the safe open. Finally, another employee was able to get the safe open.

The gunman filled a National Food Store plastic bag with money from the safe. A total of $7,534.20 was stolen, including $1,500.00 to $3,000.00 in dollar bills bundled in stacks of one hundred. Ten stacks were blocked together in cellophane and wrapped to form a brick. At this point, the gunman took some bus passes, and ordered the employees out of the office.

As they left the office, the manager saw another man with a gun in his hand, standing by a liquor display and facing the other way. So now there were two gunmen.

The four employees who were in the manager's office were ordered to lie down on the floor. The security officer and a cleaning man were already on the floor. The first gunman ordered the employees to get up and lie down closer together, with their heads next to the wall of the service counter. A seventh employee was then ordered to join the others on the floor. Ten seconds later, and with no exchange of words, the two gunmen fired shots at the employees' heads. Five to eight shots were fired. The second gunman asked the security guard for more bullets, and took them from the guard's pocket. He reloaded and went down the line, again shooting three other employees in the head. When he put the gun to one employee's head, the employee ducked his head out of the way just as the gunman pulled the trigger. The employee was shot in the hand, but pretended to be dead.

One employee was stocking shelves with two other men in the store when he heard at least six shots. He first saw a man he thought was from the cleaning crew looking out towards the street, standing at the front of the store. He then saw another man in the front of the store, leaning over several bodies on the floor. The employee who witnessed and heard this then ran back to where the other stockmen were and heard additional shots. Two of these three employees then crawled up on the roof and yelled for help to a woman walking down the street. From the roof, the two employees saw the gunmen leave the store in a car. In the meantime, one of the employees who had been shot crawled to a telephone and called the police.

Eventually a man named Donnie Blankenship[11] and Marvin Jennings[12] would be convicted of the five murders and the shooting of two people who survived. It was learned during the trial that a gun taken from the security guard was also used during the robbery and murders. Marvin Jennings was convicted of first-degree murder in the case and was sentenced to life in prison without the possibility of parole. Donnie Blankenship was convicted of second-degree murder and was sentenced to five life sentences plus 55 years. Blankenship would have to serve more than 100 years before he would be eligible for parole.

Generally, I am not a proponent of the death penalty unless it can be completely verified from numerous eyewitnesses and other physical evidence that the person is definitely guilty. I am sure more than one innocent person has been put to death because of the flaws in our legal system. If it was not for scientific DNA technology, many innocent men would still be sitting in prison on rape charges. According to the Innocence Project website, 18 people have been proven innocent and exonerated after sitting on death row.

This is one of those cases that I felt the death penalty should have been applied to both assailants. Their lack of disregard for someone else's life, the callousness of their actions, and the cold and calculated method by which they shot their victims for so little an amount of money is something I feel deserved the death penalty. If my faith is correct, they'll never feel the presence of God's love after their deaths.

The final case where I had six people dead in one incident happened as I served as a deputy fire chief in Memphis. I was sitting in my office late one night in March 2008 when I kept hearing ambulances being dispatched to an address on Lester Street. I called the Alarm Office to see what was going on, and they told me they had a bunch of people shot in a house at 722 Lester Street in the Binghampton neighborhood of Memphis. Not really being familiar with Memphis, since I had only been employed about two years and I was originally from St. Louis, I did a quick Google Map search on the address and I saw it was only about 10 minutes from my office. I immediately left my office, got into my SUV, flipped on my lights and sirens, and told the Alarm Office over the radio that I was responding to the address on Lester Street.

While en route, I heard the incident commander call for two more ambulances. When I arrived on the scene some 10 minutes later, I walked into the residence. One of my battalion chiefs, one EMS lieutenant, and about five ambulances were already on the scene. I took a quick scan, and there was that unfortunate number again. Six! I counted four dead in the front room, and two children dead in two different bedrooms. All the adults appeared to be shot multiple times. One of the children, who was an infant and was still alive, appeared to have some unusual wounds to the body. I learned later that she had been beaten with a board. The other two older children were 5 and 9, and were also still alive. They also appeared to be have been beaten, and also had stab wounds. One had been stabbed in the head with what appeared to be a knife. I actually chased some of the firefighter/paramedics from the building, since this was going to be a massive criminal investigation and I did not want evidence being damaged from too many people going in and out. I stood about 5–6 feet from the front door in the front room, which led to a central hallway, which then led to the bedrooms, the kitchen, and the bathroom. I tried not to move around either, since I didn't want to contaminate the crime scene. I teach crime scene management all over the country to firefighters, police officers, and paramedics, so I am intimately familiar with what we can do wrong to contaminate the crime scene.

After all the live victims had been removed, I got with the police incident commander on the scene and suggested we do a sweep of the house, including closets, under beds, and any other place someone might have crawled, or an assailant may be hiding. He agreed, and a sweep was done.

I concluded early on that those responsible for this carnage must have run out of bullets and resulted to other methods of murder. I also concluded that more than one person was responsible for the murders. Three of the adults were still sitting on couches, and an adult male was lying on the floor in front of the television.

I was later shocked when only one person was arrested, charged, and convicted of the six murders. I do not see how three adults would remain seated on the couch while others were being shot.

Convicted in the murders was Jessie Dotson,[13] who was related to all of those in the house. He confessed that he got into an argument with his brother, shot and killed him, then attempted to murder everyone in the house because they were witnesses. As I suspected, when he ran out of bullets, he tried to kill the children in other ways. One of the children was a two-month-old. I cannot see how a two-month-old can be a witness. His actions were barbaric, and for such, he received the death penalty.

CHAPTER 7

✠

THE MEAN STREETS

A homicide is defined as the deliberate and unlawful killing of one person by another. I can tell you that definition comes nowhere close to describing how it is done, or what a homicide scene looks like.

I'm embarrassed to say, the first-ever homicide scene I walked into, I didn't even know the person was dead. It was a small grocery store at the intersection of Ann and Ohio on the near south side of St. Louis—only about five blocks from where I grew up on Nebraska Street. Allegedly someone killed an elderly lady in her small storefront early on a Saturday morning by stabbing her. There was blood everywhere, and she was on the floor. Being the eager young rookie I was, I was the first one through the door, with my kit full of medical supplies. I was ready to save a life. Unfortunately, there was no life to save. As I found out, she had been dead for a while.

As I approached her, she was lying on the floor with her back to me, and I could not see her face. She was partially lying on her left side and partially face down. The room was not well lit, either. Still, I could obviously see that there was blood everywhere, so I opened my medical kit to get out various dressing bandages to control the bleeding, and asked her where she was stabbed. As I continued to get more stuff out of my kit, I asked her again where she was stabbed. After digging for a few more seconds, I realized she hadn't answered me. At that point, I looked up to see all the police officers inside the store giggling. With a grin on his face, one of older police officers said, "She's dead, son!" I looked over at her and rolled her slightly toward me. As soon as I saw the hollowed look on her face and the blank stare from her eyes, I knew the police officer was right. I felt like crawling into a hole. How embarrassing! I packed my bag up and walked outside.

I kept thinking how dumb I was, and how stupid that probably looked, but I got over it because throughout the next 37 years, I would make up for my first blunder. I would become extremely proficient because of the hundreds if not over a thousand homicide scenes that I had responded to. At one time, I knew every homicide investigator in St. Louis by his first name. Several would always ask about my initial impressions of what I saw based on the medical condition and/or wounds of the body. This was especially true if I noted defensive wounds, the number of entry and exit bullet wounds, whether the body was covered up or not when I arrived on the scene, plus a myriad other things I knew I could tell the homicide investigators that would be important to them.

I now formally do a lecture for police officers, firefighters, and paramedics on how to perform our jobs correctly at crime scenes while not destroying evidence. The O. J. Simpson murder trial in the early 1990s showed that it is imperative that evidence on a crime scene should be disturbed as little as possible so that homicide investigators and prosecutors can recreate what happened at the scene, and possibly capture those responsible. Prior to being educated, police officers, firefighters, and paramedics were notorious for destroying crime scene evidence.

Through the years, I have become close acquaintances with many of the homicide detectives from the St. Louis and Memphis Police Departments. In St. Louis, they usually operated in teams of three, and were very identifiable on scenes since they wore business suits. Many also wore fedoras and smoked huge cigars back in the 1980s and '90s.

One of the most respected homicide detectives in St. Louis Police Department history was Sergeant Joseph Burgoon, who is now retired. For 27 years out of a 43-year law enforcement career, he worked in homicide. Joe was one of the finest professional police officers I knew, and had a memory that was second to none. He could recall dates, phone numbers, addresses, and names from many years past without hesitation. Joe never wore the fedoras or smoked the big cigars. He was a devout Roman Catholic who had impeccable ethics. His nickname was "Father Homicide." In one of the biggest travesties I've ever seen in the St. Louis Police Department, Sgt. Burgoon was transferred to a street position by a police chief who had ties to a powerful politician. This was allegedly so Burgoon wouldn't be able to further investigate an open case that suspected the politician of a homicide early in his life.

Unfortunately, most of my knowledge of homicide scenes came from being on so many, and learning from the homicide detectives in St. Louis when they pointed out different things to me. Even without witnesses, they could generally reconstruct sequentially what happened, and who their suspect(s) might be. Most of the time, they were correct! They had an excellent record of solving and cleaning up cases, as did the detectives in Memphis.

Look at the national statistics the FBI releases every year. St. Louis ranks either No. 2 or 3 as the most violent city, and Memphis is not far behind. Back in the day when I started my career, St. Louis was ranked No. 1 for many years. That's nothing to be proud of. It's just the fact of the matter. I know other major cities like Chicago and New York might have had more homicides in a year than St. Louis and Memphis, but the FBI measures their statistics based on the number of people living in a community and the geographic space. Unfortunately for St. Louis, when it comes to homicide statistics, although the St. Louis metropolitan area is large, the city itself is only 63 square miles and (during the early part of my career) had a population of around 500,000 people. The population now is down to around 350,000 people. So proportionately, it always has and will rank near the top of the FBI list.

When I started in this profession, St. Louis had well over 200 homicides a year. In 1979 and 1981, it hit a high of 265 homicides. At least that's less than the record of 309 homicides in 1970. But when you compare all of those years by the population, the homicide index was highest through the late 1970s and early 1980s because the population had decreased. Many of those were because of the drug trade, and two rival groups that were fighting over territory.

When the United States government cracked down on the countries that produced heroin, there was always another drug ready to take its place. That drug in the late 1970s was Ts and Blues when heroin became difficult to get or too expensive. According to the National Institute of Health, the IV use of Ts and Blues (Pentazocine and tripelennamine) was a major drug abuse problem in St. Louis between 1977 and 1981. The drug (Pentazocine) was a morphine-like painkiller and, when combined with a blue antihistamine pill called Pyribenzamine, would give a euphoric effect to the user. When the two are mixed, dissolved, and shot into a vein, it has the same effects of heroin, at a cheaper price.

During the time I was assigned to the north side of St. Louis, it was the hottest area of usage for the Ts and Blues users. Drive-by shootings were common, as some young drug dealer stood on a corner and was suddenly and tragically gunned down in fights over territory. Others were shot in their cars as they sat peddling their wares. Others got their drugs on credit and did not pay up when the time came. Death is a heck of a way to be delinquent on your payment. Still others overdosed on Ts and Blues and filled up the emergency rooms.

One of our challenges as paramedics dealing with all the shooting and overdose victims was trying to get an IV started. You could never find a good vein on a Ts and Blues user. When a Ts and Blues user shoots the drug, it causes their vein to become necrotic, or die, over time. You could always spot a Ts and Blues user a block away by the black, necrotic veins on their arms. It's not possible to start an IV in a vein that is necrotic. When the veins in their arms would get "used up," they would resort to other areas of their body such as the foot, legs, and groin. Sometimes the only place left to start an IV was in the neck or the jugular vein.

But others were killed for reasons besides drugs. The number two reason I saw people get murdered in St. Louis was because of some emotion, or argument. This was true in Memphis, also. The most bizarre murder was when one brother shot another brother over an argument dealing with a roll of toilet paper. Apparently, one brother had used too much, and the other brother needed some and the roll was empty. I guess he should have checked before he sat down. But nothing justifies killing another person, especially a family member, over a roll of toilet paper.

I sometimes think I have seen every possible way that one person can kill another. Once in a while a new one pops up, and you catch yourself saying, "I've never seen that before." That was the case when I got a call for a "person down" in a residence, and we found out the person had been murdered with a handheld power drill. The killer had drilled holes in the victim's chest, and the drill was still lying next to the body, plugged in. You could clearly see the drill holes in the chest where the heart would normally be.

Another bizarre homicide occurred with someone I will call Freddie. His boss reported that he didn't show up for work. When we walked into Freddie's house after forcing his front door open, it was clear at first sight the house was destroyed from what appeared to be a major fight.

Whenever we force entry into a home because someone has set off their medical alarm or has not been seen for a while, we are always accompanied by police officers. You never know who is behind the door, or what you're going to find once you get inside. Firefighters in some cases have been shot (not in St. Louis or Memphis) by the person behind the door after they forced entry into a home because that person thought it was a burglar coming through the door.

In Freddie's case, we didn't have to worry about him greeting us with a weapon; Freddie was already dead. We found him in the rear of the house in the kitchen, but we knew something was not right when we first walked through the door. In addition to the destruction, there was blood all over the walls and floor. You could see bloody handprints on the walls and white door frames. Glass tables were broken, as well as lamps.

Somebody definitely wanted Freddie dead. Freddie had two screwdrivers sticking out of his head, there was a belt around his neck that was so tight you could not squeeze a single finger between it and his neck, it appeared every lamp in the house had been broken over his body, and every steak knife in the kitchen drawer was broken, since a flimsy steak knife will break when it hits bone. Additionally, someone had poured Louisiana Hot Sauce and Tabasco Sauce down his throat, and he had been shot in the head three times to finish things off. Somebody definitely wanted Freddie dead.

When homicide investigators see this type of murder scene, a couple of things stick out. Someone with a tremendous amount of rage wanted Freddie dead. Someone was really pissed off at Freddie. Therefore, there was some relationship between Freddie and his assailant(s). The fact that there was no forced entry into the home is also an indicator that Freddie knew who killed him. Finally, Freddie still had his wallet and his money, and it did not appear as though anything was missing from the home, since none of the drawers were open.

Several days later I saw one of the homicide investigators at another homicide scene and we got to talking about Freddie. Turns out that Freddie was recently married, but still had some girlfriends he was seeing. The new wife found out about the girlfriends and exacted her revenge.

She also had help. Her son was involved in the murder, also. When they say, "Hell has no fury like that of a scorned woman," they must be talking about Freddie's wife. She meant to kill Freddie, and she wanted to make sure he paid for his sins.

The murder of children was the thing that disgusted me the most. Sometimes it was a baby, and sometimes it was a small child. In either case, there is no justification for murder, especially a small child who cannot defend themselves.

Some were Shaken Baby Syndrome cases, where a parent or babysitter shook the infant violently because they were crying. One of the most heinous acts I saw was a man who put a baby in a hot oven and basically cooked the baby to death. Those were the cases that made me angrier than I can describe. You could not help but think of the pain the poor child went through, but then you would have to put it out of your mind since you eventually learn to desensitize yourself from the many horrendous things you've seen over your career.

After 37 years, I would like to think I am desensitized to homicide and murders. I think it's a natural process that police officers, firefighters, and paramedics go through in order to function in their career. If you internalize all you have seen and dwell on it too much, your career is probably over. I have seen rookie firefighters and paramedics quit the job and leave after their first several calls. I saw one new firefighter quit after handling his first building fire on Cherokee Street in south St. Louis. He quit right on the spot. I also saw one rookie after his first trauma case leave the hospital, catch the bus that ran alongside the hospital, go back to the station, and get in his car to leave, never to return. He quit because he could not handle what he saw. And quite frankly, what he saw—a broken leg with the bone sticking out—was not that bad, in my opinion. But, it was too much for him, so he quit.

Many times there is nothing we can do for the murder victim. Other times they have just been assaulted, and there is a chance we can save them. With those opportunities where we can maybe save someone, we try. We put all our efforts into the resuscitation of the victim.

Unfortunately, experience has taught me that if they are in cardiac arrest and it is due to trauma, there is a good chance they are going to stay dead. Very seldom have I seen someone resuscitated from a cardiac arrest due to trauma. Generally, the blood loss is so severe that whatever is bleeding internally, such as a gunshot to the lung or the heart, needs to be fixed, and the blood volume needs to be increased through IV fluids or blood transfusions, before the person can be resuscitated. Unfortunately, the only way to truly fix a hole in the heart or some other vital organ is to take the person to surgery. By the time the fire apparatus and ambulance crews respond to the scene, package the patient and transport them to the emergency room—not even including the time it takes to get them into surgery—it is too late for the victim. I have seen people with such a large hole in their chest or shot so many times that even if they were on a surgical table with surgeons standing there ready to operate, they probably would not have survived.

I have seen doctors do some amazing things in the emergency room when they "crack a chest" and reach in with their hand to see if they can plug the hole in a person's heart, but I cannot ever recall seeing someone survive getting their chest cracked in the emergency room.

When a doctor "cracks a chest," they make an incision in the side of the chest so that he/she can insert a pair of rib spreaders. The doctor then slowly parts the ribs, exposing the inner part of the chest. Typically you can see the heart and lungs. The person is usually already dead when this happens, since this could never be accomplished on a conscious patient.

The other technique doctors will use in the emergency room when a patient has air or blood in the chest from an injury is inserting a chest tube. The doctor makes a small incision and inserts a tube directly into the lung. I have seen this done on conscious patients before with little or no anesthesia, since there was no time if you have a chance to save their life. The insertion of the tube allows for the air pressure to equalize in the chest to help re-inflate the lung, or it allows blood to be removed, which also allows the lung to expand to its normal size. For the conscious patient with little or no anesthesia, it is usually a painful experience that leaves them screaming. But it is necessary to save their life.

When we attempt to resuscitate a murder victim because we believe there is a chance to save them, we have to be cautious of how we operate in the crime scene.

During the O. J. Simpson trial, Simpson's "Dream Team" goal was to create doubt in the jury's mind on how evidence was collected, and whether the crime scene had been compromised because of poor techniques. In the end, O. J. was acquitted of murder charges after the jury deliberated only a short period of time. Many attributed the acquittal to the doubt that was created on how evidence had been collected, stored, and processed.

Therefore, based on the lessons learned in this case to not disturb evidence, we have to be careful even where we park when we show up on the scene. Even a fire truck, ambulance, or police car arriving on a crime scene can ruin some evidence and allow someone to walk free from the charge of murder.

Such was the case when the body of Cassidy Senter [14] was found in an alley in north St. Louis. Cassidy was a ten-year-old girl, and the second young girl to be abducted in a St. Louis suburb within a short period of time. Police authorities were convinced they were dealing with a child serial abductor and killer after several other young girls reported an attempted abducting.

Two children walking in the alley discovered Cassidy's body. This part of north St. Louis was heavily blighted with vacant lots, weeds, trash, and many vacant homes. She was wrapped in two bed comforters and a pink curtain. Her jacket and pink sweater were pulled above her chest. Her jeans were pulled down over her ankles and were inside out. A sheet was looped around each of her ankles and tied in the middle to hold the ankles together—similar to when you see a prisoner walking in shackles.

Unfortunately, Cassidy had been beaten to death. The autopsy revealed the blows to the head from a bed slat were what resulted in her demise.

But the man who was ultimately arrested and convicted of her murder was almost never found because an ambulance parked in the wrong spot.

When the 9-1-1 call was made after finding her body, besides the police, an ambulance was dispatched to the alley. The alley had a dirt surface and was not made of bricks, asphalt, or concrete, like many of the alleys in St. Louis. Thus, when the ambulance drove up, it left tire tracks. The ambulance was a converted Ford Econoline van. It is not uncommon to take a Ford Econoline van and convert it into an ambulance by cutting off the top and raising the roof.

Security cameras on a building very close to the scene showed a U-Haul van driving into the alley during the early morning hours. The video showed the brake lights coming on and the van stopping in the alley. The footage was not clear because of the darkness, but you could see someone get out of the van and drop her body on the side of the alley. You could not make out the person.

After seeing the video, homicide detectives knew they were working with someone who had rented a U-Haul to transport the body. Now all they needed was a set of tire tracks, and they might stand a chance of finding their van and, ultimately, the person who rented it. Unfortunately and ironically, the U-Haul van was also a Ford Econoline van—the same as the ambulance. When homicide detectives examined the tire tracks in the alley, they now had two sets made by the same type of vehicle with the same size tires. Some of the tracks were on top of the other, and it was difficult to tell which were which.

However, in other places they were able to distinguish two sets of tire tracks, and created plaster casts of the tire tracks. Once they had both sets of plaster casts, they came to me and wanted to know which ambulance was on the call. Looking through our records, I was able to pinpoint which ambulance took the call, and let the homicide detectives take impressions of the tires to determine which plaster casts were from the ambulance and which were from the U-Haul van.

Shortly after taking the impressions, they knew which tire tracks belonged to which vehicle. It turned out they were looking for a Goodyear Work Horse Light tire. Armed with the right set of tire tracks, the detectives visited U-Haul rental stores in the northern part of St. Louis County where she had disappeared from, to take impressions from the tires of all the U-Haul Ford Econoline vans. It didn't take long until they found their van. It had been rented for a 24-hour period from a local U-Haul rental store in Hazelwood, Missouri—which is a suburb of St. Louis.

The renter's name was Thomas Brooks, Jr.[15] Besides the U-Haul van, other evidence used in the trial to convict Brooks of the murder included witnesses who saw the U-Haul van at Brooks' sister's home, DNA from Cassidy in the basement of the home, and his confession. Brooks was sentenced to death, but died in prison in 2000 from unknown causes before justice could be carried out.

But Brooks was almost never brought to justice because an ambulance drove into a crime scene and drove right over the tire tracks of the U-Haul van.

Besides driving into a homicide scene and being cautious, firefighters, paramedics, and police officers also need to be aware of where they are walking to get into a crime scene. They can also contaminate a crime scene by stepping on evidence.

One of the most challenging times in my career was responding on a homicide call when I knew the victim. None of the victims have been a loved one, but unfortunately, they had been close friends.

One dear friend who was brutally murdered was Sister Patricia Kelley,[16] a Catholic nun with the Sisters of Charity of the Incarnate Word. Sister Pat worked in the city of St. Louis with those who had trouble paying their energy bills.

Following the tremendous heat wave that hit St. Louis in 1980, when over 153 people died of heat exhaustion during an 18-day period, Sister Pat applied for and received a grant to helped start a program called Missouri Project EnergyCare. Her program really kicked into full swing when a blizzard hit the area in 1982 and dumped almost two feet of snow over a two-day period. The following year, the local gas utility company approached Sister Pat and, together, they formed Dollar Help, Inc. Dollar Help encouraged people to add an extra dollar to their utility payment, the proceeds of which were distributed to those who could not pay their electric or gas bill. Since its formation, Dollar Help has distributed millions of dollars in energy assistance on behalf of thousands of low-income families.

I got to know Sister Pat through my good friend Dan Emerson, who was the emergency management director for the city of St. Louis at the time. Sister Pat became an excellent friend, and at times would come to the Catholic Mass where I played the organ at St. Francis de Sales. Both being Catholic, we bonded, and I always would joke with her about the Catholic nuns who taught me in grade school and how they had the "fastest yardstick rulers in the west." I will always appreciate Sister Pat's tenacity and can-do attitude when it came to working for the poor. She was comfortable dealing with the poorest of the poor, or with the most powerful politician when she was promoting her programs.

Sister Pat was raped and murdered in her office in September 1987 in the basement of the Saum Hotel on South Grand by someone she was helping. Seeing Sister Pat as I saw her that morning was extremely difficult for me; it is one of those memories that I would like to put out of my mind. How can anyone do something like that to such a good and Godly person? For all the good this woman did for others, it was not fair that she left the world in this manner. When the time came that God called her home, she deserved to be comfortable in a warm bed, surrounded by other nuns. My only solace is that Sister Pat's killer was caught.

Another person I knew closely who was murdered was Ralph Price. Ralph was a large and congenial man who worked for the St. Louis Health Department as a courier who delivered mail to different city divisions. Ralph was also a minister and an elder in his church. He also officiated my wedding.

One day Ralph did not show up to work. My wife, who was the secretary for the director of health and hospitals for the city of St. Louis at the time, and whom Ralph worked for, became worried. She sent another courier by his house to check on him. Unfortunately, he found Ralph dead in his apartment, killed in an emotional rage by another man. It appeared as though a hammer had been used on Ralph and he was bludgeoned to death. Ralph's death hit my wife and me hard. In the case of Ralph's death, I did not make the scene, but I heard plenty from those who were present.

Preserving the crime scene for the homicide investigators after we leave is something almost every firefighter and paramedic thinks about today, but we also realize the patient is the top priority. If it comes down to preserving a piece of evidence or doing something that is going to save a person's life, we're always going to err on the side of patient. If there is a chance to save the person, that is where all our efforts are put.

There are two types of crime scenes: the controlled, and the uncontrolled. If a crime scene is outside, it is generally considered uncontrolled. Even though the area can have yellow tape placed around it to limit the number of people who get close to the evidence, it is still subject to wind, rain, snow, and even animals. If the crime scene is in a building, generally the crime scene and what can impact the evidence is controlled. No weather or other elements can tamper or destroy evidence.

If it had rained the night the U-Haul van went down the dirt alley when the murderer dumped Cassidy's body, chances are the tire tracks would not have been distinguishable, and her killer may have never been brought to justice.

One of the keys to preserving evidence on a scene is to limit the number of people who enter it. It seems like every television show or movie I watch where they investigate a murder, the key detective arrives on the scene, walks up to the yellow tape where a police officer is standing, shows his badge, and receives a nod from the police officer in affirmation that it is OK to proceed into the crime scene. The lead detective then raises the yellow tape and enters. He and his partner squat down next to the body, lift the sheet, take a look, and usually talk about the bruises and bleeding they see. It also amazes me how they suddenly notice one hair or cloth fiber on the victim's clothes that they pick off with tweezers and put into a collection bag. That's the movies, and not real-life police work.

The more people who enter the crime scene, the more evidence gets destroyed or altered. This is commonly known as Locard's Exchange Principle, which says that for everyone who enters the crime scene, they leave or take a piece of trace evidence with them. They can leave clothing fibers, fingerprints, hair, dead skin cells, or footprints. They can scratch a door frame or transfer blood or other body fluids from one area or another.

Imagine if you have six or more firefighters or paramedics, several police officers, and finally the homicide investigators on a scene. You could easily wind up with 10–15 people trampling through a crime scene.

Thus, it is our goal to limit the number of firefighters and paramedics who have to enter a crime scene. If a police officer tells us when we arrive that the person is dead, we typically send just one paramedic in with a monitor/defibrillator to examine the person. If they determine the person is viable or needs attempted resuscitation, the remaining firefighters and paramedics can enter the crime scene with caution to work on the victim.

Sometimes we can destroy trace evidence, and other times we as firefighters and paramedics do some stupid things.

Such was the case when I got a telephone call from a St. Louis homicide detective saying he needed to polygraph all the firefighters who were on the scene of an apparent suicide—but they were not ruling out a homicide.

As it turns out, a young man was depressed for several months and had been threatening suicide. He had been seeing a professional counselor, but one day his family heard a shot come from his bedroom. Family members immediately ran into the room to find their loved one sprawled on the floor, blood and brain matter coming from the right side of the head and a revolver lying on the floor next to him.

The family immediately called 9-1-1, which resulted in a response of police, a fire engine, and an ambulance. Unfortunately, all eight firefighters, paramedics, and police officers who responded to the scene entered the room.

After examination by the firefighter/paramedic, it was determined that he was dead, and there should not be an attempted resuscitation since there was no heartbeat, and the brain had been significantly damaged. Even if they were successful at resuscitating him, there was a great chance he would have been brain-dead. After recording all the necessary documentation, the firefighters and paramedics left. Customarily the scene is then turned over to the police, who have it photographed and have evidence technicians collect evidence. If the death is determined not to be a homicide, the investigators typically turn the scene over to the responding officer to write the report.

But things were different on this scene. When the evidence technician police officer picked up the revolver and opened it, he discovered the spent shell casing was three clicks over from the hammer of the gun. As it turned out, the person who had committed suicide put only one bullet in the six-bullet cylinder when he pulled the trigger. You cannot fire the pistol into your head and click the trigger of the gun two more times. It is physically impossible.

There were only two plausible answers: The first was that someone tampered with the gun after the shooting, or someone other than the person who died fired the revolver and pulled the trigger two more times.

The homicide investigators immediately asked the family members if they touched the weapon after it had been fired. All five family members denied touching the gun. The police officers who initially responded were also questioned whether they had handled the weapon. Both officers denied touching the weapon. All six firefighters and paramedics who responded to the scene were also questioned, and they all also denied handling the revolver. Based on the fact that no one admitted handling the revolver, the homicide investigators were left with no choice but to begin a homicide investigation.

The scene was processed for evidence, including checking for gunshot residue on the hands of the decedent. His hands were positive for gunshot residue, which is a pretty good sign that he fired the shot. But that was still undetermined.

All family members were brought down to police headquarters for questioning, but their stories checked out and were consistent, even though they had been questioned separately.

Next, the medical examiner performed an autopsy on the individual who committed suicide, and the death was from a single bullet shot to the head. Further evidence revealed gunpowder residue on the right temple of the decedent, reflecting that the bullet had been fired at close range.

What was still baffling to the homicide investigators was that the spent casing was three clicks over from the hammer of the gun in the cylinder. Going back to the old theory that someone tampered with the gun after several weeks of investigation, the homicide detectives decided to perform a polygraph on everyone who was on the scene. This included the police officers, the firefighters, the paramedics, and the family members. That's where I came in. The police wanted to polygraph all the firefighters and paramedics, and I made the arrangements.

Just prior to one of the firefighters being polygraphed, he called me. "Chief, I've got something to tell you," he said from the other end of the phone in a low and sultry tone.

"What is it?" I asked. The firefighter began to tell me that while he was standing there with the paramedics checking out the body, he decided to look at the gun. He admitted to me that he picked up the gun, opened the cylinder of the revolver and immediately closed it back up. He said curiosity got the better of him. Unfortunately, when he closed the cylinder, the spent shell casing was three spots over from the hammer.

I had to sheepishly call the homicide detective and relay to him what the firefighter had told me. He was upset, but he was also relieved that this investigation was coming to a close, and he could focus on real homicides. The homicide detective just needed to get a final statement from the firefighter to close out the case.

What should have been a simple suicide report turned into a two-week investigation and time wasted for homicide investigators.

Some homicide scenes I do not remember, but some will never leave my memory. Even though each homicide scene is tragic, some make no sense to me at all, and even some 30 years later, have not left my memory, and leave me shaking my head.

One of those homicides occurred on the evening of February 18, 1982. We were dispatched to Eugene and Bates in south St. Louis at the Onyx gas station for a shooting. Whenever you got a call in 1982 for a shooting in that deep part of south St. Louis, you knew it wasn't a false call. The deep south side of St. Louis in 1982 was predominantly a working, white, middle-class section of the city, where lawns were neatly manicured and edged, and people routinely swept the streets in front of their house to ensure cleanliness. Most people in this section of the city have a German ancestry, and routinely attended church on Sundays. It was rare in 1982 to have a homicide in this section of the city, let alone a shooting. That's why receiving a shooting call on a Thursday evening at the intersection of Eugene and Bates told us that there was something to the call.

I was a paramedic/captain at the time, responsible for the south half of the city. I was on the streets not far from the call when it was dispatched, so I told the dispatch office over the radio to also put me on the call.

It didn't take me long to arrive, but even so there must have been 10 police cars on the scene already. That's another bad sign, since the first officer on the scene will usually radio an initial report and either request an ETA on the ambulance, call for a supervisor, or start the homicide investigation team. This radio report usually brings other police officers, increasing the number of police cars on the scene.

As I exited my car, I got a medical kit from the rear of my station wagon and headed for where I saw the officers congregating at the front door of a gasoline station. As I approached, all the officers had grim looks on their faces. One of them said to me as he pointed, "In the back room, Gary."

The gasoline station was a small building that had a small front area, with an even smaller storage room in the back. In 1982, there was no such thing as self-service at a gasoline station. Typically gasoline stations were staffed with attendants who would pump your gas, check your oil, and take your money, all while you sat in your car.

I walked into the back storage area that was dimly lit with a single light bulb hanging from the ceiling. It was filled with cardboard boxes and other assorted items that had been stored there. In one corner of the room I saw a body, still on its knees, leaning forward into the corner, still upright. Blood poured from a single wound on the head and dripped down on his shirt while even more pooled on the floor. An officer in the room in a very low and sad voice said to me, "He's dead," as he continued to write in his notebook. Even from his backside, with this face not visible, I could see it was a young male, maybe my age, in his early 20s. A quick check of his carotid pulse gave me the confirmation that he was, in fact, dead. As I was checking his carotid pulse, the paramedics walked into the small room to join me. I told them he was dead, and the only thing left to do was to lift his shirt and put the EKG electrodes on his back so we could get a tracing of his heart and confirm that there was no heartbeat for medical/legal documentation purposes. As was predicted, he had no electrical activity in his heart, which made him legally dead. As the paramedics were getting the recording of his non-existent heartbeat, I had a chance to stand back and survey the scene. As a quick look it appeared that he was an employee working at the gasoline station and was made to kneel in the corner of the room, facing the wall, while someone shot him in the back of the head. In essence, he had been executed. It appeared he had been taken in a backroom and executed, probably because of a robbery. If someone kneels in a corner and faces a wall, they are obviously not resisting the robbery. Why execute them? He complied with the robber's orders. Why did they have to take his life? If you're the robber, are you worried about being identified? Then wear something over your face! How sadistic to shoot someone in cold blood, and how cowardly to have them face a wall while you do it. You can't even look them in the face since you're such a coward.

As we finished our paperwork, we left the EKG attached to the body with the date and time the EKG tracing was done. Our job was done. Now it was time for the homicide investigators to take over.

At another homicide scene a couple of days later, I was talking with one of the homicide detectives who was also handling the gasoline store shooting, and I learned more about the case.

The person who was made to kneel and face the corner of the small and dimly lit storage room was an innocent kid of 17 years old who was only working part-time while he finished high school. His name was Donald Voepel.[17] The robbery only netted $248 and some cigarettes. This poor kid lost his life over $248 and some cigarettes while he was probably trying to earn a little extra money for his car, or maybe to take his girlfriend on a date. I am sure they brandished the gun during the robbery. The brutality of how he died, and maybe his last thoughts when he probably knew what was coming when they made him kneel and face the wall, is something that bothers me to this day. We treat our domestic animals more humanely when we have them put to sleep.

The people responsible for the heinous crime were caught shortly after the murder. It turns out that it was two men, and a woman who drove the get-away car. Stephen Johns,[18] who was 35 at the time, was put to death some twenty years later by the State of Missouri. I have no problem with the death penalty in cases like this. When you brutally murder someone else and it is beyond doubt that they did it. Donald Voepel's parents were there to witness the execution in 2001, according to newspaper accounts. I don't know if it brought them closure, but I know it would not for me if one of my children was murdered in such a heartless fashion. I pray these parents and all the other parents of murdered children find peace with the anguish they must feel.

Sometimes some people seek their own form of justice. It was a typical hot and humid late St. Louis afternoon when a report of two people shot at Sarah and Olive went out over the radio in late June 1980. The area of Sarah and Olive at the time was known as the "Stroll." The Stroll was a well-known prostitution area, and the hotbed of the activity was in the 4100, 4200, 4300, and 4400 blocks of Olive and Washington. Some of the cross streets were Sarah, Boyle, and Newstead. Prostitutes were abundant throughout the area and, just like you see on television and the movies, they would be dressed provocatively and would stand in the street and openly persuade you to pull over so they could try to strike a deal.

Sometimes when I would come through the area on a Friday or Saturday night, you would almost need police officers to direct all the traffic that would congregate on the streets. Many times I would see a carload of nicely dressed, suburban-looking white males and females in cars driving the area and looking around. It almost looked like two couples went out to eat and after dinner decided to drive down into the Stroll area as a way of killing time. They certainly were out of place, and would have no other business in the area. Quite frankly, they had no business being there.

The Stroll did have its heyday. Back after World War II and through the '60s it was the center of nightlife for St. Louis, when one nightclub after another, along with restaurants, proliferated the area. Known as Gaslight Square, the nightclubs featured jazz and such big names as The Smothers Brothers, Lenny Bruce, Miles Davis, Barbra Streisand, Jackie Mason, Mike Nichols and Elaine May, Woody Allen, Jerry Stiller, Dick Gregory, and Jack E. Leonard. At its peak, approximately 50 businesses, including taverns, cabarets, restaurants, sidewalk cafes, and antique shops, could be found in the Gaslight Square area.

Eventually in the 1960s, Gaslight Square lost its luster as businesses started shuttering. The area went into blight and decay and became infested with prostitution, other crimes, vacant buildings, and empty lots where fires at one time destroyed a building that stood there.

Unfortunately, the Stroll cost one St. Louis police officer his life.

About a week prior, Officer Gregory Erson [19] was working as an undercover detective for Vice, arresting prostitutes, when he was found dead by other officers, slumped over the steering wheel of his car. Someone had robbed him of his badge, wallet, and gun. I knew Officer Erson when he was assigned to the 3rd District as a uniformed officer. He was always a quiet guy, but professional. He had been detailed to Vice to help them with the prostitute problem in the Stroll area.

About a week later, the call of two people shot at Sarah and Olive went out over the radio, and the Stroll would take another life. I pulled up shortly after the ambulance, and could see both paramedics each working on a different shooting victim. They were obviously going to need a second ambulance, so I told the dispatcher over the radio to send another one.

What was also noticeable was that there must have been over 100 people in and around the scene, and only two police officers trying to manage things. Many times I am amazed and also frustrated when citizens give firefighters and paramedics a hard time when they don't think we're moving fast enough when treating someone medically. Usually emotions will drive their comments. That was the case here. Apparently the two victims were known to some of the people at the scene. I told the officers we were going to need additional police officers, and one of them told me they had already radioed for help. This shooting was back in the days before policies were established for fire departments that required staging and ensuring the scene is safe and secure.

Eventually, the two officers were able to move the crowd further back, making our job easier. It didn't take too long for the second ambulance to arrive. When you have two critical patients, it's like the cavalry coming over the hill to the rescue you when you see that second ambulance arrive with two more paramedics.

Our victims were two young men who had been shot in what appeared to be a drive-by shooting. One was shot multiple times, and one had a shot to his buttocks. Numerous shell casings littered the street, which is always a sign to me that the shooter was using an automatic or semi-automatic weapon, since those shell casing are ejected from the gun as they are fired. If the shooter was using a revolver, the shell casings would have remained in the cylinder and would not have been scattered on the street. If someone is shot with an automatic or semi-automatic weapon, you can generally tell. The entrance wound is typically round or oval-shaped, and looks like it has an abrasion around it. But the exit wound is most notable. It's usually large, and very destructive to the tissue as the bullet from an automatic or semi-automatic leaves the body. Sometimes the bullet breaks apart or shatters when it hits bones, and it can create multiple exit wounds.

That was why one of our two patients had so many wounds. It was difficult to distinguish what was entrance and what were exit wounds. We found what looked like entrance wounds in the shoulder, chest, abdomen, and head. The other individual was shot in the buttocks, and his wounds were less serious.

Our man with the countless wounds was dead. Blood ran from his body onto the hot sidewalk. He was mortally wounded. There was nothing we could do for him. The other man had survivable wounds and was conscious. As he lay on the ground, we cut his pants to get to the affected area. The police officers began weaving the all-too-familiar yellow crime scene tape as clear barrier for bystanders not to cross. Usually the best source for securing yellow crime scene tape on a street corner is to tie it to telephone and electric poles.

As the paramedic accessed the wound on the buttocks of the live patient, the other paramedic crew was wrapping up their procedure for documenting that a person is dead. It is the same procedure for this man as it was for Donald Voepel in the gasoline station. We put the EKG monitor on the patient to get a flat line tracing of the heart and document the date, time, and the name, if it is available, on the EKG strip.

The wounds on the buttocks were dressed with a pressure dressing and some tape. An IV was started, the patient put on oxygen, and he was loaded on a stretcher to be taken to the trauma center. His blood pressure was relatively good, which told us there was a good chance the bullet didn't hit any critical internal organs. A low blood pressure would indicate to us that internal bleeding was occurring, and our patient would head to surgery shortly after arriving at a hospital.

All we could do for the second man was put a white sheet over him, since it would be disrespectful to leave his body lying on the street in wide view for everyone to gawk at. My experience has been, as time goes by, more people usually show up to see what all the activity is about, and you might even possibly have family members show up who received a phone call that their loved one has been shot and killed.

Later I learned that the man was Quintin Moss[20] and he was 19 years old. He was a known street drug dealer and was selling drugs at his normal post at the corner of Sarah and Olive. The second man shot was Wallace Connors.[21] Connors said a car turned left off of Sarah onto Olive, began increasing speed, and eventually someone started shooting from the car. Connors was shot in the buttocks as he tried to get away. But Quintin Moss was definitely the target. The man convicted of Moss' murder was Larry Griffin[22]. As I suspected, an automatic or semi-automatic weapon had been used—a .30 caliber semi-automatic carbine weapon.

Six months earlier, Moss had been arrested in connection for the murder of Larry Griffin's brother, Dennis Griffin.[23] Moss had been released when there wasn't enough evidence to hold him. As a precursor to his murder, Moss had told his mother that on May 13, 1980, someone had shot at him on the corner of Sarah and Olive. Four days later we pronounced Moss dead on the street at the same intersection. Larry Griffin was arrested for his murder, and it was apparently in retaliation for murdering his brother Dennis. Unfortunately, like so many homicide scenes I have been on, this murder only received a small blip in the local newspaper during a time when one of the local newspapers was keeping a running tally of the murders in St. Louis on the front page of the paper, like it was some type of baseball box score. Like so many, it was treated as though it was just another drug dealer who was killed. But in my mind, it was still a teenage life. Instead, he died in a cold and vicious manner on a hot sidewalk on the corner of Sarah and Olive—and two mothers would lose three sons—two to murder, and one to prison.

But the Stroll was not always pain, prostitution, and killings. There were some lighter moments.

I was driving down Sarah Avenue near Olive about 7:00 p.m. on a summer evening and caught a glimpse of a young white male with blonde hair running down the street in his underwear—just his Fruit of the Looms, with no shirt. Even at a distance of 100 feet I could see the look of pure terror on his face. The Stroll area was a largely black populated area, so to see a white male running down the street in his underwear was beyond highly unusual. As I finally grasped in my mind what I was seeing, I noticed the many people who were standing around on the street corner were laughing and pointing, staring in disbelief like I was, or just going about their business like it was no big deal. I immediately made a U-turn in the middle of the street, pulled up next to him as he was running down the sidewalk, and yelled at him through my rolled down car window to stop. He looked over, since he did not see me approaching from the rear, and saw someone who happened to be in uniform with a car that had emergency lights on top. He stood there trying to catch his breath, but at the same time was desperately pleading for help. I asked what the problem was, and he told me he had been robbed. Standing there in his white underwear, I told him to get in on the passenger side of my car.

He sprinted to my passenger door and jumped in as though his life depended on it—which it probably did. I told him to calm down and tell me what happened. With sweat pouring off him, he told me that he had picked up a prostitute in his car and she had him drive into a nearby alley so they could have sex. The prostitute then had him take his pants and shirt off and after he got everything off, she produced a knife from her purse and told him to get out of the car or else she was going to stab him. He made the wise decision to get out, and she drove off with his car. He said in the wrong neighborhood, with no pants or shirt on, he just began running. I told him to wait in the car as I picked up my radio and asked the dispatcher to send the police to my location for a robbery. Shortly thereafter, several police cars pulled up and I turned the scared young man over to them. I bet he never came back to the Stroll anytime soon.

Some murder scenes still leave me pondering the senselessness of the murder, and how someone can calculate the death of someone else. The brutality by which they die and the pain they encounter during the process, not only physically but mentally, must be beyond description to the average person. The events must be so surreal that it must not seem believable while it is happening, and at some point reality must set in and you realize you are dying.

I wondered if Nora Attaway,[24] who was 25 years old at the time, had those thoughts as she was attacked, probably in the dark, by an assailant in her ground-floor apartment in the 6700 block of Clayton in August 1991.

The 6700 block of Clayton is in the Dogtown section of St. Louis, just south of the Forest Park area in the western part of the city. The neighborhood known for its St. Patrick's Day parade has been described very much as a small country town where life centers around the Irish Catholic church, and where some homes have been occupied by third- and fourth-generation families. A murder in this section of town is virtually unheard of, and if it does occur, unless the murderer is caught, it is enough to shake the neighbors.

We were dispatched for a person down when neighbors discovered the beaten body of Nora Attaway lying in her apartment with the door open. Since 9-1-1 dispatchers are unable to truly determine the life status of someone over the phone when someone calls after finding a body, unless the caller describes advanced decomposition, usually firefighters and paramedics are dispatched to the scene also.

At this point in my career, I was a deputy chief responsible for EMS operations. When I was not handling paperwork in my office, I was operating on the streets, and commonly responded to calls when I was close. I was also normally dispatched to calls of high significance, such as multi-casualty events, multiple-alarm fires, hostage situations, etc.

As I arrived, I could see the ambulance and the first responder fire engine were already on the scene. Neighbors were already congregating in front of their homes, watching the activity and comparing notes to see if anybody knew what was happening.

As I entered the apartment, I could see and hear that everyone was congregated toward what looked like a bedroom. I made my way into the small room, and I could see the small frame of a female lying on the bed. It appeared she has been raped and beaten. She was obviously dead. A police sergeant saw there were too many people in the apartment and told everyone, "Unless you got some business here, step outside." The majority stepped outside while the paramedics ran their traditional EKG tracing to verify and document there was no heart activity.

It is necessary to run an EKG strip on someone who is dead—even if they're obviously dead. First, not only for medical/legal documentation purposes is it necessary, but you just never know. I have seen more than one paramedic fooled in my time who declared someone dead when the person was only suffering from hypothermia and was still alive. The stories you hear of people sometimes waking up in the morgue are true, and it happened to a paramedic I know.

The apartment really did not look destroyed or ransacked, although some things were later discovered to be missing. Police later discovered one of the rear screens had been cut, allowing entry into the apartment—so one could conclude that there was no close relationship between the victim and the assailant. She was uncovered. This is one more sign that there is no emotional relationship between the victim and the assailant. Whenever we find a murder victim covered up or wrapped in a blanket, the homicide investigators immediately suspect an emotional relationship between the murderer and their victim. As it has been explained to me, there is a phenomenon that someone who loves someone and kills them, usually has some form of regret later and has difficulty seeing their loved one murdered. To help put it out of their memory as best they can, they typically cover the body so they don't have to see them. The anger and emotion they felt when the murder was committed is now gone. All of the rage has been released. Now the regret starts. One way of repressing their guilty and regretful feelings is to not see the body.

I later learned that the police were able to lift a fingerprint off a lightbulb in the apartment that had been unscrewed. Apparently the killer hid in the dark apartment awaiting her return. The fingerprints were entered into the FBI's Integrated Automatic Fingerprint Identification System (IAFIS). The IAFIS is a large central database of millions of records that include fingerprints and other information about people. Commonly, fingerprints are entered into the system to allow police to match them with other crimes or to catch criminals.

About a year after the murder, a young man got arrested in a fight at a tavern, also in the Dogtown section of the city. During the booking process, his fingerprints were taken, and as a matter of routine, were entered into the IAFIS. The IAFIS determined there was a hit between the arrested suspect's fingerprints and the fingerprints lifted from Nora Attaway's apartment. The suspect who was arrested was Patrick Hunter Ford.[25] As it turned out, Ford lived in the same apartment complex, and could see Attaway coming and going. Ford eventually confessed to the murder, and her microwave oven and telephone were found in his apartment.

Again, another senseless act where a young life was taken for no reason!

Most homicides are senseless. I remember a road rage incident in St. Louis before the term "road rage" was even used. It involved a car accident in the 1500 block of Salisbury near the McKinley Bridge that goes over the Mississippi River.

Two cars were involved in an accident. When we got there, we had a man and woman sitting in the front seat of the vehicle, shot. One of the witnesses on the scene told me he was sitting in a bar, heard the crash, came outside, and saw a man get out of one of the cars, fire multiple times into the other car, calmly put his gun away, get into his car, and drive away. In the front seat of the other car, the man behind the wheel was clearly dead and the passenger, who happened to be his wife, was shot in the arm. We transported her to the hospital, but unfortunately had to pronounce her husband dead and leave him sitting behind the wheel of the car for the homicide detectives.

***

I have always been perplexed by murder-suicides. If you're going to commit suicide, why take the life of others? A murder-suicide leaves those left behind asking why, and with a lot of unanswered questions.

I have come to learn that those who commit murder-suicide do it for several reasons. First, it may be a pact between two people. I have seen this several times, especially with elderly couples. As they get older, feebler, and face a multitude of health problems, they decide it is best to leave this world together. Typically, the husband will kill the wife, and then himself. Another reason people commit murder-suicide is because they have murdered someone they care about in a moment of rage, and they cannot imagine life without that person, or they see no other way out of where they find themselves other than to commit suicide.

One morning we were dispatched to a report of a double shooting in the 5200 block of 37th Street in south St. Louis. When we arrived, we were greeted by neighbors who said there were two dead elderly people in the house. When we got inside, there was the typical quiet and eeriness of death hanging in the air. Everything looked clean and pristine, as though Grandpa and Grandma were waiting for the kids and grandchildren to show up for Thanksgiving.

But there would be no Thanksgiving family gathering this day. We found a woman on the first floor of the house with a shotgun blast to the head, and we found her husband in the basement, also with a shotgun blast to the head, with the weapon lying next to him. It appeared he had shot his wife, went to the basement, and then turned the weapon on himself.

Unfortunately, a shotgun blast to the head is almost 100 percent fatal. In all my years in this profession, I have only seen one person survive such an injury. That happened when he attempted to commit suicide. He had the barrel of the shotgun under his chin, and it slipped when he pulled the trigger. The gun took off the front of his face. He was grossly disfigured, but he survived.

In the case of this elderly couple, as we were doing our job of declaring them dead and going through our normal ritual of running EKG strips, the police found a suicide note on the first floor dining room table from the husband, saying he was going to kill his wife, then himself.

I have no idea what drives couples to the point that both agree to commit suicide. Maybe it's finances. Maybe it's an elderly couple growing old, with health problems, and they decide one cannot live without the other. I would like to think there is always another solution other than murder-suicide. Murder-suicide is so final. There is no second chance, and there is no returning from what has been done. There is nothing but finality.

I suspect I knew what caused the murder-suicide in one case that I responded to. It was an elderly couple who had been sick for quite a while. The husband was 93 years old, and his wife was 82 years old. Their daughter had been staying with them and taking care of them. The call was in the southwest part of St. Louis in 1988. When we arrived in the quaint and quiet neighborhood around 10:30 a.m., the daughter was obviously distraught. Her father had sent her on an errand to evidently get her out of the house. When she returned, she found her mother sitting in a chair in the bedroom with a rifle shot to the head. She found her father lying on the bathroom floor, also with a rifle shot to the head, and the gun lying next to him. There was nothing we could do for them anymore. They were mortally wounded with shots to the head.

The daughter told us she had cared for her parents, and that she had no idea her father was planning anything like this. We'll never know if the wife agreed to the plan or not, only that she was murdered by her husband. The daughter told us the couple had been sick for a while, and her father was becoming more despondent over his and his wife's illness.

It's at times like this that we realize there is nothing we can do for the dead, but we need to focus our attention on the family members who remain. That is why we tried to comfort the daughter as much as possible, and even offered to take her to the hospital, but she refused. She was all by herself, with nothing to do except plan the funerals of both her parents.

I always think of the family members who are left behind after a suicide, especially a violent death where blood, tissue, and other bodily fluids need to be cleaned up. The body has been removed, but the blood, tissue, and other bodily fluids remain. They are left with the task of cleaning up this terrible mess that was once their loved ones. I know a politician in St. Louis whose husband committed suicide, and she openly talked about how angry she was at him for doing it in their bedroom. She was left with cleaning the blood, brains, and skull off their bed, the floor, and wall of the bedroom. She was upset with him for leaving her to clean up a mess that would leave her emotionally scarred.

There are companies that now do this. I didn't know that in 1988, but if I had, I would have suggested it to the daughter. She already had enough to worry about.

I went on one murder-suicide call that had me baffled. It was February of 1992, and the weather was somewhat mild for a February night in St. Louis, in the lows 50s. It was a Friday evening, and usually Friday nights are a little busier than the others nights of the week. So when a double shooting came out, I was not surprised.

We were dispatched to the Ebony Motel in the 3600 block of Page, just off North Grand Boulevard in north St. Louis. The Ebony Motel is one of those small hotels that is one story and has a front office where you check in, then drive to the door of your room and park. It's not one of the types of motel where you would stay for a week, or even a day, as a matter of fact. The Ebony Motel is one of those motels that rents rooms in three-hour blocks for couples wishing to spend some intimate time together. So when we got a call to the Ebony Motel for a double shooting, my thoughts went to some jealous husband or wife who showed up unexpectedly and enacted revenge on not only their spouse, but the other person who checked into the hotel with them.

When I arrived, several police officers were already on the scene and the hotel manager was standing outside with them, giving a statement while he nervously smoked a cigarette. I was far enough away that I could not hear what the hotel manager was saying, but I could see he was pointing in the direction of the room, and then back to the front of the motel area. The motel room door was open, and several police officers were standing at the doorway, writing in their small pocket notebooks. I walked up to the door of the room and one of the police officers I knew said, "Nothing to do here, Gary." Once I got in the room, I could see exactly what he meant. On the bed laid the body of a middle-aged woman with multiple gunshots. She was definitely shot in the face, arms, and hands. The man was lying on the floor with a single bullet wound to the head. The gun was lying next to him.

I later learned from the motel manager that the couple had checked in around 5:00 p.m. When their three hours were up and they had not checked out and dropped off the key, the manager came looking to see if they had left. He knocked several times first and did not hear any noises coming from the room. At that point he opened the door, assuming they had left, and found both bodies laying there. To the police, with no forced entry and a single bullet wound to the head of the male with the gun lying next to him, it looked like a murder and suicide. However, there was no suicide note. I concluded the wounds in the woman's hands and arms were the result of her not wanting to commit suicide, and she threw her hands and arms up in a defensive manner. I never did hear how the case was eventually ruled.

One of the more bizarre murder, possible suicide events that occurred when I worked in St. Louis occurred in 1991. About the same time, we received one call for a shooting in a car in the Lindenwood neighborhood area, and then another call for a shooting in the New Marcus Cemetery in the 7900 block of Gravois in south St. Louis. Unbeknownst to us, the police had also forced entry into a home in the 6500 block of Marquette based on the fact that workers at a bank in downtown St. Louis were worried when one of their co-workers didn't show up for work. As a matter of routine, the police will force entry into the home to check on the well-being of someone when the person has not been seen, or there are unusual circumstances, as in the case when someone has not shown up for work.

When the police forced entry into the one-story brick home in the 6500 block of Marquette, they found two bodies. The home where the bodies were found is in an area of St. Louis where neatly manicured lawns dot the area, and neighbors watch out for each other. Finding two bodies in a home in this area was highly unusual. Police officers who I talked to later said the older couple had been either shot or stabbed, and the home was ransacked. They did point out there was no evidence of forced entry. Fire or EMS were not dispatched to the home on Marquette since the police officers who forced entry determined the older couple appeared to have been dead for a while, and the paramedics were not needed.

The call I went on with the shooting in the car was right down the street from my office, and was virtually the same time the officers were forcing entry two blocks away on Marquette. The shooting was in a car in the 3300 block of Watson. When we arrived, the police were already on the scene, and there was one body of a male lying in the back seat of a red Mustang. From all indications from our external view of him through the windows of the car, he appeared to also have been dead for a while. There was blood on his body and on the car seat that had already dried to the crusty red and black it gets. He was pale, with one eye open and the other half-closed in what I have described as the death stare. His chest was not rising or falling as would happen if he was breathing.

The police officers asked us not to disturb or open the car doors, since they did not want to destroy any evidence. Even though we like to verify and document the death, we can certainly abide with the police officer's request where we can visually tell there is obvious death. The body in the back seat of the red Mustang appeared to be a younger male in his 20s, and it looked like he had some trash bags over his body.

I later learned an ambulance was dispatched about the same time to the New Marcus Cemetery, where some workers who had been emptying trash in a dumpster found another young male who appeared to be shot.

As it turned out, the older couple in the home on Marquette were the father and mother of the men found in the red Mustang and the New Marcus Cemetery. The man in the Mustang and the cemetery were brothers. Essentially, four members of one family had been murdered. There was one remaining brother missing. Was he dead somewhere else and had not been found? Somewhere else and unaware of what had transpired? Or was he responsible for the murders?

The third missing brother was in California, and had been to St. Louis on the night of the murders. He flew back to California, where he was arrested.

His name was Emory Futo.[26] He originally claimed that he had flown to St. Louis to help his brother Nicholas with a drug deal. Nicholas was the brother found in the cemetery.

Futo told investigators three different versions of his story, but he claimed that his brother Nicholas actually killed both of their parents and their other brother. During his trial, the defense tried to argue that

Nicholas did all the killing. He further told investigators that he and Nicholas had a suicide pact. Emory said he shot Nicholas, but could not bring himself to commit suicide.

Futo also told investigators in one of his stories that his brother Nicholas said he shot his brother Joseph first, and then went to the family home on Marquette, where he killed his mother with a sledgehammer and shot and stabbed their father. Futo also said his brother Nicholas had told him how he hit their mother a few times with the sledgehammer but he had become upset with her moaning. So in order to finish her off, he wrapped a cord around her neck and strangled her to death. Futo then said that his brother told him he waited for his father to come home from work and shot him until the gun was empty, and then he stabbed him some more. Homicide detectives I knew on the case like Chris Pappas and Joe Nickerson were able to reconstruct the murder scene, and pretty much concluded that everyone died as Futo described it, except he was the one who committed the murders—not his brother.

Futo claimed after he returned to California, he blocked out any memories of the events in St. Louis because of the trauma he had been through. Eventually Futo was convicted of four counts of murder and given four life sentences without the possibility of parole after he proclaimed his innocence.

When I think of the definition of the word "evil," I think of Emory Futo. How does one kill your own mother, father, and your only two siblings? The only answer I have is that Futo was a sociopath. A true sociopath is someone who has no regard for anyone except themselves. An extreme sociopath does not care who gets in their way of what they are trying to achieve. If someone gets in their way, they will remove them from the picture with no thought at all, and with no regard for their life. In this case, Futo stood to gain about $275,000–$325,000 in life insurance benefits and stock. We'll never know if that was his motive or not. Instead, the Missouri taxpayers will support him the rest of his life.

***

The homeless are also victims of homicides. Homeless people try to find shelter, usually at night to protect themselves from the weather, especially during the winter months. Winter months in St. Louis can become challenging at times. Some go to organized shelters run by charitable organizations while others band together, find sheltering, and create their own communities.

We were dispatched to a stabbing one Friday evening on the St. Louis riverfront, about a mile north of the Gateway Arch. The caller couldn't really give an address since there was no address. All we got in terms of a location was that the stabbing victim was somewhere behind the flood wall at the foot of Carr Street.

The St. Louis flood wall is a man-made concrete wall built in the 1950s to keep the Mississippi River from flooding the city. For years, the Mississippi River would flood into industrial areas and impact business. City officials decided to erect the wall, which would have occasional drive-through gates so the Mississippi River could be accessed if necessary. The flood wall does not protect the entire length of the city along the river since the majority of the city sits on higher bluffs, and floods would have no impact. However, for those areas that would be impacted by flood waters, the flood wall stands guard. It really proved its worth during the devastating floods of 1993 when the river almost lapped over the twenty-plus-foot flood wall in some areas.

The area behind and between the flood wall and the river typically has a gravel road running along the wall. Beyond that, toward the river, is sometimes patchy dirt areas and scrub brush. Normally the flood gates are open unless they are closed because of flooding. If the gates are open, you have easy access to drive through the gates and into the no-man's land between the flood wall and the river.

When we got the call for a stabbing behind the flood wall, I suspected someone was taken there and murdered, since it is a very desolate area. After being murdered, the body was left and someone found it. When I arrived at the scene, I was shocked to see a small community of homeless people who had built shanties out of anything they could find. Some were made of wood, and some were made of corrugated aluminum. Patches of plastic were used to fill in the gaps. If it was not a shanty, it would have been a very scenic location overlooking the Mississippi River as it rolled by.

It was a February evening and it was not bad weather for St. Louis—it was about 50 degrees out. But the problem was being along the river. For whatever reason, when the wind blows down along the river, it just feels much colder. It did this night also.

The community of homeless people we encountered did not speak much English. They did point to one of the shanties with concerned looks on their faces. From their appearance and dialect, I could tell they were of Hispanic background, and were probably Cuban immigrants we had been seeing after the Mariel Cuban boatlift in 1980.

Inside the shanty we found a middle-aged male stabbed in the chest and abdomen. He was obviously dead. As I looked about the shanty with my flashlight, I could see there were mattresses, kerosene lanterns, and someone had even found a wood-burning stove that had a vent going through the roof of the shanty. To my amazement, I also saw foam insulation along the walls and part of the ceiling. I thought, these homeless people are pretty innovative, and must be pretty good scroungers to build themselves a home.

Turning my attention back to the victim, it was just me and the police officer. A quick check for a pulse in his carotid artery confirmed for me that the look I saw on his face and no rising of his chest confirmed he was dead. Based on the wound in his chest, I suspected the stabbing weapon hit his heart or a major artery, such as the aorta, and he bled to death internally before I got there. Outside the shanty I could hear lots of broken English as the homeless people tried to explain to the other police officer what had happened.

I went out to my car to retrieve my monitor/defibrillators, which allowed me to take a tracing of his heart to confirm he was dead. As I stepped out of the shanty on the way to my car, one of the homeless people with a disturbed and very concerned look on her face asked me in broken English if he was alive. I looked at her and, from the look in her eyes and the concern on her face, I knew, as I had so many times before, that the man lying inside the shanty was a relative, a loved one, or a close friend.

I suspected she already knew that he was dead, but she needed confirmation for her mind and heart. She needed to start the grieving process but was in denial, and was waiting for the definitive word. As she asked, several other homeless people also paused to hear my answer. They obviously had the same look of unease on their faces, and needed affirmation from someone in a uniform that it was all right to start grieving.

What do you say in cases like this? How do you deliver the word that a loved one, a relative, or a close friend has died? There is no easy way, because the truth is going to hurt. You can't lie, either! You could never say he is alive when he is dead. Your only option and choice is to tell them he is dead. Telling someone that someone has died is not a pleasant task. In my profession, we do not have the option of taking someone to a nice, quiet conference room, or having a priest at the ready to provide comfort when the news is delivered. In my profession, the conference room is a dirt and gravel road with a concrete wall to my left and a river to my right.

All I could tell the lady was, "He did not make it." As I told her in an indirect way that he was dead, she looked at me directly in the face and as my words sunk in, she broke into a scream and collapsed on her knees to the dirt and gravel road. The tears and screams of anguish flowed from her mouth and she clenched her fists ever so tightly next to her own face. At some point the fists opened and she buried her face in her hands. Other homeless people tried to comfort her, but she needed to release all the anguish she was feeling. The homeless people were speaking in Spanish to her and I had no idea what they were saying, but I was sure they were trying to comfort her. Some of them had tears streaming down their faces also.

All I could do was stand there. I had delivered the news that someone this person cared about is dead. He may have been a homeless man, but it does not diminish him as a person, possibly a father, a brother, a son, or a husband. He is just like you or me. A person who loved and cared about certain people in his life, and people in his life loved and cared about him. And now he was gone from their lives, killed in a cruel way in a shanty next to the Mississippi River.

Although I have become used to homicide scenes in 37 years, at the same time, I have not gotten used to homicide scenes. One is never the same as the other. The thought of what transpired there minutes, hours, and sometimes days before you arrived is beyond any description that can be put in writing. The written word would never be able to capture the emotion, the feelings, and other thoughts that went through the minds of those who were murdered. What were their last thoughts? What was the last thing they saw? Did it seem like a dream and not real? Or at one point did they realize it was not a dream and they were in real peril?

We'll never know because we cannot go back and talk to them. We can only speculate their thoughts, emotions, and any pain they may have felt.

We can only pray they are at peace!

CHAPTER 8

✛

JUST EVERYDAY STUFF

Every day brings something new working in big cities. One such event occurred one April evening in 1998. The SS *Admiral* was a large floating casino located on the St. Louis riverfront in the shadows of the Gateway Arch. I was with my wife celebrating a birthday when I got that all-too-familiar notification on my pager. The text message said, *"Admiral* has broken loose from moorings—emergency evacuation underway."

I immediately left the party and put myself en route. That is one of the responsibilities any time you get promoted in a fire or EMS organization—as the chief paramedic, I was on call 24 hours a day. I am not a big drinker, so thankfully I was not drinking this night; otherwise, I wouldn't have responded, and would've had someone else taking my calls.

It took me about 10 minutes to arrive on the scene as I maneuvered my way through the city streets with my lights and sirens. There was already a second alarm in and when I arrived, I could see the *Admiral* halfway out into the river, with its back end still moored to the shore. The front end appeared to have broken away and was sticking out toward the middle of the river. The entrances and exits that had normally been on the bank side of the river were now spun around and facing out into the river. The *Admiral* was dark, also—apparently when it pulled away from its moorings, it lost its power. The only thing visible were dim lights, probably from the emergency lighting.

In its prime, the SS *Admiral* was a passenger steamship that went up and down the Mississippi River on day and night excursions. It was a massive ship that was longer than a city block, at 374 feet long, and had an impressive steel structure. It had lots of windows and five decks, the top of which was open, and where people normally sat and watched the shoreline go by as it cruised the river. As a child, my parents would periodically take my brother and me for day cruises on the *Admiral*. At this point in its life, the *Admiral* had no more engines, and was just a floating casino with 1,230 slot machines, 59 gaming tables, 18 restrooms, and one restaurant.

About 7:50 p.m., a towboat, consisting of 12 loaded and 2 empty barges, was traveling northbound on the Mississippi River through the St. Louis port. The barges struck the Missouri-side pier of the center span of the Eads Bridge. Eight barges broke away from the tow and drifted back through the Missouri-side of the bridge spans. Three of these barges drifted toward the *Admiral* and eventually struck it, causing the majority of its mooring lines to break. The *Admiral* then rotated clockwise downriver, away from the Missouri riverbank. The captain of the towboat disconnected his vessel from the six remaining barges and placed the towboat's bow against the *Admiral's* bow to hold it against the bank.

Without engines, the *Admiral* would have just floated freely down the river toward two other bridges and other boats. The Mississippi River was flooded, and the *Admiral* would not have cleared the Poplar Street Bridge downstream because of the high waters. The Poplar Street Bridge carries Interstate 64 over the Mississippi River between Missouri and Illinois.

About the time the towboat began pushing against the *Admiral*, the *Admiral's* next-to-last mooring line broke away. The towboat and the single mooring wire that remained attached to the *Admiral* held the boat near the Missouri bank.

I thought, *This is one that you don't find in the textbooks.* I got with the incident commander, and a game plan was formulated. There were over 3,000 people on the casino boat at the time. Who knows how many injuries or deaths would have occurred if the boat had struck the bridge, damaged the hull, and/or sank in the colder spring waters of the river that night. I don't even like thinking about it.

Firefighters had already taken fireboats to the *Admiral* and reported injuries on board, so we agreed to start ferrying people off using fireboats and private industry towboats, who had also responded to the scene to assist. The plan was to take all the people from the *Admiral* to a point along the riverfront and create a funnel where everyone would pass through. The funnel point would be some commercial restaurant boats. As the people got off the fireboats or towboats, they would be triaged. The wounded would go to a treatment area, and those who were not wounded would be put on busses and taken to the parking lot where their cars were located.

Thankfully we did not have any serious injuries. Those who required a higher level of care were sent to local hospitals for further treatment. In all, about 50 people were treated at the scene, and sixteen people were sent to the hospital. Most of the injuries occurred when people got knocked down in the panic as people tried getting to exits. Overall, it was a very successful operation. Considering the logistical challenges and the number of people who had to be evacuated, the operation was done in a relatively short period of time.

When you work in fire and EMS in two major urban cities like St. Louis and Memphis, every day brings something new. Just when you think you have seen it all, just wait! Firefighters and paramedics in St. Louis, Memphis, and other major cities like to say that we have a front-row seat to the most interesting show on earth.

That "just wait" happened one Saturday morning in St. Louis in 1980. We got dispatched for a "man down" at the Gateway Arch, at the base of the north leg. The stainless steel structure of the Gateway Arch rises some 630 feet off the ground, and ironically, the distance between its legs is also 630 feet. I should know. My summer job in high school was to run the trains carrying the passengers up and down the Arch legs. I heard the speech about the Arch and its statistical facts thousands of times during my summers while stationed at the top of the Arch. The park where the Arch stands is a national park, and is officially called the Jefferson National Expansion Memorial. Being federal property, it is administrated by the National Park Service. The 90 acres of tree-lined walkways with the nation's tallest monument along the St. Louis riverfront creates a fantastic forefront for the St. Louis skyline.

In order to reach the legs of the Arch, it was necessary for us to drive on the walkways in the park. When I pulled up, the ambulance and police had already arrived. I noticed a moderate-sized group of people standing at the base of the north leg. Getting out of my car and walking over, I also noticed some of the federal park rangers in their familiar uniforms with the Smokey the Bear hats.

As I got closer, I noticed a man lying on the ground. I figured he was dead since he was motionless, and no one was attempting to treat him. But what caught my eye was the parachute attached to him. I walked up next to a police sergeant I knew and said, "Don't tell me." His reply was "Yup!" I thought he did a parachute jump and the chute failed and he landed on the Arch grounds. When the police sergeant said, "Yup," he was referring to the fact that the dead man had parachuted to the top of the Arch and then fell off.

As it turns out, it was a stunt that was tried and it failed. The parachutist's goal was to land on top of the Gateway Arch and then release his main chute. He would then BASE jump from the top of the Arch using his reserve chute. Unfortunately, the wind caught his chute and dragged him over the side and he slid down the north leg landing on his head, killing him.

There are other calls that make you shake your head and chuckle, and you can't wait to tell someone. Usually those are the calls where someone got something stuck in them. One of my more memorable calls was a guy in St. Louis who lived in the projects on the near south side of downtown and got a pipe cleaner stuck in his penis. Apparently, he enjoyed sticking things down his urethra, including pens and pencils. This particular day he thought he would try a pipe cleaner with its fine wire tentacles sticking off the main stem. Unfortunately for him, it did not give him the pleasure he thought it would. It was basically stuck, and trying to take it out was too painful for him. He decided to make the dreaded call to 9-1-1 and really embarrass himself. I am not sure how the doctor at the hospital ever got it out.

Over the years, you go on calls or hear of calls where someone got something stuck in their anus. Usually you know something is up when they walk in and look pretty sheepish and embarrassed. One particular guy had an itch that he could not reach, so he decided to tie a string to the handle of a screwdriver and insert the screwdriver into his rectum—so he claims. The bad luck for him was that the string came off the handle and the screwdriver was left in the rectum. In another case in Memphis, we had a man show up at the local fire station with a window weight lodged in his rectum. I am talking about the counterweight that is usually inside the wall of a window that keeps it in position when you raise or lower the window. According to the firefighters, it had completely disappeared and of course he was embarrassed, as most people would be.

One of the most common rectally lodged items people call 9-1-1 for is usually a vibrator. What probably would make it worse was if the vibrator was still running. But over the years I've heard of a Coke bottle, a can of hairspray, a flashlight, and even a Buzz Lightyear toy stuck in a rectum.

I will never forget the call that we got for a gunshot wound. It was in a decent area of town where some more affluent people live in the bigger homes. As it turns out, this couple was sitting in their family room watching television, and the husband decided to start cleaning his .22 caliber revolver. The gun accidentally went off and he wound up shooting his wife in the cheek of her buttocks. Of course, she got mad and went to the kitchen and got a large iron skillet and started to beat the hell of out of him. A couple of whacks to his head and then she called 9-1-1! When we got there he was unconscious, lying on the family room floor and she was running around with no pants on saying, "Look at what the son-of-a-bitch did to me!"

One of the more bizarre calls I can remember was when we got a call for a serious nosebleed. When we got there, we encountered a middle-aged man who had decided he did not need his testicles anymore. He thought it would be appropriate for him to cut them off with a pair of scissors and throw them in the trash can. He answered the door wearing a house robe that was wide open, revealing where the bleeding was coming from. It certainly wasn't his nose. He got bandaged and taken to the hospital, and I am sure after his recovery he was sent to another kind of special doctor who deals with psychiatric issues.

While there is humor on the job sometimes, it is painful to be there when someone dies in front of your eyes. I have had a couple of events like that, and they will forever be lodged in my memory. One particular lady was in congestive heart failure and was as blue as the sky on a cloudless day. We got her loaded in the back of the ambulance and I decided to go along to help, since she was critical. I can remember bending over her while she was struggling to get air while lying on the stretcher. She was in a "fight or flight" situation in her effort to survive. She was so full of fluid that she couldn't get any air. She grabbed me by the shirt and pulled me toward her. We were face to face, only inches apart when we made eye contact. She said to me, "Don't let me die," in the most desperate tone of voice. I said, "I won't." In less than a minute, she died in front of me when she went into cardiac arrest. We never got her back, and the emergency room never got her back either.

Firefighters and paramedics do grieve when someone dies on them. It's hard to accept that someone would die on us and we were not successful, but it is the profession that we have chosen: to save and preserve life. I certainly grieved that night, and I will never forget the look on that lady's face some 25+ years ago when she begged me to not let her die. Somehow I feel I let her down.

In all my calls, the worst I have ever seen anyone grieve was a father who lost his young three-year-old son at the intersection of where South Broadway, Chippewa, and Jefferson come together in south St. Louis. His grieving certainly left an indelible impression on me. The babysitter was driving a Pinto car that had a hatchback on it. She had the young boy and some other children in the car when she was hit by another car. The young boy, who was in hatchback area, was thrown from the car when the hatchback flew open. The boy was thrown into a newspaper box, where he hit his head and died instantly. The father got a call to come to the scene. Once he found out his son had died, he let out the most remorseful and pitiful cries I've ever heard in my career. Cries that actually pierced your soul because they sounded so mournful. He was so distraught that we were at a loss on how to comfort him. There was no possibility of consoling him. I decided we needed to put him the back of the ambulance to at least get him out of the view of the public, who were was standing on the sidewalks and the corners watching what was happening. I ordered the paramedics to put him in the back and away from view. After being in the back of the ambulance for about five minutes while he was tended to by the paramedics, the mother showed up with another young son. I walked her and the young son to the back of the ambulance where the father was already inside. As soon as I opened the door and the father saw the other son, through his utter and complete anguish, he hopped out of the back of the ambulance, squatted to the ground, and grabbed his other son with all his strength and energy. He was locked into a hug with his son and with his eyes closed, almost to say, "I'm never going to let you go because I don't want to lose you, either." As I watched this scene play out, I had a sick feeling in my stomach. Watching this agony play out this hard drains any firefighter or paramedic of their emotions and energy. To this day, I have never seen anyone grieve as hard as that man did for his dead son. I grieved and said prayers for this father and his son that night also.

Another time I grieved was when police sergeant William Campbell[27] was gunned down and killed outside the 6th district police station in St. Louis. I knew Sergeant Campbell from working that particular area of north St. Louis for several years and had become friendly with him. He was very cordial, and an overall nice person. He was always respectful of others. I had just been on a call with him a couple hours before he was shot. It was a teenager who was showing signs of a psychiatric disorder and was becoming violent. He was going to be taken to the psychiatric hospital but, while we were inside the home, he expressed embarrassment to be taken outside in handcuffs. It was customary at that time in St. Louis to handcuff psychiatric patients in the event they became violent. Sergeant Campbell found a solution by handcuffing the young man's hands in front of him instead of in the back, and then putting a large hat over his hands so no one could see the handcuffs. He preserved the young man's dignity.

It was May 30, 1979, and a couple of hours later we got a call for a shooting in front of the 6th District police station at W. Florissant and Ruskin Avenues by Calvary Cemetery in north St. Louis. We were only a couple of blocks away, and it was before we used staging areas. When we pulled up in front of the police station, shots were still being fired from across the street near Calvary Cemetery. I looked in the direction of the shots and by the light of the streetlights, I saw a police car ram into a person standing right in front of the iron fence of the cemetery. I thought, *Jesus, that guy is dead.* Suddenly, he jumped up on the hood of the police car and bolted over a 10-foot wrought-iron fence into the cemetery. The police officer jumped out of his patrol car and another officer, who I assumed came from the police station, aimed their guns through the wrought-iron fence and fired several shots. One officer then started to climb over the fence while the other one stayed in position with his gun pointing through the fence.

I could also see two police officers in front of the station—one lying on the grass, and the other on the sidewalk. I immediately went to the officer who was not moving on the grass. He was on his back and when I got to him, I could see it was Sergeant Campbell. *Dammit; I don't know what happened, but this isn't right,* I thought. Coming up behind me was Jerry Bappert, who had a stretcher. I could see Sergeant Campbell had numerous pellet wounds in his chest, and a couple in his face. He had apparently been hit with a shotgun blast, but it had to be from a distance from the way the pellets were scattered on his body. He was not breathing, and was apparently already dead. I felt for a pulse. There was none. *Dammit,* I thought again. I told Jerry that Sergeant Campbell was dead, and we needed to get him on the stretcher and into the back of the ambulance where we could work on him.

We loaded him onto the stretcher and raced for the ambulance. Once we got him in the back, I went to intubate him and grabbed what looked like the right size endotracheal tube without checking. I put my laryngoscope together, inserted it in his mouth, saw the vocal cords and went to insert the ET tube and I thought, *Dammit again! This tube looks too big.* But I thought, *what the hell. Let's see if I can push it through his vocal cords.*

It was a tight fit, but it went in. I then figured there was no sense inflating the bulb on the end of the tube since it was already snug. Jerry started CPR, and I hooked Sergeant Campbell up to the EKG machine. I took one look at the monitor and saw he was flat line. I told Jerry to listen to the lungs and to make sure my ET tube was in as I squeezed the bag-valve mask. Two listens on both sides and he said, "You're in." A police officer took over CPR while Jerry put an IV in so we could push some drugs. He quickly slid the catheter in and hooked up the IV before pushing a couple doses of Epinephrine. I told Jerry we needed to get out of there and head to the hospital.

Unfortunately, the trauma center was some six miles away. The police officer in the back of the ambulance said we were going to get an escort, and the route would be blocked. Jerry jumped up front and we took off. All I could see was police cars in front of us and police cars behind us. We were heading for Firmin des Loge Hospital (now called St. Louis University Hospital) where all police officers were taken when they were injured back in 1979. When the police officer said the route would be cleared, he was not kidding. All the way down W. Florissant, for some two miles to Grand Avenue and then for another four miles over Grand Avenue, there was not a single civilian car on either road. I don't know how the police officers did it, but they had every street blocked to not to allow any civilian vehicles onto these two major thoroughfares. I looked through the window into the front area of the ambulance, and at one point the odometer read 80 miles per hour. It doesn't matter! Whether you are police, fire, or EMS, we're all part of the same brotherhood and sisterhood of public safety. We all go on the same calls. We all get the same abuse. We all have the same joys, cries, laughs, and sadness.

We got Sergeant Campbell to the hospital and they worked on him for quite a while. But unfortunately, he died from his injuries. I sat outside the emergency room that night at Firmin des Loge Hospital and I just felt empty and drained. The total time it took from the time we got the call until we got him to the hospital was 17 minutes. If he had any chance, I felt we gave it to him. Unfortunately, I am speculating his wounds with the shotgun blast he had taken to the chest were mortal. It probably hit his heart and/or major arteries.

As more and more police officers started showing up at the hospital, along with members of the police command staff, I started to learn what happened. Apparently the police had brought a man by the name of Lloyd Mitchell[28] to the police station after they found him sitting in a doorway after his car broke down and he wanted to get out of the rain. The police helped him by calling his parents, and Mitchell's mother indicated someone would come and get him. Mitchell sat in the police station lobby for quite a while, but when his brother showed up to pick him up, he was gone. A short time later, police could hear someone playing on the police radio, apparently from a police car or a portable radio.

A short time later, Sergeant Campbell and another police sergeant walked out the front door of the 6th district station. When he turned to talk to someone, he was shot by Mitchell, who had a shotgun and was behind a police car across the street. Sergeant Campbell immediately went down after being shot. James Cox,[29] another police officer, was also shot at the same time.

Mitchell apparently got into Sergeant Campbell's police vehicle and was able to get the shotgun out that was locked in place on the hump between the two front seats. After Mitchell fired several shots, police exchanged fire with him, and he ran across the street toward the cemetery. He was hit once by gunfire and knocked down, only to be chased by another officer in the car and officers from the police station. We were only a couple of blocks away when we got the call, so we witnessed the last part of the chase.

That night I could not sleep. I kept going over and over the call in my mind. It almost seemed surreal what I had been a part of and had seen. Sergeant Campbell was like many public servants in police, fire, and EMS, who give their lives every year all across the United States in performance of their duties.

I am grateful that I have never been killed in the line of duty, but I have certainly been in some situations that could have gone a different way.

One night we got a call from a jumper on top of the 36-story Mercantile Bank building in downtown St. Louis. It was nighttime, but someone had seen someone from down below, or from a window of a higher building on the roof and when they called 9-1-1, they said the person was getting ready to jump. About six firefighters, some police officers, and I went up to check the roof. Security took us up the elevator as high as we could go, and then we had to walk several stories to a security door to the roof. The security door was locked, and if it had been opened, an alarm would have gone off. No alarm had gone off at the security desk in the lobby. I thought there was no way there was somebody on this roof, but we still had to check it out.

The roof was flat, with no lights. It covered about half a block and was decently sized. It was hard to see since it was nighttime. The roof was separated into different sections by a small three-foot-high wall. As everybody scattered to look, I started in one particular direction and started jumping over the three-foot-high walls without looking. I would walk up to the wall, put my hand on it, and jump over it by swinging my legs from one side of the wall to the other. After about my third wall, a little voice in my head told me that it was pretty stupid to jump over the walls without looking—especially where I could not see because it was dark. The next wall I came up to, I looked over before I jumped over, and my eyes got as wide as saucers. I would have fallen 36 stories. I came to a part of the roof that looked like it was still a part of the roof, but it was actually a corner of the front of the building that did not have any roof, but the edges of the buildings still extended out to a point to give the building a square structural look. If I had jumped over the small wall, I would have fallen and landed at the front doors of the building 36 stories below. Thankfully that little voice in my head was speaking loud and clear that night.

Another time was a St. Louis fire in 1978 in the 1600 block of Park. The fire came in about 4:00 a.m. and when we pulled up, there was brown, cruddy-looking smoke oozing from all the cracks the smoke could find in a three-story brick commercial structure, with several boarded-up businesses on the first floor and what might have been apartments on the second and third floors. I didn't really know how to read smoke so early in my career, but if I did it was obvious from the way it would push out and then suck back into the cracks of the building that we were about to have a backdraft. I was by the front door, just off the sidewalk in the street by the curb behind the 2's engine, when a company right in front of me was attempting to force entry into the building by pulling the plywood off. Suddenly, there was a loud explosion, like a huge mortar shell being shot, followed by rumbling and crashing. My immediate reaction was to turn around and start running—which I did. I got hit by several bricks, and I could hear the crashing of debris behind me. I stopped on the other side of Park Avenue and turned around to see the top two stories of bricks from the front of the building had blown out and come crashing down on the firefighters on the sidewalk who could not get away. I ran back to the sidewalk and some firefighters had already self-extricated themselves from the bricks or were picking themselves up.

But where the company had been prying the plywood off the front of the building, there was one firefighter completely buried in bricks, with only his lower legs sticking out. Firefighters were already digging frantically and throwing bricks in every direction to unbury him. It did not take much digging before two firefighters picked him up by his armpits and dragged him out and away from the building, which was rolling with flames now after the backdraft. They kept dragging him face down and I yelled for them to stop. I had no idea what type of injuries he had, and dragging him too far could cause more damage. The two firefighters rolled him onto his back and I could see he was unconscious. Blood was bubbling out of his nose and mouth when he breathed.

The unconscious firefighter was Captain Arthur Werner.[30] Captain Werner, who was 56 years old, had just retired the month before, but was so restless that he came back to work after only being gone two days. At the time of the explosion he had been back on the job for about three weeks. Six other firefighters suffered smoke inhalation or were injured that night from the explosion. Captain Werner suffered internal injuries and fractured ribs, and had to undergo surgery. This was another night that my guardian angel was watching over me.

Another day my guardian angel was watching over me occurred somewhere in the early 1980s, again in St. Louis. In the 1300 block of Ann was the vacant Golden Eagle bowling alley. My dad had bowled there in leagues just a few years before. It was a two-story brick structure, with the bowling alleys on the second floor. On this particular day, there were workers on the roof taking down a large billboard sign that was on top of the building. This building sat next to Interstate 55, and it was one of those large billboards you normally see sitting next to the interstate highways.

As the workers were taking it down, one of them became seriously injured. We had to go up on the roof and get him down. In order to do this, we had to have a truck company extend their 100' ladder to the roof. We climbed up and treated the patient. We put him in a stokes basket and, through a series of ropes and pulleys of the extended ladder, lowered him to the ground. After the patient was down off the roof, it was time for us to go down also.

I walked to the edge to climb onto the truck company's ladder. In order to climb onto the ladder, you had to stand on the very edge of the building while holding onto the ladder. While standing on the edge, you had to jump up, and swing your legs and body over the raised edge of the ladder onto the rungs. I started to do this. But this building did not have a flat surface all the way to the edge. There was a small wall of three–four bricks high that went all the way around the perimeter of the building. In order to get onto the ladder, you had to step up on the small wall of bricks while holding onto the ladder, then jump up and swing your legs and body onto to the ladder.

As I stepped up onto the small wall of bricks while holding onto the ladder, the bricks gave out from underneath my feet and I fell forward. Thankfully I did not lose my grip on the ladder and I was just dangling there some 40 feet off the ground, hanging on for dear life with two hands. As people close by rushed to my aid, one firefighter, who had just gotten on the ladder right before me, rushed back up to help me pull myself up and onto the ladder. It was definitely a scary moment. Apparently the mortar that held the bricks together deteriorated and became lose over the years. When I stepped up on the bricks, the mortar gave way and the bricks crumbled under my feet. My guardian angel was watching over me again this day.

Another time, I had to extricate a shooting victim in a home where the shooter was still inside. I entered the side door of a house where we could see the patient laying in the basement, shot and bleeding to death. There was a side door that either led you up three sets of stairs into the house, or you could turn right and go down about 10 stairs into the basement. The shooter would not come out.

A police officer saw the assailant, who was a woman, run up the stairs from the basement and into the house with the gun before he could get close enough to stop her. You could tell the guy was dying since he was as white as a sheet from being in shock. We were standing at the side door of the house on the set of three stairs leading up to a door that was closed. To the right was a set of stairs leading down to the basement, where we could see the patient dying. The police officers, with guns drawn, kept yelling for the person to come out of the house with their hands up. No one came out. Finally, we had to make a decision. The plan was for the officers to cover me as I ran into the basement. Once down there, my plan was to grab the guy by the back of his shirt and pull him up the stairs.

On the count of three I went, "One, two, three!" Down the stairs as fast as I could go. I ran to the guy and told him, "Hang on, we're gonna get you out of here." He didn't say anything. He just looked at me. I dragged him over to the steps and then, getting underneath his arms, I started dragging him up the stairs. Thankfully he was not a big guy. When I got near the top, one of the officers grabbed a shoulder and helped me drag him outside. Once outside, the paramedics put him on the stretcher and whisked him away. I read next day in the newspaper that he had died.

Eventually the lady in the house surrendered without a fight. I was always thankful she did not open the door and start shooting when I was going down or up the stairs.

There have been other close calls in my career, just like every other firefighter or paramedic experiences. Unfortunately, too many of our brother and sister firefighters and paramedics lose their lives each year. It always saddens me when I get an e-mail announcing a death somewhere in the country.

But not everything is a close call or a call that is going to challenge you. Many fire and EMS calls in big cities have nothing to do with an emergency. After all these years, I continue to be amazed at some of the things that people call 9-1-1 for. One of my favorites was a man who was having chest pain for 17 years. One night he called 9-1-1 because the chest pain stopped and he was worried something was wrong. Many people call when they run out of medicine or their prescription expires. They just want a ride to the hospital to get their medicine refilled. I've known of other people who call 9-1-1 everyday because they want you to do something in their house. One lady in Memphis would call at least a couple of times a day when she wanted to be moved from her bed to her chair and from her chair to her bed. One time she called when she wanted someone to come to her house and pour her a glass of orange juice. Then there is the dreaded call at three in the morning for someone who has not been feeling well for over three weeks. You just want to ask them – *What changed at three this morning that is any different over the last three weeks that prompted you to call now?*

A large percentage of working in big-city fire and EMS systems are the regular patients we handle on a daily basis. Some of the terms used by paramedics and firefighters to describe them include Frequent Flyers, and Customer Loyalty Members.

Whether I was working in St. Louis or Memphis, there were the people who constantly and consistently call 9-1-1, sometimes daily, to be taken to the hospital. There was Gladys, Hampton, Heroin Harry, Peter, and Soda Bottle Bill. There was Ms. Adelia, William, Andy, Darryon, and Lester. The firefighters and paramedics all know them by name. Some paramedics even allow them to call in their own patient reports over the radio to the hospital while in transit to the emergency room. Some patients already have the script in their head of what the dispatcher is going to ask, and what they are going to say. Before the dispatcher can even ask the first questions, they say, "Yes, I am conscious, I am breathing, I am short of breath, I have chest pain, and I am sweating—please send me an ambulance." The dispatcher knows who they are, and they know the call is not really an emergency, but they have no choice but to send an ambulance, and sometimes an engine company. You can't assume that they are not really having an emergency. I did see one of our regulars in Memphis who called at least once every day really have a heart attack, and had to have triple bypass surgery.

Every city has their regulars. One of our most entertaining regulars in St. Louis was a lady named Gladys. Gladys was a psychiatric patient who would wander the streets sometimes—she was a larger lady, who had a belly on her. One of her favorite tricks was to walk into a business, announce that she was having labor pains, and act like she was in distress from the labor. While someone from the business was calling 9-1-1, she would pee on herself. With urine running onto the floor she would yell throughout the store that her water just broke, and collapse onto the floor. Immediately, all good Samaritans in the store would run to assist her, since they thought that she was about to give birth. The caller, still on the line with 9-1-1, would tell the operator that the lady's water just broke. Of course, the response was immediate, and you would walk into the store and find Gladys lying on the floor. Gladys was also good at pulling this off just after she got done eating a meal and the bill came.

Sometimes you would have to deal with psychiatric patients who were not your regulars. Sometimes they were harmless, but others you had to keep your eye on, because they could become violent.

The conversation with the harmless ones was somewhat entertaining, but it was obvious they needed some psychiatric intervention. One night I had an engaging conversation with a man who tried to convince me that he was from a faraway planet called Anazarra, and that he was here to warn us of the Starfleet that was coming to attack Earth. He said that over the centuries, they had already attacked and wiped out the populations on the other planets such as Mercury, Saturn, and Mars. The fact that they were uninhabited was proof those civilizations had been destroyed. He said they had also stolen all the water and other resources off those planets for use back on their own planet of Anazarra. That fact that all those planets were barren was further proof. He further told me that he really needed to talk to the president and warn him of the dire consequences to come. I told him that I knew exactly whom he needed to talk to about his warnings. I told him there were some nice people at the hospital who would listen to what he had to say, and would take down all the information he had to tell. He agreed to that, and so he was taken to the hospital.

Many of the psychiatric patients that urban firefighters and paramedics deal with are schizophrenic, and either see people and talk to them, or have a certain amount of paranoia that also makes them dangerous. Combine the psychosis with drugs, and it can certainly create an unknown situation. Therefore, you should always be on your guard.

CHAPTER 9

✛

NOT EVERYDAY STUFF

There are significant events in my career that will be etched in my memory forever. The fire calls may come and go. The shooting calls may come and go. And the heart attacks may come and go. Some you remember—most you don't because there have been so many.

But there are seminal moments in your career that you never forget because they are so unique.

As a deputy chief over EMS, and finally the chief paramedic in St. Louis, I had the opportunity to work closely with the Secret Service over the years on quite a few presidential details. It was not uncommon for presidents of the United States to come to St. Louis, particularly around election time, mainly because Missouri was one of those states that was always in play, and it was worth a significant amount of electoral votes. Washington University has also been home to quite a few presidential debates.

Over the years, I've served on presidential details for Reagan, Bush, and Clinton in St. Louis, and I was involved in the planning for presidential visits for Bush and Obama while in Memphis. Obama made several trips to Memphis as a candidate and president. I have also been involved in vice presidential visits and first lady visits over the last 37 years. Those were usually not as large and as detailed as the presidential visits.

Normally it started with a phone call from Donald Schneider, special agent in charge of the St. Louis Field Office. Don would say, "Gary, I need you to be at a planning meeting with the Secret Service at police headquarters tomorrow morning." If I ever got more than one day's notice, it was a shock. Don never got much notice, either. Don was very professional, and I enjoyed working with him over the years.

There is a Secret Service office in St. Louis, and usually these agents would work with the 6–8 agents who would come as an advance team from Washington, DC. The advance team of Secret Service agents travels prior to the president, and conducts site surveys to assess needs for manpower, equipment, hospitals, and evacuation routes for emergencies. We would meet as a group, and receive the overview of the visit and a briefing as to credible threats. In the room were predominantly law enforcement officials from local, state, and federal agencies. I was usually the only non-law enforcement official, unless a representative of the fire marshal's office was needed, if the president was going to stay overnight in a local hotel. Usually presidents have busy schedules, especially during election season, and they would typically be in and out of town within a couple of hours unless it was tied to some type of fundraiser, which could go for hours. But if it was just a speech, especially during election time, they would be in and out and fly off to their next speech and rally.

After the general briefing, we would break up into specific groups. I was always assigned to the motorcade group because we would supply an ambulance that would follow the president's motorcade. There was always one agent in charge of the motorcade. I typically would have to supply names and social security numbers of the paramedics who would be assigned to the ambulance. Background checks were necessary for security purposes.

The motorcade group would determine routes from the airport to the event, safe houses in the event of an attack, alternative routes, hospitals that would be used for emergencies, and any other details that needed ironing out before the president's driver ever puts the limousine in gear. The designated hospitals are also visited and alerted that they are a destination hospital if anything happens. The hospitals are also required to keep a certain amount of the president's blood type in supply and reserved. Usually the designated hospitals are Level 1 Trauma centers, so there is typically no problem with the right blood supply. But the important part is that the hospitals know the president's blood type ahead of time.

The ambulance would always be the second-to-last vehicle in the motorcade; the last vehicle was always a police car. The presidential motorcades are extremely long after you get done adding aides, White House communications, Secret Service vehicles, staff, and finally oodles of media people who follow the president wherever he goes. The joke was that if anything ever happened to the president, we doubt the paramedics and the ambulance would ever see him, since they were some 40 vehicles away. I hesitate to think the Secret Service would let the president be put in a vulnerable position and wait in one position until the ambulance drove the length of the motorcade to pick up the president and take him to the hospital if anything ever happened. If history is any lesson, during the Kennedy assassination and the Ford and Reagan attempted assassinations, the presidents were whisked away in the car. That would especially be true today with the way the "Beast" is built to protect the president.

The "Beast" is commonly known as the president's limousine. I have been challenged by the agents to try and open the doors of the presidential limousine, and I can tell you there is nothing light about a several hundred pound door. If the paramedics ever would have to treat the president, it would probably be at a site where the president stopped and was away from his limousine. Even then, it would probably be a circumstance if the president could not walk and he would have to be put on a stretcher. The Secret Service agents take their job very seriously, and there is no kidding or joking with them when the president is on the move and they are involved in some aspect of protection. When they can take a breather and relax, they are some of the nicest and down-to-earth people you would ever want to meet. They are all professionals and take their job seriously, but they are also human, and enjoy joking and jesting with each other and others in the public safety profession.

The presidential limousine, along with other vehicles and equipment, is usually flown in on Air Force planes ahead of time and parked inside the airport fire station. There is a Secret Service agent assigned to the car the entire time it is in the airport fire station, and I have seen some sit in it all night to make sure no one tampers with it. Nothing is left to chance when it comes to protecting the president of the United States, and that's the way it should be.

The motorcade assembles at the airport. We usually have to be there several hours in advance. Regularly, the ambulance—and, if I had my car—is swept by bomb-sniffing dogs to make sure there are no explosives. The vehicles are also searched by agents to make sure there is nothing that would compromise the president's safety.

After Air Force One lands and while the president is doing "meets and greets" with local politicians and others, we are usually approached by the president's doctor, and sometimes a nurse who may be accompanying the doctor. Medical staff travels with the president wherever he travels. Usually the medical staff is military medical personnel. They usually just introduce themselves, but there is also business conducted, including letting us know any allergies the president has. In the case of one president, he was allergic to bee, wasp, and hornet stings, so we always had to have Epinephrine and Benadryl at the ready.

Many times I would ride in the lead car with the agent in charge of the motorcade, or drive my administrative vehicle in front of the ambulance. As I said, nothing is left to chance. The highways are shut down. The bridges over the highways are shut down, and no one is allowed on them. There is usually a five-minute advance car checking the route, and helicopters overhead check the route also.

Sometimes the motorcade moves along at a pretty good clip, and I was always amazed at the media people hanging out of the trucks filming along the route. I guess if anything was going to happen, they wanted to make sure they captured it.

When you get to the site, there are long periods of boredom as the president is inside doing whatever. Most times it was a speech. Other times it was a fundraiser, and other times it was the presidential debates at Washington University. I really messed up one time. I left to go use the bathroom while at Washington University during a presidential debate, and by the time I got back, the motorcade had left without me and was heading back to President Bush's hotel. It was a shock to come out of the building and see the entire motorcade gone, and the only car sitting there was mine.

I have had an opportunity to shake the hand of several presidents, and those will always be memorable moments. I have a picture of me shaking hands with President Clinton when he did a visit to Fox Park on the south side of St. Louis. Some years after he left office, I sent him a copy of the picture and requested he sign it. Some six months later it came back, and it does look like his signature with a small comment that says "Thanks for your service."

I know some people are critical of some decisions he made in his personal life while in office, but I think we all have some "re-dos" in our lives. Overall, I thought he was a good president, and I have been in attendance several times when he has given a speech. I am always amazed that he can talk without notes or a teleprompter. I've watched him speak for an hour or more, recalling facts and figures, while also providing deep political analysis and philosophy on different matters.

But one of the proudest moments I had occurred when I was supervising a political rally for Ronald Reagan when he was the Republican candidate for the first time in 1979. He was giving a speech at the St. Louis Arena, and we were in a vast outer area by some large, overhead roll-up doors where the candidate's limousine was parked. He finished the speech and was walking with his wife Nancy from the stage to his limousine. Two other paramedics and I happened to be standing off to the side, where he would have to walk to get to his car. As he came walking through the area where there were over one hundred people including aides, campaign staff, police officers, and Secret Service agents, he saw us and made a detour to come over and shake our hands. Reagan, Nancy, his Secret Service detail, and aides formed the group heading towards us. He came straight to us and went down the line shaking our hands. I wished him well on his campaign and told him I would be voting for him. Nancy also nodded at us and mouthed the words, "Thank you."

What I regret to this day is that no one took a picture of it. The reason I regret it is that I believe that Ronald Reagan is the greatest president of my time. He took a country that was demoralized after the Iran hostage crisis and skyrocketing interest rates, and stood firm against a menacing Soviet Union to win the Cold War. He put America back on track in eight short years. Shortly after he left office, the Berlin Wall fell, and the Soviet Union crumbled. I have read several books and transcripts on his dealings with Soviet President Gorbachev, and I can tell you that President Reagan was not the aloof and bumbling president the media made him out to be.

I would have loved to have shown that picture to my children and my grandchildren.

I knew cameras were there since I remember Reagan walking several feet away from us, and there was a police officer standing there with his German shepherd police dog. Reagan bent over to pat the dog on the head and the flashbulbs went off. He kept petting the dog and the cameras kept flashing. During the next eight years, the Secret Service agents told me that they loved working for President Reagan, since he was a down-to-earth guy who loved the military and people in public safety, such as police, fire, and EMS. I can only assume he diverted our way because he saw our uniforms.

Not getting a picture with Ronald Regan was a missed opportunity, but it would not be my only one.

One of my proudest moments was when as chief paramedic, I became responsible for all medical operations when Pope John Paul II came to St. Louis for a 36-hour visit in 1999. Being a Catholic, and having the Vicar of Christ come to our community, and me being placed in such an important role, I could not experience anything but a tremendous sense of pride and joy.

We were notified by the St. Louis Archdiocese some six months ahead of the visit. This allowed us as a city to plan and prepare. In all, the pope would be in St. Louis for 36 hours, with six different venue sites and three different papal motorcades that needed to be covered operationally.

Deputy Chief Frank Schaper was the overall operations chief under the incident management system, and underneath him were the suppression branch, hazmat branch, heavy rescue branch, and the medical branch. I was responsible for the medical branch. Under my branch, I had a chief officer responsible for each venue, and one chief officer responsible for the papal parades, along with support chiefs. The pope's first-day schedule included a welcoming ceremony at the St. Louis airport by President Clinton, and a motorcade in the city to the archbishop's residence, where he would stay the night. That first evening he went to a youth rally at the Kiel Center in downtown St. Louis where the St. Louis Blues hockey team plays, and then back to the archbishop's residence for the night.

Outside the Kiel Center for about a foursquare-block area was Papal Plaza. This was an area that was secured where people could gather and watch all the proceedings on giant Jumbotron televisions. We took the lessons learned from Centennial Park during the Atlanta Olympics, where a backpack bomb exploded. Centennial Park was the only soft target out of all the Olympic venues that did not have a security check for those who came and went. Papal Plaza would have those security checkpoints for ingress and egress for checking packages, purses, backpacks, etc. The entire Papal Plaza was ringed with barricades, and then another layer of snow fencing that created about a five-foot space between the two artificial perimeters. Police officers were stationed between the barricades and the snow-fencing every so often to prevent someone from coming into the Papal Plaza without entering through the checkpoints.

The next day was another papal parade to the Edward Jones Dome, where the St. Louis Rams play football, for an indoor Mass of some 120,000 people. From there he left and went back to the archbishop's residence to rest, and then to the cathedral basilica several blocks from the archbishop's residence for an inter-faith prayer service. When done with the prayer service, the pope departed for the airport, where there was another ceremony with Vice President Al Gore. Each site—the airport, the Kiel Center, Papal Plaza, the Edwards Jones Dome, the cathedral basilica, and the archbishop's residence—required a medical officer responsible for the operation. Each medical officer had resources assigned to them. Each papal motorcade also required a medical officer responsible for medical coverage of the crowds on either side of the street.

All of the venues were not all operational at the same time, and they ramped up and became operational at different times and different days. An ambulance with our medical director was assigned to the pope the entire time he was moving somewhere or was in residence at the archbishop's home. We also had to dedicate ambulances to President Clinton and Vice President Gore when they were at the airport. The president and the vice president details also had their special meetings and planning sessions with their advance teams from the Secret Service.

One of our biggest challenges was trying to plan for adverse weather conditions, since the visit was going to occur in late January. Months in advance in St. Louis, you don't know whether to plan for 10 inches of snow or 60-degree weather. The Pink Sisters, a cloistered order of nuns in St. Louis, prayed for good weather. I am guessing they got a direct line to God, because when I left my house at 4:00 a.m. on the second day—the big event was going to be the indoor Mass with 120,000 people that morning—I could not believe what I was feeling. A warm breeze caught my attention as soon as I stepped outside. A warm breeze of air at 4:00 in the morning in January, in St. Louis? I dreaded to see what would have happened if it was 20 degrees or less that morning.

People stood outside for hours waiting to pass through security at the Edward Jones Dome on the morning of the Mass. If the Mass-goers had stood outside as the wind whipped through the downtown buildings for hours in 20 degrees or less, we would have had a mass casualty event from people suffering hypothermia. I don't believe anything would have moved people to seek shelter. The Mass attendees would not have left the security lines if it was freezing, in my opinion. I witnessed several people who were clearly having hearts attacks sign refusal treatment forms because they were bound and determined that they were going to see the pope. I'm sure if people were freezing they would have been of the same mind-set.

At the Dome that morning, I got within five feet of the pope twice: Once as he was making his way around the stadium in his pope mobile, and another time as he slowly and gingerly made his way out of the public view to his waiting limousine in the lower levels of the Edward Jones Dome. As a devout Catholic, it was an emotional moment for me to be so close to the Vicar of Christ. I was shocked to see how feebly and slow the pope moved, but we were briefed ahead of time on his medical conditions, so it did not surprise me. Personally, I did not see how a man of his age, and with some of the medical conditions I was aware of, was able to keep the 36-hour schedule he did in St. Louis. And on top of that, he flew to St. Louis from Mexico, where he also did public events. No wonder some people call him John Paul II the Great.

I did notice that he really got energized at the Youth Rally at the Kiel Center on the first night. It was obvious he loved the youth, and it was apparent they loved him, too. Some of his Swiss Guards later told us that young people invigorate the pope when he gets around them. It was amazing to watch a man who looked so tired suddenly come to life.

One of the challenges of handling the papal detail was all the federal, state, and local resources that came to assist. Just some of the federal agencies we had to meet and work with included the Secret Service, numerous components of the FBI, the U.S. Department of Public Health, the Department of Defense, the Marine's Chemical Biological Incident Response Force (CBIRF), ATF, FEMA, and the State Department. We also had state assets and a federal Urban Search and Rescue team in a staging area. With the help of numerous fire and ambulance agencies in the St. Louis area, we were able to put together a nice contingent of 30+ fire trucks and ambulances that we either had in a staging area at St. Louis Fire Department Headquarters, or at venue sites working under the auspices of the fire officer in charge of the site.

We also had ten Humvee ambulances with drivers from the Missouri National Guard staffed with our paramedics. The Humvee ambulances were mainly used along the papal motorcade route. There were other federal assets in St. Louis during the papal visit that I cannot write about. Suffice to say, when it comes to protecting dignitaries such as the pope, the federal government leaves no stone unturned. As an example, the U.S. Department of Public Health had 10,000 atropine injectors warehoused at the airport in the event we had a nerve agent attack.

After the pope's plane lifted off, we could finally stand down and start recapping what we had accomplished. The papal visit was a major undertaking, and a lot of people worked hard to make it a success.

Speaking of Christians—one of the other events I had to cover during my career was when white supremacy groups came to town and wanted to hold parades or demonstrations. The first one I experienced was in 1977, when a bunch of Nazis got a permit to ride down the middle of Cherokee Street in south St. Louis in a couple of flatbed trucks while giving the "Heil Hitler" salute. The police prepared well, including removing mailboxes ahead of time so they could not be used as obstacles to stop the trucks or have bombs in them.

I was one of several assigned to the parade, but the "parade" was over before I knew it. A bunch of Nazis in their brown shirts and armbands with the swastikas on them drove down the street at about 50 miles per hour while standing in the back of the flatbed trucks with rails on the side. People lined up on either side of the street and threw snowballs at the Nazis as they passed. A good-sized snowfall some days earlier left plenty of "ammunition" for those who disliked the Nazis. I must admit, it was one of the funniest things I saw during my career. A bunch of Nazis racing down the middle of the street in the back of trucks trying to give the Nazi salute and they were being pelted with snowballs. Those who were not throwing snowballs also pointed and laughed at the spectacle.

I dealt with another KKK rally in downtown St. Louis. The police department set up perimeter fencing around the Civil Courts Building downtown and bused about 15 KKK members in who stood on the steps and chanted their hate messages over bullhorns. Bystanders stood some 300 yards behind the fencing with their signs and hollered back. Again, another incident with no injuries!

I also dealt with a KKK rally in Memphis in 2013 after the city council decided to rename three parks that had traditional Confederate or southern names, including Confederate Park, Jefferson Davis Park, and Nathan Bedford Forest Park. About 75 Klan members showed up, and the court building where they were going to protest was blocked off for two blocks in every direction. The city asked people not to show up, and instead go to a festival across town. The KKK stood in front of the building for about 1.5 hours and chanted over their bullhorns. We had all kinds of contingency plans in place for civil disturbances, including fire apparatus staged in and around the downtown area with ambulances.

In the end, very few people showed up to see them. The city used a lot of resources to protect them, and the Memphis City Council never changed the names of the parks.

Personally, I have never understood people who hate others they do not even know or have never met. The logic of it makes no sense. It's like saying you hate (not even dislike) a Ford car and you have never driven a Ford car, rode, or sat in a Ford car. All you know is that you hate Ford cars because of things you have heard or been taught by others. Certainly, you were not born with your prejudice and hate. Human conditions like that are not genetic. They are learned behaviors.

Humans are humans regardless of the color of their skin or what country they come from. Most people I have met, regardless of the color of their skin, want the same things: a nice home, a well-paying job, and a family that they can be a part of. They want to have good health and be able to worship how they wish. Everybody wants the same thing—a nice life, and nice things. It's pretty simple; but others don't see it that way and in some cases, they even call themselves Christians. I just chuckle to myself and shake my head when White Supremacists call themselves Christians. They don't even come close to what Jesus Christ preached and practiced.

I've handled many special projects in St. Louis and Memphis over the years. One of the most "fun" events to handle was the VP Fair Fourth of July Celebration every year under the St. Louis Arch grounds. The name was eventually changed to Fair St. Louis.

During its heyday, the VP Fair Fourth of July Celebration was usually a huge three-day gala on the 90-acre grounds of the Arch, overlooking the Mississippi River. Vendors were located all along the walkways on the Arch grounds and on the street that separates the Arch from the Mississippi River. A main stage was set up directly beneath the Arch legs, and major headliners would perform on the stage at night right before the grand finale of fireworks shot from barges on the Mississippi River. Twice a day there would be air shows featuring military aircraft and acrobatic stunt pilots.

Many years I was put in charge of these details, and although it was exhausting from the long hours for three days straight, it was a diversion from the normal routine. Usually we would work closely with Red Cross medical volunteers, who rode golf carts on the inside perimeter of the Arch grounds and handled all the medical emergencies. Once they had the patient loaded they would move them to the perimeter, where one of eight ambulances would rendezvous with them and pick up the patient. The heat and humidity on the Fourth of July weekend in St. Louis can be unbearable, so to help with the heat relief we would sometimes set up public transportation buses as cooling stations on the perimeter of the grounds and, in other strategic locations, engine companies would be set up and water would be flowing out the nozzle tip on the ladder, creating a shower effect. Many of the kids, and even adults, found the showers refreshing.

But even with all the precautions in place, people would suffer from the heat since they did not dress or prepare properly. The one I will never forget is the new mother who brought her two-day-old infant to the Fair wrapped in a wool blanket. When we got to the baby, it was barely alive and suffering from heat stroke. I never knew if the baby survived or not.

In some of the earlier years before fair management started turning it into more of a family affair with different entertainment, we would usually have someone shot every year, knifed, or assaulted after dark. One year we had someone start shooting wildly into the crowd in an attempt to get away from some motorcycle gang members. The gang members were chasing him and he shot five people, two of whom died. I was close by, and it was pure pandemonium when I pulled up on my golf cart. A throng of people were holding and beating the individual who allegedly did the shooting. One lady was going crazy and grabbed my arm so hard that I found bruises that resembled her fingers on my arm the next day. I thought my arm was going to break the way she was grabbing it.

There was always something every year at the fair, including the time someone messed up and a guy did a bungee jump and the cord broke. He landed some 90 feet below in the airbag, and was not hurt seriously. And then there was the time I could have died. I was sitting on a small Coast Guard boat watching the fireworks on the river when a malfunction occurred and blew the foot off one of the workers on the fireworks barge when he was lighting the tube. We could see the "short-shot" and the explosion on the barge, and we knew something was wrong. Shortly thereafter, a radio message came from the towboat handling the fireworks barges that they had someone hurt and needed an evacuation. We raced our small boat to the barges and when we got there, the Coast Guardsman piloting our 18-foot small boat told me to get up on the bow, and the barge workers could pull me up and onto the barge. I moved to the bow of the boat, but if you have ever tried to stand on a boat when it is bobbing in the water, you know it is impossible to keep your balance. I tried to balance myself as the small boat inched over to the barge. In the light of the moon, all I saw below me was the dark and muddy water of the black river running past me. With no lights out on the river, it looked even darker. The barges were sticking way out of the water and we were well below the surface of the barges in our small Coast Guard boat. As we inched closer to the barge and finally got next to it, the barge workers were laying on their stomachs, reaching over the edge to my extended arms to pull me up.

As I tried to reach for their hands, I vividly remember looking over my shoulder and seeing nothing but dark and black water running between the barge and the small boat. I thought *Hell no! This is about as stupid as it gets. They drop me and I am a goner. I'll probably be sucked under the barge and passed through the props of the towboat on my way out the backside.* I immediately crouched down to my knees and told them this was not going to work. I told the Coast Guardsmen that I was going to call in a medical helicopter and they could land on the barge and take him off. That is exactly what I did!

My career, especially in St. Louis, was filled with all kinds of interesting details. There was the World Series in 1982, 1985, and 1987. Somehow, it was not planned, but I wound up in the Cardinal's dugout when they won the 1982 World Series in St. Louis. I was at Busch Stadium in uniform during game seven with the Milwaukee Brewers, since I was working that shift. I was walking and talking to a police officer who was a friend. The next thing I knew, we made a right turn and were heading down the tunnel into the dugout with some other police officers who were walking in front of us. I thought this was pretty cool, and I was not going to say anything. As it turned out, those were the days when it was common for fans to run out and jump over the walls onto the field after a World Series win. Today, that does not happen. In 1982, the police officers were being sent onto the field to at least try to help the players back into the dugout. I was standing there, about 10 feet from Manager Whitey Herzog, when the next thing I knew pure pandemonium broke out, and all the police officers ran onto the field.

I ran up the couple of dugout steps onto the field and I stood there like a kid seeing something in awe for the first time. All around me, hundreds of people were running onto the field, players were racing to the dugout, and 360 degrees around me, some 60,000 people were screaming. Fireworks were going off, and there was complete chaos everywhere I looked. I just stood still. I had nowhere to run to, and certainly did not have anything to do out there. I saw Cardinal players trying to make their way to the dugout while also congratulating each other. Standing there with a catcher's facemask was Officer Rich Banahan. As it turned out, catcher Daryl Porter threw off his facemask and ran to pitcher Bruce Sutter after the last strike. Rich was later able to present Darrell Porter's facemask back to him.

It was another exciting night in St. Louis the night the St. Louis Rams won Super Bowl XXXIV in 1999. Although the game was in the Georgia Dome in Atlanta, the St. Louis downtown area around the Edward Jones Dome became a big festive location, with people acting wildly in the streets, driving around blowing horns, or hugging and kissing complete strangers in and around the Dome and the nearby entertainment district. Again, nothing unusual or serious happened that night. The Super Bowl parade several days later was also a challenge, as some 500,000 people crowded into downtown St. Louis for the first-ever St. Louis Super Bowl parade.

But it wasn't always fun when it came to special details.

One day in 1993, we were called down to the St. Louis Office of Emergency Management. All top city officials were there from different departments, and this was usually a bad sign. When the meeting began, we were briefed by a representative from the Corps of Engineers who told us the Mississippi River was on the rise, and it was expected to crest at flood level the next week. The impact of the flooding would be a record for the St. Louis area, and would impact all along the riverfront and residential areas in the south part of St. Louis. The Corps of Engineers had it down to a science. They were able to show us contour maps of what areas would flood based on the flood stage of the river.

The entire eastern border of the city of St. Louis is the Mississippi River. In the southern end of the city, a large storm water channel called the River des Peres empties into the Mississippi River. So whenever the Mississippi rises, the River des Peres backs up. The River Des Peres runs through residential areas, so if the channel rose over its banks, it would also impact the residential areas. During my lifetime, I never saw the River des Peres rise above its banks and impact the heavy residential area around it. But this would change in 1993.

The Corps of Engineer maps showed large amounts of residential areas of south St. Louis that would flood each time the foot level of the river rose. They knew exactly the foot level the river would be at, even a week out. Parts of the eastern border of the city were protected by a huge concrete flood wall that stands some 20 feet high. At different points there are flood gates that are normally open to allow access to the river and the areas behind the flood walls, but during flooding they are closed. The gates would be closed during the 1993 flood. So the flood wall protected most of the industrial parts of the city along the river. If the flood wall had not been there in 1993, the devastation would have been unimaginable to the industrial sections of the city. But the residents along River des Peres were not so lucky. There was no flood wall, and no flood gates to protect them.

Those areas were going to flood. So the city leaders concentrated their efforts along the River des Peres. Coordinated by the city, sandbagging operations would begin the next day after our initial meeting, for some 2.5 miles on the River des Peres channel on both sides of the river.

Again, I was responsible for the medical operation of this endeavor that would see me work out of a command post in Carondelet Park, which was near the flooding, for 41 days. The city ordered a voluntary evacuation of the affected areas, and reinforced it by cutting off the electricity. Some people chose not to leave. Some had nowhere else to go. Others did not want to leave their homes vacant for the possibility of looters. Some of these people had medical problems and we would have paramedics go and check on them daily.

Another major part of my operation was supporting the sandbagging operations. Hundreds, if not thousands, of volunteers showed up to sandbag. They would park in a staging area miles away from the operation and then transit buses would bring them to the sandbagging operation. The buses ran constantly for people who wanted to come or were ready to go home. Once filled, the sandbags were loaded onto city dump trucks and taken to where they were stacked by other volunteers alongside the River des Peres. The major problem with the sandbagging operations was the heat. July and August in St. Louis can be stifling, and 1993 was no exception. With heat indexes approaching and sometimes exceeding 100 degrees, the challenge was making sure the volunteers did not suffer from heat exhaustion or stroke.

As the flood waters continued to rise, there were three record crests. Sometimes the water would dip a couple feet, and then with more rains to the north, the water would rise even higher. Just like a symphony that rises to a crescendo at the end of the performance on the last song, the flood of '93 did the same thing. As the end approached and the waters got higher, more activity ramped up for us. Eventually, the voluntary evacuation became a mandatory evacuation.

Some unusual events occurred during the flooding. One happened when I was leaving a briefing at the Emergency Operations Office one morning and I heard a call go out on one of the bridges that goes from downtown St. Louis to Illinois for a "jumper." Being in the downtown area, I decided to go on the call. When I arrived on the Poplar Street

Bridge, there was a man sitting on the side rail with his legs and feet dangling over the river. One push off and he would have fallen into the river. As police officers attempted to talk him out of jumping, he blasted back at them with nothing but expletives. There was no conversing with him. We all begged him to come back on the other side of the rail. He kept talking out of his head. By this time, a fire boat was in position under the bridge if he jumped. Almost on cue once the boat arrived, he pushed off and fell into the river. I ran to the side rail to see him come up from the water and the firefighters in the fire boat grabbed him. This was my first trip to the side rail, since I didn't want to get too close to him, but one look at the water and I thought, "Jesus, this guy didn't fall that far—maybe 25 feet!" No wonder he survived. It was like going off a high diving board feet first. I had no idea the river was that close to the top of the bridge. I've seen people go off these bridges before and fall over 90 feet and die. Jumping from that height and hitting water is just like hitting concrete. I've watched several people jump from the bridges over the Mississippi River over the years, and none have survived.

As I said, the river was inching higher and higher and was due to crest on August 1, 1993. As the highest crest of the river moved towards St. Louis, we watched on television as levees broke north of St. Louis on the Mississippi and Missouri rivers. Unfortunately for St. Louis, the Mississippi, Missouri, and Illinois Rivers all come together in a confluence just north of St. Louis, and the waters of all three rivers would join and flow past. One person from the Corps of Engineers told us in a briefing that at its peak, a little over 1 million gallons of water would be flowing past the Arch every second. He said at that rate, Busch Stadium would be filled to the brim with water in about 70 seconds if it were a bowl. We all gasped when he used that analogy.

The challenges became even greater near the end. Near where the River des Peres empties into the Mississippi River was a Phillips petroleum tank farm with 51 tanks, each containing 30,000 gallons of liquefied propane. Officials from Phillips knew the tank farm was going to flood, so they allegedly filled the tanks with propane to weigh them down, and then used steel straps with huge bolts to secure the tanks down into the concrete cradles that they were resting on. One evening, a firefighter who had been on fire watch kept hearing loud popping noises coming from the tank farm area. He and Phillips representatives soon learned that the tanks were starting to rise out of the water and as they did, they snapped the huge bolts from the concrete cradles. As a result, three-inch pipes that ran beneath the tanks began to twist like a string would under a helium balloon bobbing in the wind. Eventually stress fractures would show on the piping and liquefied propane would escape, vaporize, and then dissipate into the air. That evening there was enough propane vapor in the air that the simple ringing of the telephone in a small building on the tank farm caused a fire and explosion in the building. Propane is highly flammable, and the slightest spark can ignite it.

An emergency meeting was called that night and we met until about 2:00 a.m. The decision was made to do a mandatory evacuation of a one-mile radius of the propane tank farm in five hours, at 7:00 a.m. This would affect some 1,200 homes and approximately 20,000 people. This also included several nursing homes and other facilities for the elderly that would have to be evacuated. Computer modeling showed that if just five of the tanks were to release their entire product simultaneously, it would create a cloud of propane 12 feet high and over half a mile in size. If that propane found just one ignition source, it would look like an atomic explosion going off. Residents were warned, and given several hours to gather their things and move out. All electricity and gas to the area was going to be cut that morning to prevent possible ignition sources. My responsibility entailed creating a medical branch that would handle the evacuation of residents who were not ambulatory, and also the nursing home patients. That was a period that I did not get any sleep for 58 hours. Eventually, Phillips Petroleum brought in a private company that, with the assistance of the St. Louis Fire Department, slowly bled the tanks of propane and used high-volume water monitors to dissipate the propane vapor into the air. It worked and, after about a week, people were allowed back into their homes.

While we were meeting about the propane tank farm in the emergency operations center, three riverboats that were moored along the downtown St. Louis riverfront broke from their moorings as the river rose. All three floated down river and thankfully did not hit a flood wall and crack it. If they had, they would have sent the entire Mississippi River flooding into the industrial areas south of downtown. A floating Burger King restaurant was one of the boats that broke away, and its top deck got torn off when it hit the Poplar Street Bridge. It was corralled by towboats eventually. The other ship was an old World War II minesweeper that hit the bridge and drifted to the shore and sank. The third was a helicopter barge that was also rounded up by towboats. If one of these boats had hit the flood wall and cracked it, it would have been a complete disaster.

Near the peak of the flood, I climbed a ladder that was up against the 20-foot-high flood wall just south of the downtown area to see how the river looked on the other side. When I got to the top and peered over, my jaw practically hit the flood wall. The water was only a couple of feet below the flood wall. I couldn't believe this two-foot-thick wall of concrete was holding the entire river back. The pressure against the walls must have been tremendous, but it did hold. The flood walls were built to hold back the Mississippi River at the 52-foot level, and at its peak the Mississippi River crested at 49 feet and six inches on August 1, 1993— with just a little over 2½ feet to spare. Normal flood stage is 30 feet. So the river was almost 20 feet above flood level on August 1.

Each morning, all city officials would meet in the emergency operations center at the Office of Emergency Management. We would get a briefing from those around the table, and the Corps of Engineers would provide us with an update. On the day that was to be the highest and final crest, the water would lap over the sandbags on the River des Peres in south St. Louis. We had built the sandbags as high and as fast as we could, and that was still not good enough. Julian Boyd, the director of public safety at the time, said with a grim look on his face at the end of the briefing that morning, "It looks like the river is going to win. The river is going to crest over the tops of our sandbags along River des Peres." There was silence in the room. We continued to watch the communities to the north of St. Louis along the Mississippi River and to the west along the Missouri River as the crest moved downstream. The entire Chesterfield Valley in west St. Louis County flooded at one point when the Monarch levee failed. Interstate 64 was shut down for about five miles as a result, since it was under water. I can still remember as a news helicopter hovered over a quarry as the Missouri river eventually inched over the top and water fell into the quarry like a waterfall. I also watched as the Missouri river unearthed thousands of bodies in a cemetery in Hardin, Missouri. We all knew all that water was heading our way and would be upon us in a day or two.

But the river did not win in St. Louis. Something very fortunate happened for St. Louis, albeit unfortunate for others, just as the river was peaking in St. Louis on the morning of August 1, 1993. A levee opposite St. Louis on the Illinois side of the river failed, and 47,000 acres of land flooded, completely swallowing up the towns of Valmeyer and Fults, Illinois. Not knowing the levee on the other side of the river had failed, I can remember looking at a Styrofoam cup floating in River des Peres and thinking it was weird—it was flowing the wrong way. It needed to be flowing into the city at the crest instead of back out toward the Mississippi River. That levee failing on the other side of the river in Illinois saved St. Louis from disaster. The best part was that no one got killed in St. Louis as a result of the flooding.

I did experience major flooding in Memphis also in 2011. Unusually heavy spring rains in April plus the snowmelt created flooding conditions all up and down the Mississippi River. The most severe flooding was from about the middle of Missouri going south. Homes and business all along the river, all the way down to New Orleans, were affected by the flood. Thankfully, as a deputy fire chief, I was not directly responsible for the operation. One of my division chiefs took responsibility. In all, 1,300 homes had to be evacuated in Memphis, and our Fire Training Academy was completely cut off by flood waters. The academy itself was on slightly higher ground and, although the water came up to the doors and the academy looked like it was sitting on an island, water never got inside the academy building itself. I took several boat rides out to the academy and to our USAR warehouse. I was amazed at the number of snakes that were in the water and hanging around the building. I almost stepped on a baby water moccasin at the USAR building when it was hidden under a handrail on the walkway. They are aggressive little things, and it never made an effort to run. It just stayed there, reared back, and was ready to strike. Again, thankfully no one got killed in Memphis as a result of the flooding.

My career was also filled with other peak events in St. Louis and Memphis history. For the 25 years that I worked in St. Louis, a tornado never hit the city—although it seemed like we had multiple tornado warnings every year. I went to work in Memphis and within the first seven years of working there, two tornados hit the city. One was tragic when the tornado hit the southeastern section of the city in 2008 and plowed through an industrial area and hit the Hickory Ridge Mall, doing a great deal of damage to Sears, Macy's and the front entrance itself. I first responded to the mall, but once we had that all cleared and everyone accounted for, I responded to an industrial section about a mile away where a factory had collapsed on workers. Although a bunch of workers were trapped and rescued, three employees unfortunately died in the factory, and it took us several hours to dig them out.

Another tornado touched down on July 30, 2009. The tornado touched down just east of Interstate 40 and Appling Road. It damaged some baseball fields, and then kept going east into a shopping area and damaged several businesses. The tornado then crossed Germantown Parkway and damaged a motel, restaurant, and gas station before moving into a residential area. As I drove through the area on my way to the shopping area, I noticed damaged homes, trees uprooted, and other trees that were snapped in half.

I assumed the operations chief position under the incident command system, and immediately set up three different geographic divisions. Then I placed a battalion chief in charge of each one of those areas who would call for the necessary resources from the staging area. Their main function in each geographic division was to check on people, cars, and homes to make sure people were all right. There were many damaged cars thrown about the parking lots, and my fear was that someone had been in one of those cars and had been killed. Thankfully, unlike the other tornado, no one was killed this time.

I was also involved in other significant weather events during my career. The first one occurred during the summer of 1980.

On July 1, 1980, as a precursor to what was to come, the temperature grilled St. Louis when it rose to 105 degrees. The temperature then dropped the next day, but it would not last long. Only July 7 the temperature reached 99, and 101 the following day. The temperature shattered the 100-degree mark for the next 9 out of 14 days, and eventually reached 107 on July 15. In all, it was 100 degrees or hotter on 18 days that July and early August in 1980.

Eventually the heatwave would kill 153 people in St. Louis, but I suspect it was much more. I was on plenty of calls where we found an elderly person dead in a chair, sitting in front of nothing but a fan, with the entire house closed up. The main criteria for determining if it was a heat death was to see if their body temperature was 105 degrees or higher. Some we checked had body temperatures of 102 or 103, but they were not ruled as heat deaths because it did not break the magic mark of 105. I still have the image locked in my head of walking into the large walk-in cooler that measured some 20 feet by 30 feet at the St. Louis Medical Examiner's Office and being stunned by the amount of bodies stacked two and three high on top of each other on the floor. There were no more stretchers, and the only place to store bodies was on top of each other. "We're running out of places to put the bodies," said Rose Marie Green of the St. Louis medical examiner's office to a St. Louis newspaper. The newspaper story also said stench smacked visitors at the front door of the medical examiner's office.

The EMS call volume during this period was off the charts. Not only did you have all the deaths, but you had people who survived but still had heat exhaustion or heat stroke. You had those who had some medical conditions such as asthma exacerbated by the heat.

To make things worse, the city-owned hospital lacked air conditioning in the general wards, and the military had to be brought in with truck-size air conditioners that pumped cold air into the wards.

Most of those who died during this heat wave were the elderly, most of them in brick structures with the black flat tar roofs that I wrote of earlier. The bricks would remain hot at night, and so did the house. They were elderly, and many kept their doors and windows shut for fear of burglars. This was true especially at night. I went on calls and pronounced people dead who had a window air conditioner running, but it was pumping out hot air. I went on other calls where people had air conditioning but did not turn it on because they lived on a fixed income and could not afford to run their air conditioner. With some of the victims, in order to cool them down, we would take frozen peas, or chicken, orange juice, or whatever they had in their freezer and put it under their armpits or in the groin area to cool the blood down that was going through their body.

One victim was cooked on the sidewalk at the intersection of Olive and Jefferson. The man was found lying on the sidewalk, and when his body temperature was taken it was 106 degrees. He was unconscious, so he was intubated, cooled down with cold water, and taken to the hospital. I do not know if he ever survived.

Many dead and suffering people were found by mail carriers who reported the mail had not been picked up in several days, or that they could smell something coming from the house.

That was the case in the 2100 block of Chippewa. We pulled up and you could smell the pungent, rancid, and distinctive odor from the street. One neighbor told us the car in front of the house had not moved for 14 days. As we were standing there waiting for the police to arrive before we could enter the home, someone pointed out that it looked like the dark shades over the windows were moving. We thought initially that maybe a fan was on. Upon closer examination, we discovered they were moving all right, but they were not shades—they were flies that completely covered up both front windows of the brick home.

We put on air tanks to go into the house and, to our complete and utter surprise, we found a man and a woman. The man's wife was still alive in the house, laying next to him on the bed. The remains that she was laying next to did not even resemble the shape of a human anymore. The only way I can describe what the body looked like is if you take five-gallon buckets of green, red, purple, yellow, black, blue, and orange jelly and throw it on the bed and stir it all up. It no longer resembled any human shape at all.

The lady was talking, and was obviously delusional. She had been living in this house the entire time with a decaying and rotten body in untold heat. I guess I would be out of my mind also. I can still remember us loading her on the stretcher and her looking back at her husband and saying, "Are you going to take him, too?"

Funny thing about this heat wave—my parents told me this was nothing compared to 1936. They could remember as teenagers sleeping in the parks at night since it was a little bit cooler there than sleeping in the hot houses. There really was no such thing as air conditioning back then. When I did a little research, I found that 420 people died in St. Louis during that heat wave.

But they say if you don't like the weather in St. Louis, just stick around for a little bit.

That came true in 1982, when a record snowstorm hit the St. Louis area. In what was called the Blizzard of '82, a record 18–20 inches of snow fell in a 24-hour period in the St. Louis area. The night before the storm I was at a friend's house, and when we left it was snowing and thundering at the same time. I now have learned when you hear thunder and it's snowing, you are in for a ton of snow. The city was shut down for about three days, and the National Guard came in with front-end loaders to help clear downtown streets. Firefighters and paramedics could not get to work, and those who did reported to the closest station. Eighteen inches of snow might not be a big deal to some of our friends in Wisconsin and Minnesota, but St. Louis is not prepared for this amount of snow.

I spent most of those three days assigned to Dan Emerson, who was the city's emergency management director. Many people laughed at him when he got a vehicle with four-wheel drive when he became director, but they weren't laughing at him now. Many of those same people were calling to see if it could get them a ride somewhere. Dan could not! He was busy trying to coordinate relief efforts in the city. The emergencies that you would not think of are amazing during events such as this. Imagine all the people who could not get out and get their prescriptions refilled and needed medicine. The 9-1-1 lines and Dan's office were besieged with phone calls like this. Calls also came from people who were stuck on interstate highways and their cars could not go any further. Many people just abandoned their cars on the highway and tried walking somewhere.

Fire trucks and ambulances, even with chains on their tires, had a tough time navigating streets as 18" of snow and sometimes higher with snow drifts made finding the way difficult.

After about a day, with snowplows working around the clock, the major thoroughfares started to resemble a passageway. But the snow was also piled up even higher on cars sitting on the side of the road. The major problem all three days was trying to access people who had a medical emergency. If they lived on some secondary street where the snowplows had not gone, we had trouble getting to them. In order to accomplish getting to these patients, a call went out for people with four-wheel drive vehicles who were willing to volunteer. A paramedic or a firefighter with a radio was put with each one of these volunteers, and they were stationed at various points around the city. When an ambulance could not access someone on a secondary street, the four-wheel-drive vehicle would pick up the ambulance crew and their medical equipment at the closest access point with a major thoroughfare and drive into the address, and then help with moving the patient back to where the ambulance was parked. These four-wheel-drive Samaritans also volunteered to deliver medicine, food, take people to kidney dialysis, and drop off blood where needed. They were major heroes during this snow emergency.

The sad part is the abuse of the ambulance service that occurs during snow emergencies like this. People who really do not need an ambulance, but don't want to drive, call for an ambulance to take them to the hospital. Others, who had shoveled out a parking spot for their car, would openly tell you they called for an ambulance because they did not want to lose their parking spot.

These people tied up ambulances that were really needed elsewhere. Four people died that first day from shoveling snow, and over the next week another dozen would die of storm-related causes, mostly from heart attacks by pushing snow or vehicles.

CHAPTER 10

✚

THE CONCLUSION

I thought when I first started writing this book, I would not have enough to write about or remember enough to fill a book. I was wrong! I could easily write another thousand pages with many of my experiences—what it's like to be a firefighter, what it's like to be a paramedic, or just what it's like to work in our profession. So some years ago I thought I would encapsulate all or many of my experiences, thoughts, emotions, and feelings into one compressed description of our profession. What follows is that description.

I have witnessed the miracle of birth; I have held a baby in my arms as it took its last breath; I sometimes do not eat meals on time; I have laughed with my patients; I have cried with my patients; Patients have vomited on me; I have comforted a father who held his dead son in his arms and grieved with the greatest sorrow I have ever seen; I administer medications; Sometimes I work on Christmas; I have compassion for my patients; I control bleeding; I cut my patients out of wrecked cars; I have been called an ambulance driver; I have had people try to beat me through an intersection when I am driving with lights and sirens; I have said a short, silent prayer for a patient I just delivered to an emergency room in critical condition; I start IVs; I work shift work; I have sat for hours in my ambulance while on a standby; I read EKGs; I have fought fire; I work a second job on my off-days to provide for my children; I have worked past the end of my shift when I had important plans after I was scheduled to get off work; I have intubated patients in darks alleys, windowless basements, and cramped bathrooms; I have had doctors yell at me for taking too long to arrive at the hospital, even though the patient had to be extricated from a third floor; I must continually go to school and educate myself; I love my job; I have seen the worst that one human being can do to another; I have ventilated a building; I have seen an elderly lady lay for days with a broken hip because she had nobody to check on her; I have seen a mother burn to death after running back into a burning building to save her child; I splint broken bones; I cook the meals in my fire station; I laugh with my brother and sister firefighters; I bandage cuts; I have concern for my patients; I sometimes get upset at people who do not get out of my way when I am driving my ambulance; I must use all my senses; I am the godfather to my partner's first-born child; I have performed CPR; I work in intense summer heat; I work in severe winter cold; I have seen what a shotgun blast can do to a human body; I have tried to reason with a person sitting on a window ledge threatening to jump; I have carried a hose up more than 10 stories; I lift and carry patients who weigh more than me; I have helped a doctor crack a chest; I have caught a cold from my patients; I have accidentally stuck myself with a needle; I take blood pressures; I install car seats; I put out car fires; I slide a brass pole; I have been cussed out by a patient; I have resuscitated people who have walked out of the hospital; I have rappelled off the side of a building; I have seen what a bee sting can do to someone who is allergic to bee stings; I have peeled a steering wheel off someone's chest; I have not finished many meals; I have fallen through a floor; I sit on the ramp and wave at people who honk their horns; I constantly train on the equipment on my apparatus; I climb ladders; I have treated stab wounds; I've had to tell a son that his father died; I have had a patient thank me; I have seen the effects of not wearing a helmet when a motorcycle crashes; I have been criticized for showing up late at a call; I have held a young child's hand while his mother was loaded on a stretcher into an ambulance; I immobilize neck and back injuries; I have gotten lost in a smoke-filled building; I have driven home after my shift wondering if a patient survived; I have let a father cut the umbilical cord; I have climbed down dark holes; I have hugged my children after coming home from a shift; I administer medication for pain; I listen when a patient tells me they are dying; I deal with the homeless; I have laughed with my partner about some call we remembered last week; I have had a citizen file a complaint against me; I have driven an elderly lady to the hospital in the front seat of my ambulance as CPR was performed on her husband of 56 years in the rear of the ambulance and listened to her fear of the unknown; I have gone an entire shift without eating a meal; I have pulled a firehouse prank of a newly graduated recruit; I have smelled a burned body; I shower when I can; I read all the latest fire and EMS journals; I have a license to practice medicine; I have loaded a hose after a fire; I have decompressed a chest filled with air; I have listened to my partner's frustrations; I have chopped a hole in a roof; I have cried after a call; I have hugged family members after a terrible shift; I have made a child smile; I would not dream of doing any another job; I am a professional; I am a firefighter/paramedic.

NOTES

1   Lavenia Goree, *St. Louis Post Dispatch*, July 19, 1985.

2   Don Miller, *St. Louis Post Dispatch*, June 16, 1978.

3   Robert O'Donnell;, *People* magazine, May 15, 1995.

4   Bill Lemmon, *St. Louis Post Dispatch*, August 10, 1977.

5   LaVerie Sutton, *St. Louis Post Dispatch*, August 10, 1977.

6   Leon Sutton, *St. Louis Post Dispatch*, August 10, 1977.

7   Robert Marshall, *St. Louis Post Dispatch*, August 10, 1977.

8   Mike LeBrun, *St. Louis Post Dispatch*, October 13, 1998.

9   Joe Pruente, *St. Louis Post Dispatch*, December 17, 1981.

10 Nevelyn "Wilbur" Stokes, *St. Louis Post Dispatch*, April 19, 1999.

11 Donnie Blankenship, Associated Press, April 24, 1989.

12 Marvin Jennings, State of Missouri vs Jennings, NOS. 55682, 58698.

13 Jessie Dotson, *Commercial Appeal*, November 9, 2010.

14 Cassidy Senter, State of Missouri vs Thomas Brooks, 960 S.W. 2d 479 (Mo. banc 1997).

15 Thomas Brooks, State of Missouri vs Thomas Brooks, 960 S.W. 2d 479 (Mo. banc 1997).

16 Sister Patricia Kelley, *St. Louis Post Dispatch*, September 29, 1987.

17 Donald Voepel, State of Missouri vs Stephen Johns, 679 S.W. 2d 253 (Mo. Banc 1984).

18 Stephen Johns, United Press International, October 24, 2001.

19 Officer Gregory Erson, St. Louis Police Department press release dated March 20, 2009.

20 Quintin Moss, State of Missouri vs Larry Griffin, 622 S.W. 2d 854 (Mo. banc 1983).

21 Wallace Connors, State of Missouri vs Larry Griffin, 622 S.W. 2d 854 (Mo. banc 1983).

[22]   Larry Griffin, State of Missouri vs Larry Griffin, 622 S.W. 2d 854 (Mo. banc 1983).

[23]   Dennis Griffin, State of Missouri vs Larry Griffin, 622 S.W. 2d 854 (Mo. banc 1983).

[24]   Nora Attaway, *St. Louis Post Dispatch*, August 26, 1991.

[25]   Patrick Hunter Ford, *St. Louis Post Dispatch*, October 28, 1992.

[26]   Emory Futo, State of Missouri vs Emory Futo, No. 73500.

[27]   William Campbell, *St. Louis Post Dispatch*, May 31, 1979.

[28]   Lloyd Mitchell, *St. Louis Post Dispatch*, May 31, 1979.

[29]   James Cox, *St. Louis Post Dispatch*, May 31, 1979.

[30]   Arthur Werner, *St. Louis Post Dispatch*, October 26, 1978.

CPSIA information can be obtained
at www.ICGtesting.com
Printed in the USA
BVOW03s1822260617

487867BV00001B/16/P